The ANIMAL SMUGGLERS
and other wildlife traders

The ANIMAL SMUGGLERS
and other wildlife traders

JOHN NICHOL

Facts On File Publications
New York • Oxford

First published in the United States of America by Facts On File, Inc.
460 Park Avenue South,
New York, New York 10016.

Library of Congress Cataloging-in-Publication Data

Nichol, John.
    Animal smugglers.

    Bibliography: p. 194.
    Includes index.
    1. Wild animal trade.   2. Endangered species.
3. Rare animals.   I. Title.
QL82.N53   1987   333.95′4   87-9072
ISBN 0-8160-1834-0

Printed in Great Britain

10 9 8 7 6 5 4 3 2 1

CONTENTS

FOR JUDY

Colour Plates

Preface

A book about animal smugglers and the trade in wildlife is a difficult thing to write as there are so many subjects to cover. All these topics are interrelated and it is not practical to tackle them one after the other in systematic fashion, so although I have imposed a certain order, which on the face of it seems reasonable, the business just is not like that and, inevitably, I have had to go off at a tangent pretty frequently.

This volume is not supposed to be a textbook on the wildlife trade for conservationists, though I hope it will be of use to them. It is the result of my own experience and observation, supplemented by considerable research, which I hope will be read by people who do not watch wildlife programmes on television, as those who do are already aware of all the problems to which I refer. I have friends on both sides of the fence whom I respect greatly but I do not mind telling them that some of their actions are naïve or harmful or just plain silly.

When I do that they just disagree with me!

I certainly do not disapprove in principle of taking animals from the wild to keep in captivity with a view to breeding them and learning from them, nor even of keeping an animal to enter in shows, although I feel a bit uncomfortable about it. The variety of birds or reptiles or whatever in one of the Fancy shows is what stimulates many who see them to look at animals more closely.

What I really do object to is the trade in animal products. A dead animal is forever and to make parts of it into a briefcase or perfume or a fur coat seems obscene to me. One cannot blame the villager in South America who kills a crocodile, sells the hide and eats the meat. He is exploiting his environment in a most sensible fashion. It is the person who buys the end product that I find offensive. I don't mind if he owns 35 Rolls-Royces to prove that he is rich but the days have long gone when he could respond to my arguments by saying that each of us had an opinion that was different but equally valid. Today the evidence that the destruction of our plants and animals is also causing our own destruction is overwhelming, and such wholesale destruction should not be tolerated any longer.

A great part of this book refers to incidents and people in South Eastern Asia. There is a good reason for this. Similar happenings are to be found all over the world but only by concentrating on one particular area was I able to cover all that I wanted to in a reasonably sized book, so when you read of an animal being exploited in a particular way in Thailand, it should be borne in mind that the same sort of thing is happening in Tanzania and Sierra Leone and Brazil and Mexico. What also should be borne in mind as you read on, is that the things I talk about are happening today. It is very easy to be misled by government statements that claim to have ended a given trade, or by dealers who state that they no longer deal in a particular animal. Only recently some colleagues with whom I was then working refused to believe that animals were being traded illegally despite the evidence before their eyes. Customs and other officials kept saying that there was no such trade and some dealers insisted that their stock was nowadays all captive-bred, and they were believed, even though one of those particular dealers had stock worth around £50 million and 90 per cent of it was illegal. Much of the information contained in this book would not normally be available to investigators. All the dealers are well aware that some people approach them purporting to be in the business in order to obtain material for damning reports on their operations. Such innocents are invariably rumbled pretty quickly. When that happens they are either shown the door or they are fed all sorts of rubbish to give an entirely distorted picture.

But just to give an idea of how much some dealers feel they have to lose, let me tell of a case I came across a few months ago. Some young graduates were investigating the local scene in the capital of a tropical country that is famous for exporting wildlife. They posed as traders but got nowhere as they could not talk the right language, by which I mean the language of animal dealers the world over. One evening in their hotel one of them mentioned their lack of success to an American journalist who was also staying there. She declared that she was sure to be able to infiltrate the business, and would report to the researchers as soon as she had any news.

The next day she started work. Three days later she paid a visit to one exporter, saying that she wanted to buy animals. Obviously she must have roused suspicion as that evening she received a phone call, supposedly from the girl who had first mentioned animal smuggling, asking her to meet in half an hour on the corner of some street. Off went the journalist but when she arrived at the rendezvous there was no-one around. It was dark and quiet and frightening and she was just thinking of leaving when she was grabbed from behind by two men who laid her in the road. She was held in place while a car was driven over her legs. The men climbed into the vehicle and drove off leaving the poor girl in agony until someone found her in due course and she was taken to hospital. She did not investigate that particular animal dealer again but left for the States as soon as she was able.

There is much money in animal dealing, and a fair bit of my information for this book came from people I have known for many years who told me and showed me things on the strict understanding that they would not be identified. So, where appropriate I have either used no name or I have changed names in order that some informant cannot be recognised.

So to those who maintain that illegal wildlife trade is non-existent these days, let me just say that I have built up contacts around the world who send me up-to-date reports by every post. One newspaper cutting arrived today which starts, 'A bird smuggler was stopped at the airport today and, on being searched, was found to have forty two cockatoos in his luggage . . .'

A note on animal names:

Where I have written of animals generally, I have used a small initial letter, e.g. cockatoos, but where there is the full common name of a species, each word within it has a capital initial, e.g. Black Palm Cockatoos.

These full names can then be checked in the index for their scientific names.

1. Introduction

It all started when I mentioned the parrot sausages. 'What are parrot sausages?' asked someone, and I had to explain.

Years ago when I had been collecting animals for zoos, I had become involved in the odd, sometimes confusing, and frequently shady world of animal dealing. Over the years I got to know just about everyone in the business from the trappers and hunters, through the middlemen to the exporters, in countries as far apart as India, Senegal and Colombia. And in Europe and Britain, and to a lesser extent North America, I became friends with importers and collectors of exotic animals.

The world was different then and animals of all sorts were being traded in huge numbers. It was not uncommon for consignments of 30,000 birds to leave Senegal, and one dealer in India used to offer considerable discounts for quantities of finches over 100,000. In those days there were very few restrictions on the trade and the existing ones affected only a few species that were considered a health hazard to domestic animals, so, for instance, one could not import gallinaceous birds—poultry and the like—into the United Kingdom for fear of fowl pest. Twenty-five years ago there was no talk of conservation, natural habitats weren't being exploited and not a murmur was heard about the depletion of natural resources.

Then the whole situation began to alter. The first time it really struck me that this traffic was having an effect on wild stocks was when I visited India nearly 20 years ago, and asked a friend where all the monkeys were that could previously have been commonly seen.

'Oh,' he said with a shrug, 'they're in your country.' It seems incredible nowadays that no one had given a thought to the effects the business might have, but then the numbers seemed limitless. Several things started to happen about the same time that were to change the whole trade completely. World populations began to increase steeply after a setback during the Second World War, so that more land was cleared for cultivation, and a period of prosperity meant that people had money to buy a lot more—not just exotic pets, but new furniture, wood panelling in the home and, for the first time, new cars. All this purchasing power meant a sudden demand on the wild, for animals, timber and rubber. For the first time television sets appeared in the home, and before long natural history programmes were being shown which stimulated people to want to travel to ever more distant locations actually to see the animals that they had watched on the box. But when they arrived in their chosen resort they discovered that the Garden of Eden was having to compete with logging industries, large industrial estates and factories. On returning home, these now rather concerned tourists created the first of a whole legion of societies dedicated to conserving some aspect of the natural world.

Over the next two decades the whole situation deteriorated so that by the end of the 1970s numbers of both plants and animals were disappearing faster and faster.

By then, many countries had brought in legislation to stop, or at least control, this depredation, and then in the mid-1970s a number of nations signed an agreement in Washington to standardise the international trade in endangered animals and plants so that everywhere might follow the same system. However, CITES (Convention on International Trade in Endangered Species) was as full of holes as a fishing net, and although over the years more and more countries have ratified CITES, and indeed it has done a lot of good in many cases, it is a Convention that is largely abused or ignored by signatories that are either uncaring or are making so much money from the trade that at least one blind eye is turned to its restrictions.

Wherever there is a demand, a way will be found to supply it and if the demand cannot be supplied legally, there will always be plenty of people to meet it in other ways.

I dare say that people have always smuggled animals or animal products since first a peasant killed a deer on the King's estates and carried off the meat to sell in a distant market, but with the advent of CITES the whole proposition suddenly became much more attractive. Animals that had previously been cheap suddenly became expensive, and animals that had been expensive became unobtainable, so a new generation of animal smugglers started to bring a variety of species to Europe and America from their countries of origin. To start with it was easy—customs controls were not too strict and officials in any case were not trained to be able to differentiate between one animal and another. But as law enforcement improved, the smugglers had to adopt ever more ingenious techniques to evade discovery, and today the illegal trading in animals is a sophisticated business. The public face of officialdom in every country either maintains that the problem is non-existent or that it is very minor, and whenever someone is caught much is made of it. The reality is that only small-fry are ever caught and the big men in the business continue to trade as they have for years, quietly and without any fuss. Most people are totally unaware of the trade. John Tonge, a courier who was caught in 1985 when he attempted to smuggle some parrots through Felixstowe, is quoted as saying that when he was asked to smuggle birds '... I just laughed, "Who'd want to smuggle bloody parrots?" I thought!'

Unfortunately, whenever a case is reported in the press it is written by a journalist, which means that it is generally full of sensational inaccuracies and that doesn't help the situation at all. The exaggerations are included to cover holes in the reporter's knowledge. The real animal smuggling scene needs no embellishments to make it fascinating and exciting.

The smuggling of live animals and animal products is a business that involves many people, because despite public protestations to the contrary, there are very few dealers or collectors who would not become involved in an illegal deal if circumstances were right. The one thing that can be said about the trade is that it is world-wide.

One thing that cannot be said is that the story is simple. It is incredibly multifaceted, covering as it does the subjects of health and customs legislation, cruelty and destruction of habitat, changing lifestyles at both ends of the trade and conservationists on each side of the legal fence. Sometimes the story is sad and the wastage of life is terrible, sometimes it is about the boring shuffling around of paper to 'legitimise' consignments, and sometimes it is comically unbelievable, which brings me back to where I began, at the parrot sausages. Though birds are now frequently smuggled like this, the first time I saw it was in Germany. I was staying with a friend in Duisburg who was an animal dealer, well known among collectors as someone who could obtain the more difficult species. I asked him how he managed to get hold of animals that elsewhere in Germany were difficult to find.

'Come, I'll show you,' he said, and led me upstairs.

The building where he kept his stock was an old tall house and as we climbed ever more rickety stairs past floors full of Squirrel Monkeys and pythons and pigeons, he explained that all his illegal stock was kept on the top floor which we had to reach by squeezing past sacks of seed and old airline crates. Once we had negotiated this obstacle course I discovered that the room beyond was packed with cages. At first I thought that they were all empty, but then I saw that in one block in the corner there were about a dozen Amazon parrots of different species and a pair of Leadbeater's Cockatoos.

'Aren't all parrots prohibited for sale in Germany?' I asked.

'Oh yes,' he replied with a laugh, 'but that makes them far more valuable. As you can see, I do not have many just now but I will be getting a new consignment in the next few days. I will show you.'

He was as good as his word. Some days later just as the sun was setting he picked me up from my hotel in his opulent grey Mercedes and, as it got steadily darker, we set off through the streets of Duisburg. Leaving the town behind we headed towards the Dutch border. About an hour after midnight we turned off the road into a small wood and switched off the engine. My friend locked the car, and taking a cloth bag from the boot, he led the way through the wood and across flat country for over a mile before we waded a ditch, struggled through a wire fence and continued for another quarter of an hour across fields until we came to a narrow road. There, parked in an overgrown layby, was a car, containing – it soon became obvious – a courting couple.

Their enthusiasm didn't inhibit Hans-Georg, however, from knocking on the window. Instantly the couple separated, and with no sign of embarrassment climbed out of the car to greet us, for the man was our contact. The woman, who was his girl friend, provided a pleasurable excuse for being parked in a deserted layby while they waited for us. They were both Dutch, as during our walk we had strayed into Holland, and while they drove us to their house they discussed the business of trading in animals. At that time there was a ban on parrots coming into Germany as an anti-psittacosis measure, whilst Holland suffered no such restrictions, so whenever parrots were needed in Duisburg an arrangement such as this was set up on the telephone. At the Dutch dealer's premises we took off our wellingtons and sat down to a very late supper after which we went to pick up the birds that were to return to Germany with us.

From the bag that we had brought with us, Hans-Georg extracted several pairs of women's tights and a reel of sellotape. The first bird was selected and it was removed from its cage and held on the table while the beak was sellotaped shut and then it was inserted head first into the foot of a pair of tights. A short piece of tape was twisted round the tights behind the tail, and the process was repeated again and again until several pairs had been filled. With this consignment of birds carefully laid in boxes in the car, we all set off for the layby where we had met the Dutch dealer. We bumped off the road until we were again hidden by the high bank, and climbed out into the chilly night. Without a word being spoken the strings of parrot sausages were hung round Hans-Georg's neck, and with handshakes all round we set off on the long trudge back to the Mercedes. The expedition was totally without event, and soon after dawn we were unpacking the birds in the attic in Duisburg.

Nowadays things are different. I'm sure that today it would not be possible to make that journey so easily, and though that same business still exists I heard recently that Hans-Georg had died about five years ago. The technique is still in use and a few weeks ago it was being used across the Mexican–United States border.

Animal smuggling is a complex business, and the only way to write a book about it is to cover the many facets one by one. But by its nature it is a secretive trade which ebbs and flows constantly across the ever-changing quicksands of supply and demand and legislation, and what many people cannot understand is that there are not usually any firm answers to the questions that are frequently asked by those who are not involved.

2.The Mainly Legal Trade: Live Animals

There is a perfectly legal world trade in live animals, and though it is no longer conducted on the scale of the 1960s, when airlines regularly carried more animal passengers than human, it is still considerable.

The greater part of the animals are transported by air, and can be conveniently divided into two groups: the wild animals on the one hand, and the domestic farm animals and pets on the other. The trouble with transporting large animals is that they are heavy, and freight rates are usually charged by weight, so although high quality cattle are moved around the world by air, the numbers involved are usually low as the individual animals are destined to form the nuclei of breeding herds. However, in recent years much work has been done to try and reduce the cost, and nowadays what is sometimes done is to remove a tiny embryo from a pedigree cow, implant it into the uterus of a much smaller animal and then ship that abroad. The same system of course can be used with horses, although the technique will not solve all the problems of shipping these animals, since they are frequently moved around the world in order to take part in races.

Apart from the need for new stock for breeders, most farm animals are transported for slaughter. Civilised countries nowadays try to ensure that animals that are to end up as meat are killed in the country of origin, but that is by no means always the case, and Britain, for example, exports live cattle and horses to the continent for the meat trade. Live rabbits are a considerable part of the business. They are driven to the east coast ports of England whence they travel by sea to the continent to be slaughtered and frozen and then sent to Korea. There the inedible bits such as the heads, the guts and the feet are processed to make food for poultry, the meat is chopped up, re-frozen and shipped to the supermarkets of Great Britain where you can buy it marked 'Produce of Korea', even though it might have originally come from down the road. The skins are made up into fur coats and again exported to the West—labelled 'Fun Furs', though I dare say it's not a lot of fun for the rabbits.

But though an awful lot of rabbits are involved in this trade the numbers cannot possibly match the vast quantities of sheep that are sent from Australia to the Middle East each year on enormous, unstable-looking ships that are specially converted for the purpose. Each carries thousands of sheep in quite appalling conditions and many die on the way. Although I had seen photographs of these vessels I had not appreciated just how big they were until I actually saw one in Singapore earlier this year. I asked what it was for and was told that it was to make regular trips to Saudi Arabia. 'But what,' I persisted, 'will it carry?'

'Oh, sheep,' was the response, and after a pause, 'Or Koreans.'

It seemed an odd remark but it turned out to be perfectly true. Ships were being converted in Singapore in such a way that they could indeed either carry sheep, or communities of Korean workers who were on contract in the Middle East, in which case the ship became a self-contained town, complete with shops, barbers, workshops and everything else.

Common humanity and animal welfare will always come a poor second to profits, but it does seem sad to me that when animals are being sent to be slaughtered they are treated so badly, though it must be said that such treatment might be well within the law. Personal pets that are being exported fare much better.

Although cats and dogs generally only travel in ones and twos, the airlines handle quite a few of them every year as people emigrate or move to a new country to work. Although it must be a worrying business for Fido and often involves a long quarantine at the end of the journey, there are not usually many problems involved.

Wild animals on the other hand are a totally different kettle of fish, and in order to attempt to make sense of the whole story, perhaps now is a good opportunity to examine how a consignment of animals reaches the final consumer. Even many dealers and collectors of animals are not aware of the complexities of the business.

There is really no such thing as a typical consignment. One dealer said to me recently, 'After thirty years of unpacking boxes of birds it is still exciting to see what is going to emerge.' This is because of so many variables along the way, from the hunter's experience, the season of capture and the weather, the availability of food, delays in transit, the knowledge of the importer and much else; but bearing all these things in mind, this is what typically happens.

The trapper usually lives in a small village a long way from any sort of civilisation, and he knows from long personal experience or from the experience of his family before him the sort of animals that the dealers want for export. The majority of these are common species that are collected in large numbers and are generally available throughout the year. In addition, he knows that there is also a market for a great number of species of animals that are a lot less common, or more secretive, or live largely solitary lives and can therefore only be trapped in ones or twos.

The trapper might also know that the dealer has a particular requirement to fulfil an order—say, a rare animal or a baby or an animal of a specific sex, so that when he leaves home in the morning he must keep all this in mind. He sets off, carrying nets and traps, ropes and cloth bags and various baits, and the first thing he does is to visit all the traps that he set the previous day. If he is lucky he will find what he wants in a small proportion of them, but it is more likely that there is nothing, or else animals that have no commercial value for him. If he has caught something he will extract it from the trap and place it in a cloth bag and tie the top so that it cannot escape. If the animal is such that it would escape from a bag, it will instead be placed in a tiny cage. If the captive is a bird it is less likely to flap about and injure itself if it is in darkness, so provided it isn't too small the trapper might very well seel it. This involves inserting a needle and thread through a lower eyelid, taking the thread over the top of the head and through the other eyelid and pulling them closed before knotting the thread and cutting it off. This is an old falconry technique that is not practised nowadays in Britain, but is commonly used by bird trappers.

When all the traps have been cleared and baited and reset, and any new traps put in place, the trapper might very well decide to collect a variety of passerine soft-billed birds for which there is a ready market. He will remove a small owl from one of his bags, and attach it by its jesses to a suitable perch in a clearing between the trees. The owl is an old professional just as is the trapper, and it sits quietly, taking no active part in the proceedings. The trapper moves off and starts to tie together several lengths of bamboo that he is carrying with him until he has a pole about 20 feet long. Sticking out from the top end are three, 1-foot-long twigs. Each year just after the rainy season when plants are putting forth new growth and the sap is rising, the trapper prepares himself a new lot of birdlime. Recipes for this are legion but by far the most efficient is made from the latex of the rubber tree mixed with that from the breadfruit tree. It is quick and easy to prepare, doesn't smell and is efficient to use and, unlike all other types of bird lime, it can be cleaned after use and recycled. In this case it is applied to the three twigs and the trapper hides behind a bush to wait.

Before long, first one and then a host of small birds are zipping in and out of the branches around the owl, mobbing it. Their concentration is only on the owl which they dive-bomb repeatedly with many harsh alarm calls. The trapper patiently eases his pole towards the birds and gently touches one on the breast. It adheres instantly, and the pole is pulled back again. The bird is removed with the loss of some feathers and the operation is repeated so that by the end of the day the trapper has many of his bags full of birds. He retrieves his owl, dismantles his pole and returns home.

Around his house he has a variety of containers for his animals. The birds need to be removed from their bags, their eyes unseeled, and any remaining birdlime removed from their feathers with a little paraffin before they are placed in cages and fed. Many of these birds have highly specific diets, and the basic food that the trapper provides will not suit them. Trapping animals is difficult, but conditioning them to captivity is the really hard part and many die before learning to take a substitute food, often simply because they do not recognise it as such. A flycatcher that forever grabs insects on the wing can sit in a cage knee-deep in maggots and starve to death, even though they are nutritionally just as good as the flies they will hatch into.

Eventually the birds are caged, the mammals are crammed into small crates and the snakes and frogs are dropped into deep earthenware jars, and for the trapper the day is finished unless he intends to trap nocturnal species of animals.

By morning when he is ready to set off to check his traps again, many of the previous day's catch are dying, and by the following day most of them will be dead. But enough survive to enable him to make a living, and for each he will be paid a few pennies.

In due course when enough animals have been accumulated to make it worth his while, the trapper will box them up and set off on a journey to the middleman who lives in a nearby small town. The journey to his premises will be partly on foot and partly by whatever means of transport is available, be it canoe, bus or cycle-rickshaw, but the journey is almost always less than about twelve hours. The trapper is not employed by the middleman, he simply gets paid by results, and unless an animal is really rare the trapper knows in advance more or less what he's going to be paid for his stock because from beginning to end of the journey from jungle to pet shop each animal has a fairly fixed price. After the transaction the trapper returns home while the staff who work for the middleman cage and feed the new arrivals.

These premises, whilst unbelievably squalid, are more sophisticated than those of the trapper, and the cages here tend to be made of wire netting rather than bamboo.

Large numbers of animals are collected, and once again due to stress, injury, lack of hygiene and careless feeding, the losses are high, but after a week or two there is enough stock available to make up a consignment for the exporter, and once again the animals are crated and sent off with someone accompanying them. The middleman is not rich so he is unlikely to own a vehicle, and the boxes and baskets travel by cart to the nearest railway station to be loaded onto a train for a journey to the exporter's establishment in a large city. The journey will take a number of hours during which the temperature in the guard's van might very well rise to over 100°F and mortality along the way is not uncommon, but in the end the stock that has survived is housed in cages at the dealer's premises.

These holding stations vary enormously. Some are well maintained, and the stock is cared for as well as possible, though overcrowding is always a problem. In some cases the staff are most knowledgeable about animals and are really interested in them. There are still losses, of course, as there are at every stage, but by now all the weaker animals have died so that the remainder are the real toughies.

The variety of species in these places is really exciting to someone who is interested in animals, and although most of the animals are common there are always rarities and sometimes one comes across colour variants; indeed some dealers specialise in them. Siam Farm on the outskirts of Bangkok in Thailand is one such. The company is the biggest dealer in Thailand and on my various visits I saw a fascinating range of colour forms of otherwise common animals. There were blue, and also yellow (lutino) Ringnecked Parakeets, cinnamon Jungle Crows, albino Spectacled Cobras and Pigtailed Macaques and, most beautiful of all, Golden Indian Pythons. Generally I don't care for colour variants but these snakes were quite exquisite.

Siam Farm is a good example of a dealer who keeps his stock in the best conditions that he can. On the other hand the premises of some dealers can only be described as squalid, and sometimes they are located in bird markets, though these are disappearing as legislation makes it harder for them to operate. 'Bird market' is a misnomer really since one can obtain almost any sort of animal in these places. Each stall is a black hole filled to the ceiling with tier after tier of ramshackle cages, encrusted with cobwebs, faeces and heaps of putrefying food. As you might imagine, losses here are enormous and I've seen tea chests full of dead Tiger Finches, tiny birds smaller than a wren—can you imagine how many of those are required to fill a tea chest?

Whether the consignment that we have been following ends up at Siam Farm or the Jakarta Bird Market in Indonesia, in due course the dealer needs to ship the animals abroad. Special export crates are made up. These will be the best accommodation that the animals have yet seen because the boxes have to be a certain type and standard to be accepted by an airline.

The dealer has received his order and payment from his customer, has booked cargo space on a particular flight and has advised his customer when to expect the shipment. He obtains a certificate from the relevant veterinary surgeon to say that all the animals are healthy and not suffering from contagious diseases, and ensures that all other necessary documents such as CITES permits are in order. Then on the day of shipment the animals are packed into the crates which are fitted with food and water containers, filled for the journey, and the boxes are taken by van to the airport. When they are loaded onto a plane the crates should be placed in such a position in the hold that the airflow is not restricted, they cannot fall over, and they are strapped down so that they cannot move. With the temperature somewhere around 80°F the loading is completed and the cargo doors are closed.

All the passengers returning to the West from their holiday in the exotic Orient fasten their seat belts and the plane takes off. The animals in the hold can settle down to an uneasy rest after they have become accustomed to the noise and movement. But then, several hours later the plane lands for a refuelling stop and the cargo doors are opened again in somewhere like Abu Dhabi where the temperature is still as high as when the plane first took off. An hour later, after taking on more cargo, the plane leaves for Europe. When next it lands in Paris or Frankfurt or Amsterdam and the doors are opened to admit a cold blast of air, the temperature might well be below freezing and the poor animals in the hold have to sit for an hour while cargo is loaded or unloaded. Many flights, however, terminate in one of these towns so if the consignment is destined for the UK or the USA, the crates are unloaded onto a trolley which is driven across the open apron to a cargo building, and thence, perhaps several hours later, they are packed onto another plane.

Eventually they arrive at their destination and are again driven across the airport to the cargo terminal. Now, assuming that all the papers are in order and the consignment can be cleared through customs, the crates are either collected by the importer who packs them into his van, or else they are sent on by a domestic airline (or by train) and finally by road vehicle.

On arrival at the importer's premises the stock is unpacked into quarantine cages. These are certainly the most hygienic yet, and the variety of food is probably greater. There is more room too and the whole place is heated to a suitable temperature. And here the animals feed, rest and recover from the journey, or else die, to be thrown away together with the bodies of those that failed to arrive alive. The quarantine period varies from country to country, but eventually after some weeks they can be released for sale. Some of them might now be picked up by a retailer from the other side of the country and in his cages they will stay until sold to the final customer.

At each stage they need to be caught up from their cages and placed in small boxes for their journey and at each stage you get losses, but finally the animal that started life in a jungle on the other side of the world arrives at the home of a collector and is released into a roomy cage for the first time since capture. If it survives the first two or three days in its new home it will probably do all right, and if it is lucky and the owner is a caring, knowledgeable person, the animal will from now on be better off than ever it was in the wild, and certainly will be better cared for than it has been up till now.

Due to the ever-increasing costs of airfreight, quarantine, food, housing and

Animals and other cargo are carried on open trailers across a snow-covered airport soon after leaving the tropics (W. Newing)

the wages of staff, wild animals are no longer cheap, which isn't at all a bad thing, because nowadays they are not bought on impulse from pet shops by people who wouldn't know an Avadavat from a Neon Tetra. Instead they end up with collectors who really want them so that they are properly looked after and more and more frequently are bred in captivity.

3. The Mainly Legal Trade: Animal Products

The difference between the trade in live animals and in animal products lies in the last sentence of Chapter 2. Both trades are very wasteful, but with the former the final consumer buys the animal because he cares about it. If you visit collectors you soon discover that they all have quite extensive libraries on animals and often a lot of houseplants, and they watch all the natural history programmes on television. Whereas the purchaser of a fur coat is not at all interested in the animal from which it came.

The trade in animal products is colossal, which is something of which one tends not to be aware in Britain since such products are rarely to be seen, but one only needs to visit countries of origin to discover how much is going on. But the animals that are used to supply the trade all come from the same areas, whether they are to end up as fur coats, briefcases or medicinal products, and the wild populations won't be able to sustain these depredations much longer. And what seems sad is that none of these products is necessary for anyone—they are all luxury goods. Just have a look at what I'm talking about.

Animal	Areas of origin	Products
Elephant	Throughout Africa and Asia	Ivory, bone carving, feet for waste paper baskets, tail hair for bracelets
Rhinoceros	Throughout Africa and Asia	Horn, skin, toenails for medicinal use
Wildebeest	East Africa	Tails for whisks
Leopard and Tiger	Africa and Asia	Teeth (ornaments), skins for fur coats, skulls, bone for ashtrays, medicinal use
Jaguar	South America	
Lynx	North America	
Ocelot	South America	Skins for fur coats
Other small spotted cats	Throughout the tropics	
Pangolins	Thailand	Skin boots and wallets
Monkeys	Throughout the tropics	Skins for rugs, skulls as ornaments, teeth as jewellery
Bears	Asia	Skins as rugs, claws as jewellery, gall bladder for medicinal purposes. Whole bear for food
Civet	Ethiopia	Anal glands for perfume
Musk Deer	Asia	Musk glands for perfume
Seals	Canada	Skins for souvenirs
Birds of Paradise	New Guinea	Stuffed birds of paradise, plumage for ornamentation and for making pictures of birds of paradise
Hornbills	Asia	Skulls for medicinal purposes and as ornaments
Toads	Asia	Skins for bags

Frogs	Asia	Frogs' legs for restaurants
Pythons	Asia	Skins for coats, boots, wallets, purses,
Cobras	Asia	belts and to be stuffed so that they look
Rat Snakes	Asia	like Pythons, Cobras and Rat Snakes
Crocodilians	Throughout the tropics	Skins for bags, wallets, etc.
Monitor Lizards	Asia	As for snakes, feet as keyrings
Marine Turtles	Throughout the tropics	Complete as souvenirs, meat, skins for boots, eggs for food, tortoiseshell for trinkets
Beetles	Central and South America	Jewellery, mounting in glass cases
Butterflies and Moths	World-wide	Wings for tourist souvenirs and for mounting in glass cases
Scorpions	Throughout the tropics	As souvenirs embedded in plastic
Spiders	Throughout the tropics	Dried, as souvenirs

The trade routes in wild animal products are similar in many ways to those used in the live animal trade, in so far as the hunter will collect a number of specimens to take to a middleman who then supplies the exporters. After that the consignments usually travel by sea. The point in the journey at which the raw material is processed to become the final product varies according to the individual item. Skins are generally tanned and made-up in the country of origin, whereas tortoiseshell is often carved in the consumer country.

Everyone who is in the business of dealing in either live or dead animals complains bitterly that trade isn't what it was 20 years ago and undoubtedly that is true. Public awareness, stringent conservation laws and dwindling resources are certainly having their effect, and in talking to the dealers it is surprising how many of them are saying that the only way to go forward is to breed animals in captivity to supply the market, and looking at advertisements in the trade press the variety of animals available has certainly dropped over the years. But having said all that, there are an awful lot of animals still being taken from the wild each year. People outside the business have a host of misconceptions about it, but to a great extent the live animal business is similar to the trade in baked beans or umbrellas. Most animals have a fixed price and are traded in the same way, and the dealer himself is just as much a businessman as the chap who manufactures bicycles. And like him they have fingers in other business pies. In Bangkok, the managing director of Siam Farm, Mr Komain Nukulphanitwipat, sells Green Tree Pythons and Goffin's Cockatoos, but insists that it is his hobby. Most of his money comes from his other businesses, including selling airbuses, on each of which he gets five per cent. Even so his animal business was estimated to be worth US$1 million annually six years ago and it is certainly bigger now. On the other hand, Terence Loh Peck Soon of Universal Tropical Enterprises in

Singapore, who also has other businesses selling leather and automobile spare parts, says that he earns far higher profits from cockatoos than carburettors. And the whole business is like that—there are no definite answers anywhere.

Part of the reptile list from Siam Farm. They also stock mammals, birds, amphibians and invertebrates (J. Nichol)

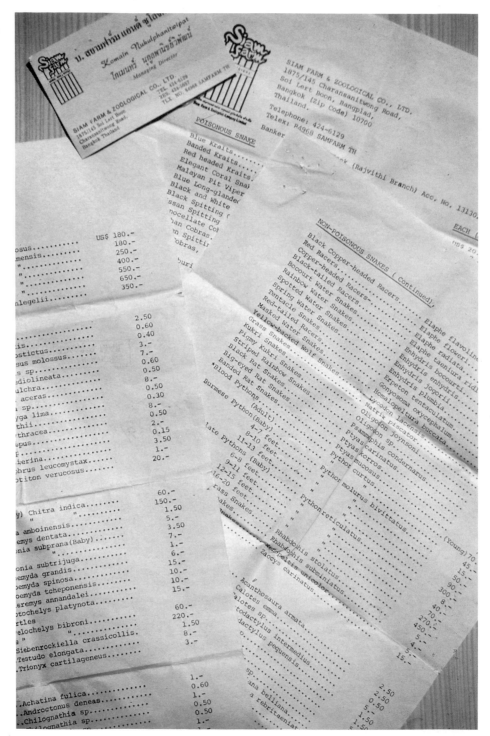

4. The Mainly Illegal Trade: Live Animals

Talk about animal smugglers, and people think of the chap who gets caught with a parrot hidden in the door panels of his car. In reality that is only a tiny part of the picture, which is complicated by the fact that every country has different laws regarding wildlife trading, different degrees of conscientiousness in applying these laws and, in many cases, different languages and animals.

So, although many animals are actually smuggled in the above sense, many others are traded ostensibly legally by altering or forging documents, laundering them through another country, or just plain lying about them. All these ploys are made easier because laws are made by lawmakers and written by civil servants rather than by people who understand animals and the trade. Ask any government official in any country whether animal smuggling is going on and he will invariably say 'Oh yes, the odd thing does get through, I'm sure, but we are extremely vigilant and I'm convinced we're on top of the problem.' One official in the United States even expressed considerable surprise at the subject being raised. 'It just doesn't happen at all over here,' he affirmed, in a country which more parrots enter illegally than there are holes in the nets that trap them.

Let's have a look at the ways animals are traded illegally. Perhaps the easiest of all arises because nowadays more and more animals are being bred in captivity. Most people who do this are perfectly honest, but for the dealer in illegal stock the practice is a godsend. Almost invariably countries state that if an animal has been bred in captivity it can be traded without any problems. So what could possibly be easier than to breed 50 parrots a year and say that you've bred 100? No government administration has the personnel to check these claims even if they care enough to want to do so. But the dealer who has bred the 50 birds simply makes up his stock with additional supplies from the wild and, just to blur the picture even further, several dealers in a city will lend each other young birds in the rare event of an investigation. Life is made a little more difficult in those countries which demand that captive-bred stock should be close-rung, which means that a ring without a seam is placed on a bird's leg within the first few days of its life. The ring has certain data such as the year and the breeder's name printed upon it. But a law like this is only a minor hiccup as there are several ways around it. One can, for example, trap birds young enough and ring them just as one would a captive-bred bird, or indeed one can even close-ring an adult bird. It is done everywhere in the world, and someone who has been in the business for a few years can tell you how it is done. Lastly one can forge rings, for when shipping out a consignment of 2,000 birds—200 each of ten different species, what harassed official is going to open every box, catch every bird and check every ring?

Thailand's Suchino Corporation exports very large numbers of animals each year. The country is a signatory of CITES and has national legislation to implement the Convention though it is flouted quite openly everywhere. However, to make life as easy for themselves as possible, Suchino only export from Thailand what is legal. Most of their stock is trapped and held in neighbouring Laos whence it is shipped to the West. Laos does not recognise CITES, but in order to simplify things for the customer each consignment is accompanied by a document which states that all animals in the consignment are captive-bred. They rarely are, and many of the species have never been bred in captivity anywhere in the world.

The next wheeze for legalising shipments is to forge documents. Most consignments for export need two types of documentation. The first is a veterinary certificate which states that the animals have all been examined and are healthy, and the second is one or more bits of paper to certify, in effect, that the animals are legal and are not being shipped in contravention of any laws, either in the country they are leaving or in the country in which they were trapped, which might very well be different.

Veterinary certificates have never been a problem. In many exporting countries they can be bought from a veterinary surgeon, blank and pre-signed. Where these are not available it is simplicity itself either to print some with the heading of a mythical practice, or in these days of sophisticated and inexpensive copying techniques, to paint out the details on an existing certificate and run off a pile of xerox copies so that they are blanks and can be filled in as needed. And lastly one can buy documents from someone else. The best way of explaining this is to relate an example that I witnessed recently. A consignment of birds was shipped from Burma to Singapore perfectly legally. Neither the exporter nor the importer did anything at all crooked, but the export documents from Burma are not terribly specific, simply stating, '100 parrots, 100 mynahs . . .' and so on. For consignments leaving Singapore, however, the scientific name of each species has to be typed in. The birds in this particular consignment were very common species and destined for the local market in Singapore.

On arrival the whole lot were bought, together with the documentation, by an exporter who flogged them to the pet shops for more or less what it had cost him. He wasn't interested in them. What he wanted was the documents that had come in with the consignment. Armed with this he could ship out anything he wanted. After the words '100 parrots' he had only to type in '—10 Black Palm Cockatoos, 10 Eclectus Parrots' and so on. Hey presto, the birds had all suddenly become legal, on paper at any rate.

Such doctoring of bits of paper is easy, but that's not to say that the animals themselves are not actually smuggled. They frequently are.

Singapore was at one time the centre in the Far East for the exporting of wild animals, but not any longer. The most important exporter in the country is certainly Terence Loh Peck Soon, followed by Doctor Kwek of Avifauna Ltd, a medical doctor who earns a lot more from his parrots than his patients. And the once well known Wee brothers, Christopher and David, still have a shop in Serangoon Road from which they export a small amount.

The position of Singapore has been taken over by Bangkok and Jakarta. Ten years ago there were several dealers in Bangkok but they have all faded away leaving the field clear for Siam Farm and Suchino, and both of these firms deal on a very large scale.

The other country in the area which is now a major exporter is Indonesia. The three dealers, who between them handle most of the stock from the area, are Chuck Darsono, Firma Hasco, which handles only birds, and Frankie Sulemain, who started in business a long time ago when he taught Terence Loh all he knows in Singapore before a difference of opinion between them took him to Jakarta. Sulemain handles all sorts of stock.

Indonesia is an interesting place because, despite the government's public communications about a caring attitude towards conservation, there are heaps of wild animals leaving the country regularly. It is difficult in the West to try and make people realise that our way of thinking about animals is totally alien to the people in countries such as Indonesia. I don't know how else to explain it except by saying that they think of wild animals in the same way as we do, say, of empty potato crisp packets. We would sell crisp packets if there was a market for them, otherwise we don't give them a thought. They are always around wherever we look, we wouldn't think twice if someone destroyed one, they'll always be there and if they weren't it wouldn't matter at all to us—in fact we probably wouldn't even notice for a long time. They're just an unimportant part of life. Consequently the Indonesians find it incomprehensible when foreigners start jumping up and down about the subject. In many countries the people who are responsible for such things only do it because of their public image abroad and not because of an interest in the subject. One of the senior government officials with this responsibility is the brother-in-law of one of the biggest of the bird dealers!

Not long ago, Garuda Indonesia Airways, the national airline, printed a poster showing someone with a cockatoo and wording to the effect that when Garuda flew consignments of these cockatoos they handled them carefully. Garuda was pleased with the poster and no one noticed that they should not be carrying the birds since it was illegal to do so. Swift complaints from the West resulted in the government insisting that the airline withdrew the poster immediately and that they check before they did something like that again. They mustn't put up posters like that, they were told—not that they mustn't carry birds like that.

Indonesia is extraordinary when it comes to smuggling because if you look at a detailed map of the area you will see that it consists of a multitude of islands scattered about like confetti between mainland Asia and Australia. When you actually go to the area you realise that there are even more islands than you thought, though some of them are little more than foliage-covered rocks. In the north the islands are very close to Malaysia and Singapore, whence a hydrofoil service to one of them takes only 25 minutes, and in the south they are not far from Australia. Legions of small boats ply throughout the region and so it is the easiest thing in the world to bring Australian and New Guinea stock to the bird market at Jakarta.

From Jakarta and Lampung it is just as easy to take it across to Singapore, or from Medan in the north of Sumatra across to Penang in Malaysia. The Indonesian authorities admit that a bit of this trading goes on but they are powerless to stop it. A friend of mine was told in Jakarta that the government was very worried about the smuggling of animals and that if he could stop it he would be an 'Indonesian Hero'. The PPD (Primary Production Department) in Singapore, claims it doesn't happen, and customs officials at Pasir Panjang Wharf, where it all arrives, insist that the trade is non-existent. Yet the dealers freely talk about the illegal consignments arriving there, and in fact go and collect them when advised by phone that a shipment is arriving for them. It must be said that legal consignments also come in, and when asked about them a customs man pointed to a large freighter that was staggering past some miles out to sea, and told me that they arrived on ships like that and were unloaded onto bumboats off shore. But that's certainly not true, as I subsequently observed a consignment of birds being packed in Jakarta for delivery to Singapore, and I watched them being loaded onto a small, ramshackle boat that I certainly wouldn't have trusted to take me to Singapore, and was told by the dealer that this is how it was always done, and I have no reason to doubt his words. I watched the boat putter off northwards towards Pasir Panjang without there having been even a cursory glance by authorities, which were noticeable only by their absence, and that particular consignment included a number of species that supposedly enjoy strict protection and which should not be traded at all because of their rarity. So the consignment was illegal on several counts.

Smuggling on this scale is completely open as no one is in the least bit interested in trying to stop it. I saw a dealer's premises in Singapore with birds worth about £50 million at UK prices, and 95 per cent of them were illegal and had been brought in from Indonesia and Australia; indeed many arrive quite openly by air, flown in from Jakarta on Garuda flights.

Not very far from the airport at Changi lives a lady who has been trying for years to get the illegal trade stopped, but she complains bitterly that whenever she approaches any relevant government department she is met with either a determined wall of silence, or total indifference. What Marjorie Doggett really objects to is not just what she sees as the immorality of the trade, but the cruelty involved. When animals are sent abroad in normal export crates they naturally suffer stress, and other factors on the way also affect their well-being, so that when they arrive at their destination some will not have survived the journey and some will be unwell.

In the trade this is known as 'transit disease'. Medically there is no such thing but it is a convenient way of saying that the animals are ill because of overcrowding, hunger, thirst, general bacterial infection, cold, fear or whatever. None the less, animals shipped legally travel much better than those that are smuggled.

There are really three ways of doing the latter. The exporter can hope that customs officials are not very good at identifying species, and simply label an animal incorrectly. It used to happen a great deal, and I remember watching a dealer many years ago arguing fiercely with a customs man that the birds in a particular crate were not parrots (they were in fact lovebirds—a type of parrot—and at the time it was illegal to import them into England), but parrot finches. He got away with it, too. Nowadays the inspectors are much more knowledgeable, but it does still happen.

Another way of sneaking animals in and out of countries undetected is to make them look like something else—or at any rate prevent them from being instantly recognisable. This is being done regularly with birds of paradise, for example, shipped from New Guinea via Java to Hong Kong and Japan. The cocks are readily recognisable by the brightly coloured plumage and the long ornamental feathers (which they moult and regrow annually), so the latter are carefully pulled out and the birds are dyed black. When they are dry they are included in a consignment of mynahs or crows. I've not watched it being done, but I've seen the treated birds awaiting export, and birdmen in the market have explained the process and stated that it is commonplace, and indeed quite a few

Animals at a dealer's premises in Medan, Sumatra, whence they are smuggled to Malaysia (W. Newing)

One of the four holding stations of the biggest dealer in Singapore (J. Nichol)

birds of paradise turn up elsewhere in South East Asia, so obviously they get out with no problems.

The same technique is sometimes used with mammals though I feel that this must be a rarity. I talked some time ago to a dealer in Bangkok who is breeding all sorts of animals on a commercial scale, including Cotton Eared Marmosets. She told me that what she would really like to do is to set up a breeding colony of Golden Lion Tamarins, which are extremely rare and therefore very expensive. I asked her if she had any and she said not, but added that she had imported one pair which had been dyed black in with a consignment of other South American primates, but sadly one had arrived dead and the other died shortly afterwards. A few weeks later while chatting to a dealer from Bolivia he told me that he shipped out the occasional Golden Lion Tamarin the same way.

And the third method of sending animals illegally from one country to another is to hide them in a secret compartment, but it is not nearly as common as it used to be in commercial, air-freighted consignments around the world because of modern sophisticated detection techniques, though it does happen regularly. Large secret compartments would be easily discovered, so they must be made as small as possible with the result that animals confined to these tiny cells have virtually no room to move on a flight that could last more than 20 hours, and the lack of space also means that the food with which they have been provided ends up glued to the fur or feathers, and so do the faeces. When the poor old beast reaches the other end he is in quite a state.

On a few occasions customs men have been alerted to the presence of hidden animals by unexpected scuffling noises, and in order to prevent this, animals are sometimes deliberately packed so that they are completely immobile. This might mean dressing an animal in some sort of straightjacket or bandaging, or inserting it into a container that prevents any movement. The Environmental Investigation Agency have records of squirrels that were shoved into short lengths of plastic tube with the ends sealed, leaving only airholes. The animals died *en route*, and from the photographs it is clear that it must have been a pretty tight fit inside the tubes.

Another system is used to import illegal animals into countries like Britain which has very strict laws that are strictly enforced—so much so that if you talk to dealers in Asia, Africa or South America about sending stock to England they all complain about how difficult life is being made for them by the British authorities. They moan about the UK more than anywhere else; in fact they find that doing business with English importers is so difficult that they often refuse to enter into negotiations at all, preferring to send stock elsewhere. The great problem with shipping animals illegally is that it is usually the importing country that kicks up the fuss. Third World countries are not usually bothered about what species go out (regardless of what the law says about them), and when the United Kingdom began to get tough some years ago, dodgy items began to be shipped to Germany, Holland, or especially Belgium, where all the big European animal wholesalers are to be found.

But slowly Germany and Holland started to tighten up, and eventually Belgium got such a bad name for flagrant disregard of the generally accepted standards of animal trading that even they had to make some gesture of conciliation, so that now, even though it is still the biggest wholesaler of animals in Europe, it is much tighter than before. The result is that animal exporters say that they would far rather send consignments to France, or preferably Spain, where the authorities have a more realistic approach to their business.

Yet the European Economic Community as a single body has ratified CITES, so it should in theory be as difficult to get illegal animals into Spain as it is to get them into England. And this raises a nice point. On the northern coast of South America is the country of French Guiana. It is not run as a colony of France but as a 'Department', which is, if you like, similar to a British county. This means that French Guiana in South America is a part of the EEC, and this makes a mockery of the whole idea of the European Community all accepting CITES because it is simplicity itself to trap animals in French Guiana which are proscribed for importation. They are now 'in France' and can be traded within the community fairly freely. In days gone by when Guyana, Suriname and Brazil were exporting animals nothing was coming out of French Guiana. Suddenly to the world of wildlife trading it has become important and will become more so. Furthermore, the country has a long, unprotected border and animals from other countries can now be smuggled into French Guiana from places like Brazil which forbids the export of any fauna.

It is because of this discrepancy between countries like Belgium and France on the one hand and England on the other that the smuggling of animals has largely changed. The old habit of hiding them in a secret compartment for the long haul from the Far East or South America, has now given way to the new system where they arrive openly, or at any rate fairly openly, in Paris or Brussels and it is from there that they are smuggled through the ports and coastline of East and South East England.

Protected Mountain Horned Agamas are shipped from Thailand to Europe (W. Newing)

A German dealer's computerised list which runs to many pages (J. Nichol)

```
Günter Enderle                                            West-Germany

Exotische Ziervögel    Amtliche Quarantäne-Station      Nekton Produkte
                       Eigene Zucht-Station              Import – Export

                                                         Kieselbronner Straße 28
    Günter Enderle · Kieselbronner Straße 28 · D-7530 Pforzheim    D-7530 Pforzheim
                                                         Telefon (07231) 5 50 51
                                                         Telex: 783 404 enpfd


                                    17.02.86        SEITE    6

  ÜLBUL-ARTEN
  --------------------------------
  4544      PYCNONOTUS JACOSUS        RED WHISKERED BULBUL      21,00/S
  454413    PYGNONOTUS SINENSIS       LIGHT-VENTED BULBUL       37,00/S

  LIEGENSCHNAPPER-ARTEN
  --------------------------------
  46311     PHOENICURUS AURORENS      DAURIAN REDSTART          90,00/S

  ANGAREN-ARTEN
  --------------------------------
  471115    ANISOGNATHUS FLAVINUCHA   BLUE-WINGED MOUNTAIN-TAN. 140,00/S
  471142    TRAUPIS BONARIENS.DARWINI BLUE-AND-YELLOW TANAGER   145,00/S
  47121     RAMPHOCELUS C.CARBO       SILVER BEAK. TANAGER       80,00/S
  47129     RAMPHO.F.ICTERONOTUS      YELLOW-RUMP.TANAGER       175,00/S
  471312    TANGARA SCHRANKII         GREEN A.GOLD TANAGER       85,00/S
  471315    TANG.PUNCTATA ZAMOR.      SPOTTED TANAGER            85,00/S
  471316    TANG.ARTHUS GOODSONI      GOLDEN TANAGER            105,00/S
  471318    TANG.CYANIC.CAERULE.      BLUE-NECKED TANAGER        85,00/S
  471319    TANG.P.PARZUDAKII         FLAME-FACED TANAGER       120,00/S
  471333    TANGARA NIGROVIRIDIS      BERYL-SPANGLED TANAGER    120,00/S
  47142     THRAUPIS PALMARUM         PALM TANAGER               90,00/S

  YRANNENARTIGE VÖGEL
  --------------------------------
  47273     PROGNIAS NUDICOLLIS       NAKED-THROATED BELLBIRD   950,00/S
  47281     CEPHALOPTERUS PENDULIGER  LONG-WATTLED UMBRELLABIRD 1.750,00/S
  47524     DIGLOSSA CYANEA           MASKED FLOWER-PIERCER     110,00/S
  47534     DIGLOSSA HUMERALIS        BLACK FLOWER-PIERCER      110,00/S

  ÓLIBRI-ARTEN
  --------------------------------
  48253     CAMPYLOPT.HYBERYTHR.      RUFOUS-BREAST.SABREW      190,00/S
  48261     FLORISUGA MELLIVORA       WHITE-NECKED JACOBIN      190,00/S
  48381     THALURANIA FURCATA        FORK-TAIL.WOODNYMPH       160,00/S
  48424     OAMÖPHILA JULIA           VIOLET-BELLIED HUMMINGB.  180,00/S
  4851111   AMAZILIA A.ALTICOLA       AMAZILIA-HUMMINGBIRD      190,00/S
  485112    AMAZILIA FRANCIAE         ANDEN EMERALD             90,00/S
  485141    AMAZILIA AMABILIS         BLUE-CHESTED HUMMINGBIRD  170,00/S
  48517     AMAZILIA TZACATL          RUFOUS-TAILED HUMMINGBIRD  90,00/S
  48651     LAFRESNAYA LAFRESNAYI     MOUNTAIN VELVETBREAST     240,00/S
  48662     COELIGENA TOURQUATA       COLLARED INCA            280,00/S
  48684     HELIANGELUS EXORTIS       TOURMALINE SUNANGEL      220,00/S
  48711     ERIOCNEMIS VESTITUS       GLOWING PUFFLEG          210,00/S
  48722     LESBIA NUNA               GREEN-TAILED TRAINBEARER 230,00/S
  48741     METALLURA TYRIANTHINA     TYRIAN METALTAIL         160,00/S
  48771     AGLAIOCERCUS KINGI        LONG-TAILED SYLPH        220,00/S
  48832     RHODOPSIS VESPER          OASIS HUMMINGBIRD        170,00/S

  OTMOTS
  --------------------------------
  495219    MOMOTUS MOMOTA            BLUE-CROWNED MOTMOT      180,00/S
```

On the one hand individuals who want particular species for their own collections go over to the continent, collect them and return with the animals hidden about their person or in their car, and on the other hand dealers either do the same, or more frequently get couriers to do it for them. The couriers get paid in stock rather than money, but it enables them to clear a healthy profit for a couple of days work. It is not big-time dealers in Britain that work in this way but rather the whole host of cowboys who operate around the fringes of the business. I know one who regularly travels from his home to Manningtree on the Essex coast to stay overnight before making the short drive the next morning to Harwich to catch the ship to Holland, where he loads up with reptiles and amphibians, and returns a day later. Most of what he brings back is dead straight but how many customs men could tell a Mountain Horned Agama from a common Asian tree lizard? And if he declares a nice fat consignment of animals like a good boy, the chances are that he'll get away with those that remain in the car while he's showing the rest to the inspector. And it's a lot easier to hide a silent, non-moving, 6-inch-long lizard than it is to hide an African Grey Parrot. He usually gets away with it.

The best time of the year for this sort of activity is the summer when there are lots of tourists on the move, and at least one person deliberately goes over as a tourist in one of those day coach trips to France, where instead of making immediately for the hypermarket he meets his opposite number to pick up his animals. This friend has already done the hypermarket bit and the animals have been hidden in packs of groceries. When the coach leaves France for the return trip the doctored collection of duty frees looks just like that of everyone else, and who on earth checks through the luggage of day trippers to France?

It is tempting, but it would be a mistake to dismiss this aspect of the trade as only referring to the odd animal here and there. Last year I know for a fact that people brought into Britain Papuan Green Tree Pythons, Chipmunks, Madagascan day geckoes, African Grey Parrots, marmosets and Indian Starred Tortoise babies, all from the continent.

5. The Mainly Illegal Trade: Animal Products

Previous page: When this picture was shot in Calcutta it was legal to sell pythons but not their skins (D. Whiting)

At a stall in the handicrafts market in Jakarta an American woman was examining a small, stuffed marine turtle that was one of dozens on sale as souvenirs.

'If I buy this,' she asked the sales assistant, 'will I be able to get it into the States OK?'

'No problem,' affirmed the girl. 'We sell these all the time to American tourists.'

The tourist was dubious and in the end decided to leave the turtle where it was. She was right to be cautious because she would not have been permitted to import the turtle legally into the United States regardless of the salesgirl's assurances, and yet tourists throughout the tropics are told that they can take with them all sorts of things that are strictly forbidden. In Delhi I was offered a Leopard skin. It is an offence to trade in this product in India, and I would certainly not have been permitted to import the thing into Britain.

'Oh yes, you can,' the shopkeeper assured me, and it was only when I asked him why there was no head on the skin that he changed his tune. The head was bulky, and yes I was quite right, it was illegal but without the head the skin could be folded very small to fit into my suitcase. As a matter of interest I asked if he had a Tiger skin. The answer was that he hadn't, but given a day or two he could get hold of one for me. 'Anything is possible in India, Sahib,' he added with a grin. Tigers in India have just been clawed back from the edge of extinction by a decade of careful conservation work.

Very many tourists, finding themselves in exotic locations, are not as careful as the American woman over her turtle, and buy wildlife products that are banned, usually because they don't know, but sometimes because they calculate that they can smuggle the things back home anyway. The items are confiscated when discovered, and if you think this is a minor problem you should see the Customs & Excise warehouses where these confiscated items are stored. They are huge and creaking at the seams with snakeskin shoes and sealskin pelts, with tortoiseshell combs and Leopard skin purses and such a variety of things as you could never imagine.

Marine turtles have been recognised as becoming rarer for quite some time

Some of the hundreds of stuffed marine turtles for sale in Indonesia (W. Newing)

and, as a result, the trade in items made from them has been illegal in most countries for a number of years, yet such things can be obtained all over the place. On the north bank of the Rio Grande in Texas is the town of Brownsville and from here one can go on a day trip in a car across the bridge to Mexico. Just the other side of the border anybody can buy turtle skin boots. When the proprietor of the shop was asked if it was legal to import them into the USA, she replied, 'Put them in your case, no one will search it.' She was quite right, no one does, and the drive back across the bridge is uneventful.

Someone once said that the Chinese will eat anything with four legs except a table and anything with wings except an aeroplane. That seems to be about right and what animals they don't use as food they turn into powders and potions for the pharmaceutical trade. By way of illustration of the range of such medicines I was shown elephant appendix which is used in the treatment of kidney complaints, Tiger bone to relieve backache and gall bladder of bear to reduce a high temperature and cure a variety of liver complaints. Rhino horn is available all over the place. I don't know how on earth we in the West got hold of the idea that it is supposed to be an aphrodisiac. Various bits of rhino are used for a whole lot of ills, but a particular Chinese pharmacist impatiently brushed aside my comments about rhino horn and potency. That was nonsense, I was firmly told, there certainly were products to stimulate the libido, but rhino horn was not one of them. Rhino horn is primarily employed as a febrifuge and for treating illnesses in babies.

Rhino toenails and bits of skin are also handy things to have, but best of all was a complete rhino. In days gone by, I was told wistfully by a pharmacist in Thailand, a live rhino would be imported by all the shopkeepers who would club together to buy bits of it as it was far too expensive for one. I imagine there would also be a problem storing a whole rhino since customers only buy these products by a fraction of a gram at a time. But when such an event did occur it seems that just about everything was used from the blood and meat to the urine in the bladder. One would have to be pretty ill to partake of the last as rhino urine is eye-wateringly pungent. 'But alas,' the pharmacist added sadly, 'such a thing does not happen often these days.'

Not just rhino horn, but skin, toenails and even urine is sought by Chinese pharmacists everywhere (D. Whiting)

Though he might find it difficult to get hold of a complete rhino there is clearly no problem obtaining rhino horns, and these together with all the other animal bits and pieces may be found in Chinese pharmacies the world over. In New York ships arrive daily to unload container after container of goods, many of them from the Far East. There are so few customs officers at the container terminal, and so much cargo arriving that anyone wanting to smuggle something into the States via the port stands a pretty good chance of getting away with it. The Customs Department knows well that Chinese pharmaceuticals arrive in quantity but they are pretty helpless to stop them as the relevant containers, together with plenty of perfectly legal ones, are not opened at New York but are shipped instead under customs seal to Canada. There, with even less chance of being detected, the container is unloaded and the hidden pharmaceuticals are removed for packing into smaller containers for retail sale. They are then taken back to the USA by road without any harassment at all to end up in Chinatown in New York and elsewhere. The silly thing is that most of these products are useless. You might as well chew your fingernails as rhino horn. They're the same stuff and neither will do anything for your health. But an illogical, historical demand for these products continues to thrive, and though young Chinese don't use them it is going to be a long time before the trade dies out.

I had known for years that the Chinese people ate snakes as food, but I was not aware until recently that a cobra's blood and the contents of its gall bladder were considered to be efficacious in inhibiting the onset of old age and also for the treatment of various eye complaints—not forgetting the reducing of fever: have you noticed how many of these things are good at reducing fever? To provide for this market there is a considerable trade in live cobras throughout the Far East. Hong Kong imports crates and crates of the things from Thailand and in many towns I had been told that Bangkok was the place to see the drinking of cobra juice—but it took me a fair while to discover where it actually took place.

In the centre of Bangkok is a lovely little recreation area known as Lumpini Park. It is popular with the townspeople who visit it to hire boats on the ornamental lake, eat in the open-air café or simply sit around on the grass or fly kites as people do in parks the world over. The trees are full of mynahs and orioles, the bushes are the homes of countless lizards of several species and the lake contains so many fish that it resembles an English pond full of tadpoles in the spring. Each morning just as it begins to get light, people arrive to jog around the perimeter road, and by seven o'clock there are hundreds of them. By the time they have finished shedding a few ounces of fat and buckets of sweat they are ready to put it on again by having a drink and something to eat, and while they were running, many small food stalls so typical of Asia have been erected on the pavement outside the railings on the north side of the park. Here the runners can buy a fizzy drink at one stall, or chicken rice at another, or joke, the thin rice porridge that the Thais have for breakfast, and at another stall you can get your daily fix of cobra juice.

Mister John, who runs the stall, lives in a shanty village a few yards further along the road, and actually within the north-eastern corner of the park. The whole, squalid, fascinating complex is illegal, all the inhabitants are squatters, and though there is talk of clearing the area my guess is that it will be there for a long time yet. Each morning Mister John and his two helpers, Anan and Siriwat, squeeze out through the hole in the fence that is their front door and load up their trolley with crates of snakes, tables and chairs and crockery for the customers, and set off for their pitch along the road. In a few minutes they have set up and are ready for business. The prices on the cages state that cobras cost 150 baht (£4.50), Russell's Vipers and various non-venomous snakes are 100 baht (£2.70) and Reticulate Pythons and Indian Pythons are 1,000 baht (£27.00).

Left:
Thailand exports many cobras to Hong Kong; the demand is enormous (D. Whiting)

Right:
Dried meat and other cobra products are sold as health foods (J. Nichol)

As the joggers finish their exercise, some of them come to Mister John's stall for a slug of cobra juice to set them up for the day. The customer chooses a cobra (it's usually a cobra), or he leaves it to the staff to select one. Much showmanship goes into the choosing as one snake after another is hauled from the cages and tormented to try and make it raise its hood. By this stage in their lives the poor old beasts have put up with so much handling and abuse that all they want to do is to slide off, but eventually one is selected and it is taken to a gallows that has been erected on the pavement next to the cages. A noose is placed round the snake's neck and Siriwat or Anan crouch on the floor pulling down on the tail to hold the snake immobile. The belly is then swabbed from one end to the other with cottonwool soaked in surgical spirit, and with a scalpel Mister John slits the snake open from throat to vent, then carefully with a pair of forceps he delicately picks the portal vein from the abdominal cavity and nicks it with a scalpel so that the blood flows into a wineglass, and afterwards the gall bladder is also pierced and the two warm liquids are stirred together with a good slug of brandy and handed to the customer who is sitting on his stool beside the table. Over the next few minutes he sips it delicately while chatting to his friends, some of whom come to drink cobra soup which is served in little porcelain bowls from the stockpot which is simmering away at one side. It looks like chicken noodle soup without the noodles, and in fact tastes very similar. While the customer is taking his medicine the skin is peeled upwards off the still kicking snake and the body is cut free at the neck. If the customer wants the meat it is given to him in a plastic carrier bag. If he doesn't, it goes into the soup. I asked one customer why he came every day for his cobra juice and he told me that not only was it good for him but it gave him a nice, warm feeling inside.

By half past ten the joggers have all gone off to their offices and the snake stall is packed up and taken home. The skins are salted to be collected later by a chap from a tanning factory who takes them away to be made into boots.

While I was talking about this sorry business with Pisit Na Patalung of the Wildlife Fund, Thailand, he told me of an occasion some months previously when he was at Suan Chatuchak, the weekend animal market. A Chinese man started to bargain with the stall holder for a largish Reticulate Python, but when the deal was agreed the customer asked that only the tail of the snake be hauled out through a small gap in the door. This done he grabbed the tail firmly and carefully wiped it with a clean handkerchief. He then opened a penknife, and cut the tail right off. He dropped it on the floor and placed his mouth round the stump, and while everyone watched in disgust he sucked the blood from the python until it was empty (and, naturally, dead). Then with a gentle dab of his lips with the hanky he thanked the stall holder and departed. Pisit said that two of the watchers vomited during the business, and he finished by asking me, 'How can someone do a thing like that?' I had no answer for him.

The killing of pythons is illegal in Thailand, and by now the killing of cobras will also be illegal. The reason for the relevant legislation is that all these snakes are important predators on the rodent populations in the agricultural areas. At about the time I watched the scene at Lumpini Park there was a locally-made television film being screened in Bangkok. I talked to the producer, and asked him if he could let me contact some of the snake men that had appeared in the programme. He refused point blank, explaining that if he helped me and I made the story public in the West, Thailand would appear in a poor light. 'People from your country use stories like this to make Thailand appear ridiculous,' he told me.

It was in Java that I went into the Cobra Shop and Restaurant and bought a small packet of dried, minced cobra. With it came a sheet of instructions on how to cure all sorts of ills by eating the stuff, but I prefer to think that if I add water to it I will end up with instant cobra. In this same restaurant the skins of the snakes are made up into the usual souvenirs but this was the only place I came across a Disco Cobra. After death it had been mounted in the usual position with an erect hood, but two tiny red lights had been inserted for eyes, and the lead emerged from the cloaca. When the thing was attached to disco equipment the eyes flickered in synchronisation with the rhythm of the music.

Although many people find it difficult to relate to a cobra, these lovely reptiles are every bit as important as cuddly mammals are to the environment. Snake catchers tell me that there are nothing like the numbers about these days as there used to be, and farmers say that rodents are destroying much more of their crops than before and they are aware that this is due to the dearth of snakes.

When it comes to elephants it is much easier to interest people in their plight. I was telling a friend recently that I had been talking to Dr Esmond Bradley Martin some time ago. He asked me who Esmond was and I explained that he is an American who lives in Nairobi and who almost certainly knows more about the ivory and rhino horn trade than anyone else.

'Oh,' said my friend dismissively. 'Up-market animal welfare. It's easy to persuade people to save elephants.' And though he's probably doing a disservice to Esmond, he's right. Elephants as a 'cause' are easy to sell. Like everyone else I was aware of both a legal and an illegal trade in ivory, but I had not been aware of the scale of the business until recently. Nor had I realised that shops throughout Africa, and particularly Asia that sell ivory also have a healthy sideline selling the teeth and claws of Tigers and Leopards. They are everywhere in ivory shops but by far the biggest heap that I came across was in a shop called Buddy's in the Oriental Plaza Shopping Precinct in Bangkok, where there were handfuls of them on display. Most Tiger teeth are sold just as they are but they can also be bought with the root of the tooth carved into the form of a seated Tiger. I watched a young lad doing this in an ivory workshop with a nonchalant professionalism that was impressive. He sketched in a few guide lines on the tooth with a pencil, and in a very few minutes, using an electric grinder like that of a dentist, he had produced a super Tiger. He was equally adept at carving ivory and in a short time, using pretty basic equipment, a tusk was chopped into bits that in turn became carvings and rings, bracelets and pendants.

The Chinese woman who was the proprietor waddled into the workshop where I was watching the manufacture of the ivory pieces, and handed me a glass of Coca-Cola, signing to me that I should go with her into her house to sit down and drink it in comfort. To enter her sitting room I first removed my shoes according to custom, and then spent the rest of the visit wishing I hadn't since in addition to the mats, the floor was also covered with dollops of noodles, prawn heads and rice, part of the lunch which was still congealing in bowls on the table. The room was full of lurid Chinese calendars and red and gold ornaments, while next to a small shrine in one corner of the room, the fish in several tanks swam slowly back and forth in the murky water and blew bubbles at us. I perched on the edge of a dark brown, geriatric leather sofa, whose stuffing leaked from numerous rips, and tried to ignore the squidgy bottoms of my socks while I chatted to the woman via a good friend, Somsak, who acted as interpreter. As we spoke she threaded one ivory bead after another onto nylon line to make necklaces. The beads were graded according to size, each in a polythene bag on the low table. As one never sees ivory in bulk in Britain I was surprised to see so many thousands of beads in one place, and said so. The woman smiled and waddled across to a metal filing cabinet by the end of the sofa on which I was sitting. She pulled open the top drawer and beckoned me over. You know how big the drawers in filing cabinets are—this one was full to the brim with plastic bags full of ivory jewellery. One bag contained rings, another heart pendants, a third earrings and so it went on. The drawer below was full of ornaments of all kinds especially carvings of elephants, and the two lower drawers had a mixture of all sorts including many more of the beads that I had seen on the table. Before I had finished examining the contents of the filing cabinet the woman slopped across the room to pull open a six-foot door which I discovered led to a walk-in cupboard packed from floor to ceiling with a variety of containers that held unfinished ivory, including offcuts and scraps. The raw material is so expensive that even the tiniest bits are made into something.

When we were once more sitting down to finish the Coke, I asked where the ivory came from. Did it arrive from Africa? I asked, assuming that most of it arrived from ports like Mombasa; but I was wrong. The woman told me that only very rarely did they import African ivory, and then only when a particularly large tusk was required to fulfil a special order. African ivory was too expensive but Asian Elephants just don't grow tusks as large as those from Africa. I asked where the tusks came from. Mainly from Burma and Indonesia I was told, but it was getting more and more difficult these days to make a decent living in the business because it was illegal to export the ivory from both those countries, or to import it into Thailand. Consequently one was nowadays having to pay ever higher prices for the raw material, and higher bribes to relevant officials so that one could be sure of a constant supply of raw stock. Did that mean that none of the ivory the woman handled was legal? 'Oh yes,' she replied. 'It's all legal, because if you pay the appropriate people the correct sums of money they make sure that it has all the legal documents you could possibly want.' After further questioning I finally discovered that in fact some ivory really is legal, but not very much.

I was interested to know how the ivory actually travelled. Apparently from Burma it is carried over the hills across the border, and from Indonesia it enters Malaysia by boat from the east coast of Sumatra and from there it travels all over the place, as far even as Hong Kong.

I was later told that Burma not only forbids the export of ivory, but also of elephants unless they are aged or so clapped out that they cannot work, so in order to export ivory 'legally' to Thailand and India, traders have to resort to a ruse: an elephant with a good set of tusks has a nice rusty nail or a bamboo splinter dipped into a nicely rotting something or other so that there's a good chance that it picks up some infective micro-organisms, and hammered into the sole of an elephant's foot so that the animal soon becomes lame and ill. It is then registered as no good, and at that stage it can be legally exported, so the wretched animal is then marched sometimes hundreds of miles until it is handed over across the border to be slaughtered for the ivory. I imagine that very often the poor beast must be more dead than alive on arrival, but to the ivory smuggler that doesn't matter—it is only being used to transport its own tusks.

The African ivory trade has featured in many publications and although the greater part of it is legal there is still a considerable trade in tusks that are not. Not so long ago a couple of friends of mine were in Abidjan in the Ivory Coast, and coming across heaps of tusks in the market they started to photograph them, but as soon as the locals realised what they were doing they vanished, leaving the tusks unattended until shortly afterwards an individual who purported to be a government official, although he did not offer any identification, moved on the photographers, telling them that it was forbidden to take pictures of the ivory. About this time I was shown a copy of a letter from a woman in Belgium who had travelled on a plane from Burundi to Brussels together with various Belgian luminaries. While waiting to board her flight she was idly watching cargo being loaded, and noticed that the luggage included a few tusks and one very sorry looking Chimpanzee. As she was one of the party, albeit a very minor one, she was able to discover that these items were gifts to members of the party and had been shipped without any documentation at either end. When she complained and began stirring things up she was leaned on fairly heavily and told that she would face considerable problems if she took the matter any further. As a result, in the letter I mentioned, she says that her conscience won't allow her to drop the matter, but begs that nothing further be done as she was frightened. She ends by saying that the chimp died a few days later.

Whenever I read reports of countries banning the trade in wildlife of one sort or another, or hear conservationists congratulating themselves that their work has resulted in legislation prohibiting the export of endangered wildlife, I find myself surprised again and again at their naïvety. Illegal dealing happens and in many Third World countries bits of paper are totally meaningless.

Though much of the ivory from African Elephants is obtained through legal culls, poaching still continues (D. Whiting)

The legislation concerning ivory and skin trading is being openly abused around the world and colossal quantities of the latter are bought and sold each year. The majority are cat skins and reptile skins, although there are those of other groups of animals available in the market. One can still buy Colobus Monkey skins made up into the most attractive rugs and coats, both of which are totally useless as the fur is so long that it soon becomes matted. It needs constant grooming by a monkey inside it to keep it looking as it does at the point of sale.

Eel skins are an up-and-coming product as the number of available reptiles continues to decrease. Last year South Korea exported US$25 million worth. From November until June each year about 3,000,000 eels are said to be skinned alive, and sold for a dollar each—they say that if the skin is removed after death it is too tough to be usable.

There is a fair old business in bird skins, and firms, mainly in West Germany, are willing to supply skins of all sorts to taxidermists. Their lists include species that are protected and name birds from all over the world. Birds of paradise skins are exported from Indonesia to countries throughout South East Asia so that they can be mounted as up-market souvenirs. Since they are expensive, mounted birds of paradise are much sought after in that part of the world—an area which firmly believes in ostentation and the display of wealth.

But even though 3,000,000 eel skins a month sounds a lot, this figure is small compared with reptile skins that are used for wallets and briefcases, belts and watch straps. The trouble with reptile skins is that it takes a remarkable customs man to decide whether they come from a legitimately farmed or hunted animal, or from an endangered species when the two types are mixed in a consignment arriving at a port. Not all such skins are traded openly and in September 1985 a hidden consignment of snake skins was discovered in southern India as it was being loaded onto a ship for Singapore. The shipment was said to be comprised of 400 tins of cashew nuts, but when they were opened, in fact only 140 of the tins contained nuts. The remainder were packed with snake skins, with added pebbles and sand to make up the weight. And if you think that a few cans of skins hardly seems worth the effort, you might be surprised to know that the lot was worth US$1.6 million.

Not so long ago most of the snakeskins used in the manufacture of luxury leather goods came from pythons and boas, and also cobras. The scene is now changing as pythons and boas disappear, and as enforcement officers become more adept at identifying species. Snakes with a bold pattern are fairly easy to spot. Your problems start when there is no pattern at all to help you. So nowadays, in addition to those three groups of snakes, Elephant Trunk Snakes, sea snakes and rat snakes are also being used. But more and more of the reptile skins that one sees are from marine turtles, monitor lizards and crocodiles.

The Directory of Crocodilian Farming Operations was published in December 1985. It gives details of more than 152 farms, in 24 countries, who claim a stock of over 160,000 animals. Most of these establishments are without doubt dead straight, but I met a dealer recently who had several dozen wild-caught crocodiles in stock. Since most of the firm's business was in birds I was surprised, and asked where the crocodiles were going and without any hesitation I was told that they were for the local crocodile farm which bought regularly from this company, and yet this particular farm claimed in publicity literature that it took no animals from the wild.

It is not only good business to breed captive animals when wild stocks are decreasing, but is good conservation also since one is not further depleting natural populations and can, in addition, return animals to the wild from captive stocks. And crocodile farmers, being businessmen, exploit their potential to the utmost. To take one particular establishment as an example, one of the big crocodile farms outside Bangkok offers a variety of entertainments for the tourist and it is vigorously promoted in all the tourist literature. It is a good job that there are other things to see than the crocodiles as they are not the most exciting beasts in the world from the visitor's point of view. The reality of a crocodile farm is pretty squalid. There is pen after concrete pen containing a small pond full of 'Brown Windsor Soup', and a heap of motionless crocodiles. One lot of such enclosures holds foot-long reptiles, the second lot houses animals twice that size, the third, three-foot-long crocs and so on until you come to a large enclosure full of monsters. There are even pens for 'seconds'— crocodiles with no tails, or missing feet or malformed jaws, or all three.

And that's it!

Occasionally one of them will clamber all over his friends and drop into the water with a splash, or another will haul itself lethargically back onto the concrete from the pond, but once you've got over the astonishment of seeing 30,000 crocodiles, that's it. Of course, the idea of letting you see all these animals is that you then can't resist the idea of buying something made from crocodile skin, so you rush off to the souvenir soup to buy a briefcase at a 'special price just for you', or if you're really sick, a stuffed hatchling or a keyring with the foot of a baby croc hanging from it.

So for your further delectation and entertainment, ladies and gentlemen, the Samutprakan Crocodile Farm presents . . . a zoo. There are several surprisingly good aviaries displaying Asian birds, fairly well labelled, and a few Victorian cages full of cramped, paranoid mammals, and a gibbon island. Gibbons are super, active animals that live in social groups, and an island is a good way to display them. But this gibbon island was competely treeless, planted instead with a number of poles, each with a gibbon-sized kennel on the top. And to each of these was chained a single gibbon. It could climb up and down its pole but each chain was short enough to ensure that it couldn't reach a neighbour.

When the visitor has become bored with all this he can watch the performing elephants, but the highlight of the visit is the crocodile wrestling show. You've never seen such a con in your life! A long concrete island is surrounded by a moat in which live a couple of dozen assorted crocodiles which range in size from about six feet long to about eleven feet. Most of them are pretty scabby, and when you watch the show you begin to understand why. At the time the performance is billed to start a young lad dressed in scarlet pyjamas enters the arena and splashes through the murky water to climb onto the island where he wanders about looking as though he's wondering if he's in the right place. Eventually he picks up a short length of bamboo and trudges through the water again to grab a young crocodile by the tail which he drags backwards until he plonks it on the island. Everyone laughs. He begins to repeat the process with another, but the first, having done all this before and not being stagestruck takes the opportunity to slope off unobtrusively back into the water. Everyone laughs again and the ringmaster mutters in Thai under his breath what I take to mean, 'Oh dear, he's gone back in the water.' Anyway, everyone who hears thinks it is funny. The second crocodile, now in centre stage, has its top jaw hauled open

This crocodile farm near Bangkok has a stock of 30,000 animals (W. Newing)

and tapped with a stick so that it closes with a loud 'clock'. This time everyone 'oohs'. The move is obviously popular so it is repeated ad nauseam, with this and other crocodiles, who are prodded and pushed, and who are obviously most reluctant. They just sit where they are waiting for the end of the performance. The climax of the show is 'The Large Crocodile'. Not so many liberties are taken with this one and it is too heavy to haul around, but by dint of much prodding and shouting it is eventually induced to climb onto the island and 'clock' its jaws a few times. Then the star of the show opens the animal's mouth and sticks his head in before ending the act by lying along his partner's back and waving to the crowd. Everyone cheers. I watched the audience during this show. The Asians loved it. The Westerners either looked totally bored or faintly embarrassed. But it was noticeable that after the show the souvenir shop did increased trade, which is what it was all about after all.

I didn't find the place a lot of fun, but the bit that bothered me most was that by the exit there are kept several animals with which the visitor can pose for a photograph. There is a placid, old Reticulate Python, and a baby chimp, and most impressive of all, a full-grown Tiger. He looked magnificent, lying in a sort

Chained to its pole this gibbon cannot reach the others that share its island (W. Newing)

of summerhouse with the teenage girl who was his keeper. The Tiger had a chain from the wall attached to his collar, and from a distance I thought that it looked inadequate to restrain a belligerent duck, and I thought that either the Tiger was quite exceptionally tame or that the proprietors were irresponsible. Naïve, of course, I should have realised nothing is what it seems in the East. The animal was lying on a bed of straw and as I approached I was cajoled by the keeper to take a photo. 'Tiger very tame,' she assured me.

That Tiger wasn't going to hurt anyone. Its feet were simply floppy stumps half hidden by the straw. It couldn't even stand. I should have taken a photograph but I felt too sick and felt I had to at least make a show of not encouraging the practice.

Poor Tiger, I could walk away from the place. He literally couldn't.

The majority of crocodiles at that particular farm were of two species, the Siamese Crocodile and the Saltwater Crocodile. Most of the skins (apart from those used within the country) go to Japan, or to Italy or France. The skins of the latter animal are also exported from Jakarta to Japan. Indonesia says that the trade is declining, but figures from Japan show that this is not so, and this is one of the problems inherent in the trade, namely that figures are generally obtained from either the dealers themselves or from official sources, often customs departments, and in many countries both groups of people will happily cook the books if it is in their interest to do so. Doubts arise when the figures from the exporting country fail to tally with those of the importers. Take as an example the figures for 1983. Japan claimed to import about 19,000 kilos of skins (and assume a minimum skin weight of 1 kilo), while Indonesia says that it exported

650 skins. I know I'm bad at maths but that doesn't look right to me.

Throughout the world the legal trade in crocodile skins involves about six species, to a total of about 2,000,000 skins annually. Of these, about three-quarters are of a single species, the South American Spectacled Caiman, but it has been estimated that at least another million caiman skins, despite protection from the law, leave Bolivia, Brazil and Paraguay each year. In the summer of 1985, Mendal Hermanos, a firm in Colombia, was fined just over US$6,000

Performing elephants at the crocodile farm are of far more interest to the local people than to the tourists, who generally walk past

Crocodile wrestling seems to be popular with everyone except the crocodiles (W. Newing)

for the illegal export of animal skins worth an estimated US$32,600,000.

Many South American skins end up in the USA, but they certainly do not travel a direct route. From Brazil, whence a lot of them originate, the skins are taken by small boat either to the north-eastern border of Bolivia or to the Leticia peninsula in Colombia. They again travel, often overland, to the nearest port whence they are shipped to Panama where the consignments are consolidated to be sent by sea, mainly to Italy. In that country they are processed and made up into handbags or whatever, for sale in the USA. The finished items are extremely expensive and come complete with 'designer labels'. Even some of the best-known manufacturers are not averse to handling illegal skins and have been fined in the USA for this type of offence. I was amused to see someone recently in an office of one of the world's best-known conservation bodies not only wearing a lizard skin watch strap, but also looking through a ring binder which was covered in crocodile skin.

It seems to me that more people are wearing reptile skin products nowadays than for quite some time, and I find this surprising in an age where hardly anyone in the Western world can fail to be aware of the problems and pressures on the flora and fauna with which we share the globe.

But the odd thing is that when one starts to investigate the fur trade, although there are heaps and heaps of spotted cat skins being traded in the Third World countries, both as skins and as coats, it is very rare actually to find someone in the consumer countries wearing one. The climate has changed since the war so that what was once thought glamorous and opulent is now looked upon with disgust, so that the people who might be inclined to wear such furs no longer do so for fear of abuse; but clearly the things are being sold somewhere.

I went to a press launch for a conservation campaign in 1985 that was attended by Prince Charles, Sir David Attenborough and everyone who is anyone in the conservation world. And because one of the aims of the event was to raise money, tickets had been sent to a lot of wealthy people who turned up to hobnob with the mighty. I had to leave early and when I went to collect my coat the cloakroom was full of expensive furs. There were no spotted cats but plenty of sable and mink.

The world's largest consumer of wild cat skins is the Federal Republic of Germany, where in contrast to Great Britain you can go into a shop and buy a spotted cat coat off the rack quite openly. Stores in towns such as Munich have a large range of furs, and throughout the country you can buy everything from pussy cat to Leopard. Brazil, Colombia, Argentina, Bolivia, Paraguay and probably Venezuela are known to forbid the export of cat skins and these are the countries from which skins have traditionally been exported.

The word 'probably' in the last sentence is not there accidentally and should be noted as it encapsulates very nicely the whole business of conservation legislation. In so many countries, even where there are known to be such laws, trying to pin down civil servants and enforcement officials is like trying to read an airmail copy of *The Times* in a high wind. The whole conversation is punctuated by 'Ah, but' and, 'Well, you see'. Nothing is ever what it seems and I have known people who, after talking to dealers and officials, and looking at premises with stock for sale, have been convinced that nothing illegal is going on even when surrounded by forbidden goods and in the face of overwhelming evidence to the contrary.

Double the number of Tiger Cat skins were exported from Paraguay in the year following the banning of all wildlife for commercial trade, and these, together with Ocelots, Margays, Geoffroy's Cat and some Jaguar are the animals most under pressure for the export fur trade, though one should not forget those that are killed for the domestic market. In every single South American country one can buy, for example, Ocelot skins and these never enter the official trade figures.

The reason that most spotted furs come from South America is that it is the only large chunk of rain forest that has not been plundered to any extent, though this is changing now and it won't be long before populations of all these animals are in real trouble.

Leopard and Cheetah skins still find their way out of Africa, and throughout Asia Tigers, Leopards, Clouded Leopards, Snow Leopards and Leopard Cats are still killed with depressing frequency. I went to New Market in Calcutta to see what skins are available these days. An old friend of mine, David Whiting, had stirred things up a few years ago when he had managed to get some dealers in illegal skins arrested after posing as a potential buyer, and I was interested to see if anything was still openly on display. It wasn't. Several shops had ancient, moth-eaten old Leopard and Tiger skins rolled up in corners, and the odd mangy wallet that they half heartedly tried to sell me but nothing else. It was obvious that this stock had all been around since David's raid, and indeed, once they saw that I wasn't impressed with what was on offer all the dealers admitted that it was old stock, but despite my hinting that I was interested in such things no information was forthcoming. Until, that is, I went to a grotty little stall that hadn't seen a lick of paint or a good clean for a million years, and which was lit by a flickering, fluorescent tube which emitted a faint khaki light due to an encrustation of fly droppings—light just enough to throw the shadows of the many cobwebs onto the wall. This magnificent emporium revelled in the name 'Lovely Corner', and here I struck gold, or at any rate fur, when I spoke to a

Crocodile skins are sold as leather and much of the meat is used as food (D. Whiting)

man about buying fur. He politely explained that he couldn't possibly display skins as it was forbidden, but if I was seriously interested he would take me to his home (which also turned out to be his factory), to show me his stock. Upon my agreeing he called a young boy from another stall and asked me to follow him. The communication network of these people in the markets is quite something because after dodging through the shoppers after my guide, past the fruit stalls and the site of the old bird market, I arrived near a Post Office where the boy pointed to a waiting taxi. The Sikh driver leaned out of his window.

'Come, Sahib,' he called softly, 'I taking you to see Tiger skins.' I can never understand why people go to great expense to discover the thrill of canoeing down the Amazon on a skateboard or leaping off a mountain top with a hang glider to land in a river full of piranhas, when you can experience the same heart-stopping fear by going for a ride in a Calcutta taxi. Eventually I opened my eyes and metaphorically took my foot off the brake to find that we had arrived at the Tiljalan Road factory of the man I met at 'Lovely Corner'.

Within a couple of minutes he had pulled out a dozen or so brand new Leopard skins which were in superb condition, and one Tiger skin (complete with head) that was a bit scruffy although it was a new skin. It was the only one in stock, I was told, but if I cared to return the next day he could have some more for me to look at. If I wanted a quantity I could have them at a special price. I don't know how he thought I was going to smuggle the things, but obviously someone must buy them.

In Indonesia too, Tigers are hunted for their skins, the hunters being very careful to strangle the tigers so that the skins are not damaged. This is achieved

Leopard and Tiger skins
can be easily bought in
India if you know where
to go (J. Nichol)

by trapping the animals with a noose (though this is not done too often as the animal can do itself a fair bit of damage while fighting the noose) or by trapping it in a cage to prevent movement and then actually strangling it by inserting a noose through the bars.

I hunted through the shops in Singapore but could find no furs anywhere. I am sure that there must be some, though I expect most of them go for export. I'd love to know where the Tiger and Leopard skins from Thailand go. Someone did a survey and discovered that over 300 shops in Bangkok alone sold claws and teeth from these animals, but apart from the odd handbag and wallet there were no skins to be found.

In New York an American colleague was researching this subject for me, posing as the girlfriend of a wealthy man who wanted to buy her a fur coat. At each showroom she was shown the same range of perfectly legal furs, and each time she explained that she didn't know anything about furs but wanted 'something different'. And at every place she drew a blank until in one particular warehouse she came across a single full-length spotted coat hanging on a rack in a corner. She wasn't sure whether it was a Jaguar or a Leopard but when she expressed interest she was firmly steered away while the salesman explained that it was a one-off job for a special order. When she looked in that direction again it had gone.

Greece is a funny country from the point of view of the fur trade because you can go into any one of a number of shops in Athens and buy a Leopard skin coat quite openly; the country specialises in work on bits and pieces of fur. The industry is centred on a little town in the top left-hand corner of Greece, known as Kastoria. Here in this old-fashioned little place by the side of Lake Kastorias it seems that the whole community is involved in this peculiar industry. It is odd because it employs all the substandard pelts, rejected in the great international fur auctions, and also buys in remnants left after the manufacture of garments. Here they are all gathered together and the usable pieces trimmed from the rubbish and turned into a variety of small articles from fur collars to wallets and handbags. It must be successful because the industry employs a lot of people.

Leopard skins can still be bought under the counter (D. Whiting)

The other interesting place with regard to furs is Afghanistan. One doesn't think of this backward country in terms of furs but it has a thriving trade turning furs into garments. However, since Afghanistan isn't rich in fashionable fur-bearing animals it imports quite a number from India and Pakistan, mostly illegally. Being where it is, the country inevitably processes some skins of the now very rare Snow Leopards, and what with this and the considerable numbers of less endangered animals that are killed to supply the trade, there are moves afoot to try and stop the industry. The Afghani government says that it is happy to do this provided that alternative work can be found to provide employment for the villagers, so feasibility studies are at the moment going on to see if Muskrats or something similar are suitable and can be bred in captivity to replace the wild animals.

I suppose that everyone must be aware that there is a trade in animal skins, but other ways in which animals are exploited are legion and often unbelievable. Would you believe that if you go into a tourist shop in Rio de Janeiro you can buy a dolphin's eyeball as a souvenir? You can even phone off an order for one, quote your credit card number and it will arrive by post. One dealer has been quoted as saying that he can supply 500 within a week, which means the death of 250 Amazon River Dolphins—and it's not even as though there is any money in the trade. The eyes only cost a couple of dollars each.

And if you think that is an unlikely tale, what about the story of musk? The Musk Deer is a small deer that lives in inaccessible places well up in the mountain ranges of Asia. The poor old male has a gland on his abdomen filled with gunge that has a high value in the perfume industry. For this the deer are killed, even though nowadays the stuff can, and is, synthesised. Purists say that only the real thing is suitable for the very best perfumes. Other mortals can't tell the difference. To supply this trade about 4,000 male Musk Deer are killed annually, mainly illegally. But when you are hunting musk it is difficult to tell from a distance whether an animal is carrying a musk pod, or even whether an animal is a male. The result is that more of these very shy animals are killed than need be, and it has been estimated that up to half of the Himalayan population could be killed annually. A scheme has now been proposed which suggests that local people could trap the animals instead of killing them, remove the musk and release them again. This idea certainly hasn't come from anyone with practical experience of Musk Deer. All deer are touchy animals, even the Red Deer that are farmed in Scotland and they must be one of the most placid of all deer, but to try and do what is suggested to the highly strung, hysterical Musk Deer is asking for trouble. I can't see it working and nor can any of the deer-y friends to whom I've spoken, which is sad because I'm all for ideas which enable wildlife to be harvested without putting the existence of wild populations in jeopardy.

When I was researching material for this book I came across a brand new smuggling story that I had not heard of before. As everybody knows, it is now against the law to import any mammal into Great Britain unless it goes into quarantine for six months. This is a common-sense law to protect us from the introduction of rabies which is such a terrible disease that you would think that no one would ever contemplate taking risks over it, yet people do, and by far the worst offenders are those wretched pet owners who enter the country with their cat or dog and either don't want to pay for the quarantine, or can't bear to be parted from the animal for six months. Periodically someone is caught with an animal in a handbag as they come through customs control at the airport, but you can bet that some get through.

One can imagine how worrying it must be for your amateur criminal trying to sneak Fido into the country, trying to keep him quiet and hoping that he won't wriggle at the critical moments. To relieve his owner of this worry there is now a way of paying someone to bring an animal into the country illegally. I first discovered this when a friend of someone I know, who lives in Majorca, came across the system. There it is apparently well established that if you are an expatriate returning to England you can arrange for your pet to be taken back for you. When I started to ferret about I discovered that there were certain people in Belgium who would do the job for a consideration. I don't know what happens between Spain (or anywhere else for that matter) and Belgium—whether you need to arrange for that step to be done by someone else in the chain, or whether you take it to Belgium yourself, but from that country I was told that the whole thing was so well established that one only had to approach the people who operated fishing boats and other small craft out of Ostende in any of the small towns along the coast to find someone who would do the job. I asked the Ministry of Agriculture, Fisheries and Food if they had heard of the story but they pooh-poohed it. 'Oh, I'm sure the odd animal comes in secretly, but if there was anything more I'm certain we would have heard of it.' Where have I heard that before?

I felt that the attitude was a bit naïve, because if you think about it, this is an obvious market that would find a supplier sooner or later, but without any more information or contacts I was sceptical about finding a smuggler easily in Belgium within two or three days. And then I thought that if the tale was true, that time scale must be realistic because the average, frantic pet owner, would probably work on that basis—arrive in Belgium and spend that amount of time hunting for someone. After that I guessed that most would give up and either

abandon the idea or try and bring the animal in themselves. The reality was simple. Most of the people approached said that they thought it could be done, but they didn't themselves know anyone who could help. In time persistence paid off, and in one café there were several people who would be willing to undertake the project for £1,000. Attempts to discover where an animal would be landed came to nothing. The pet would be delivered to the owner's home— no one was saying any more than that, but East Anglia is such a maze of small rivers and creeks that I can't imagine that landing a dog from a small boat would present much of a problem. As long as there is someone who wants something badly enough there will be someone else who is willing to meet that demand.

The tusked male Musk Deer is shot to provide the perfume industry with musk (D. Whiting)

A trapper of Musk Deer setting a snare (D. Whiting)

6. The American Scene

The illegal animal trade into the United States is such that it needs a chapter to itself. Most of what is smuggled into the States is birds, and most of the birds are parrots, for though plenty of Americans keep other animals, the country has gone parrot mad.

It all began, so they say, with a television series in which the hero, 'Biretta', had a pet cockatoo. There had always been parrot fanciers but the series started the man in the street keeping parrots and other birds. Nowadays hundreds of thousands are imported each year. Most of them arrive quite legitimately through the hosts of importers, most of whom are found in California and Florida, but there is a steady trade across the border from Mexico.

I had read reports in the press about the problems that America had with illegal immigrants from Mexico and all the measures that were being taken to curtail these visitors. There were stories of border patrols and wire fences and sophisticated television cameras fitted with image intensifiers to record activity during the hours of darkness. The reality is laughably different. In places, the river along the border, the Rio Grande, is little more than a widish stream, easily fordable, and made even easier by small stone dams across it at intervals. People cross readily with little hindrance and the border guards know. They stand on the north bank and explain that the little groups of Mexicans across the river are intending to cross as soon as the patrol has moved on, and that is exactly what happens. They depart and the immigrants quickly cross the river. The Mexican border guards are even more accommodating. They deliberately turn their backs on the groups as they approach the river. And if people can cross the river that easily, imagine how simple it is to take birds across, and that is what happens all the way along the border. Brownsville in Texas is well known by the bird smugglers as this is the most easterly point for the operations. Birds are taken across in this area from Matamoros in Mexico for the eastern half of the USA. Another acknowledged crossing is from Cuidad Juarez to El Paso at the State border between Texas and New Mexico, and at Nogales, where, I was told by a border guard, the parrot smuggling operation on the Mexican side is run by a senior army officer in the garrison in Nogales. Birds from here are destined for the dealers in California.

The staff of the United States Department of Agriculture and the Fish and Wildlife Service along the border are perfectly aware of what happens and constantly try to combat the trade but the truth is that the border is just far too long, too easy to cross and there are nothing like the personnel to be effective. There are some USDA and Customs officials who are extremely keen on trying to stop this trade. They are as efficient as they can be and some of them have made their names by combating the bird smugglers, but there are limits to their effectiveness. They rely to a great extent on tip offs. These almost always come from someone within the business, and at one time whenever a consignment was intercepted the birds were killed by officialdom, but when this came into the open advance information on smuggling operations stopped. People who know and care enough about the birds to want the trade stopped were not willing to talk if the end result was going to be the death of the birds. So the government changed their policy of mass destruction, and instead built huge warehouses at points along the border and in some of the towns where the trade was big business, and staffed them with bird keepers. Today when a smuggler is caught, his birds are put into quarantine in one of these buildings, and after a suitable period has elapsed they are moved to other holding cages. A good idea so far, but then it gets silly. Periodically the birds are auctioned, and very often they are sold for knockdown prices to the dealers and collectors, and it is not unknown for one dealer who knows that a competitor has an illegal consignment arriving to shop him to the law, then when the birds are auctioned he can often buy them for a tiny fraction of the price they would have cost him to import, and without any of the hassle. And another thing that happens is that the original importer can have the birds bought at auction for him, so although he has paid for the birds and paid a fine, he now has a stock of legal birds for which otherwise he might not have been able to obtain a permit. It's a crazy situation, but goodness knows what a sensible answer is.

The losses involved are terrific because first of all, most of the parrots thus imported are youngsters that have been removed from their nest. This has very often meant the death of one or both parents which are frequently killed either for food, or plumage, or both, and not infrequently the chopping down of the nesting tree as well to get at the birds, which can result in the death of some or all of the chicks. The babies are taken by Amerindian villagers to be hand-reared, and anyone who has tried to hand-rear birds knows how many die, but eventually the survivors are taken away and start their long journey from South America to Mexico, usually overland in cramped conditions, so that by the time they arrive in San Diego or Miami only the strongest are still alive. But the poor old parrots' problems are then still not over. The dedicated aviculturist and conservationist does not want a bird that is too tame since it is likely to breed much more readily if it is not. The person who wants a single bird for his apartment, however, wants a pet bird, a tame bird, and more than that a bird that will perform all sorts of tricks to impress his friends. So to supply this chap and everyone else similarly inclined, many American pet shops specialise in that sort of product. To watch a healthy adult parrot being brainwashed into condition by the trade is not fun.

A parrot is not a domestic animal and has not been reared through generation after generation to fit in with the whims and living conditions of a human being. It is wild and, therefore, is quite likely to object to doing things to order, and if it does object it can make an appreciable hole in a finger. Remember that some species open Brazil nuts with their beaks and one or two can even chew through chainlink fencing if they set their minds to it, so in order to ensure that a parrot isn't going to do this to the owner it is put through many—what do the Russians call them?—Re-education Lessons, by an unscrupulous dealer.

Once again the demand for tame birds is so great and the supply from the wild is getting more difficult to obtain that nowadays there are quite a lot of establishments that are breeding parrots on a commercial basis, so that they can supply birds that have been lovingly hand-reared from the moment of hatching.

It is not surprising that large numbers of birds are being imported illegally when import restrictions render free trade ever more difficult, not to mention export restriction as the number of countries clamping down on the removal of native wildlife increases year by year. The cost is also an important factor to consider because although the actual cost of importation is not colossal, the necessary legal quarantine period puts the price up enormously. None the less plenty of birds are imported legally. There are currently 81 USDA approved quarantine facilities for commercial importations of birds, located as follows:

39 in California   7 in Louisiana
18 in Florida   6 in New York
2 in Hawaii   2 in Texas
7 in Illinois

The whole animal business is a funny one, because while there are huge numbers of birds entering the USA from Mexico, another trade is taking place in the opposite direction. I thought that it had stopped years ago but I recently discovered that the thing was still going as actively as ever. The problem is that the USA prohibits the export of many species of birds that have a commercial value elsewhere so what happens is that during the migration periods, when such birds are flying south, mile upon mile of mist nets are set up in Mexico just across the border from the States. Then smoke bombs or fires are lit all along this line but on the northern side of the river and far enough back to ensure that there will be a number of birds between the smoke and the border. Given a wind that is blowing towards Mexico all the birds in the way of the smoke take off and head south to get out of it. They land up in the mist nets and are caged for export. Before me I have a photograph of a consignment that was intercepted near Brownsville which included Indigo Buntings, Lazuli Buntings and cardinals—all North American species.

This poor old parrot can live for weeks in this cage till it ends up in the West (W. Newing)

It would be wrong to think that conservation is the only reason for forbidding the importation of animals. One of the best reasons of all must be to prevent the spread of diseases that can be transmitted to man by other species of animals, and rabies is perhaps the best example of this. It is often thought that only dogs carry rabies but in theory any mammal could do that. Bats certainly do, and rabid Vampire Bats occur in South America. Rabies is not the only such disease. Old World monkeys carry an organism known as Virus B which causes encephalitis in humans, and the USA is one of the largest importers of non-human primates for research.

It is incorrect to think that mammals are the only animals which can be responsible for the transmission of disease. Birds are known to carry ornithosis which is not necessarily lethal to man, but is jolly unpleasant all the same. Not so many years ago the condition was known as psittacosis as it was thought that only parrots (psittacine birds) could cause the disease, but it is now recognised that any avian species can do that and it is said that 90 per cent of the pigeons in Trafalgar Square, London suffer from ornithosis, so next time you pose for a photograph with Landseer's lions behind you and a row of birds up your arm just remember that.

In December 1985 the American Medical Association published a report on the incidence of *Salmonella* in terrapins that were being exported from the USA. Each year between 3,000,000 and 4,000,000 Red Eared Terrapins are exported from the south-eastern corner of the country, and of the sample tested for the report, 89 per cent were found to be contaminated with *Salmonella pomona*. The various serotypes of the genus can cause salmonellosis in humans and indeed death. In Puerto Rico, 12 to 17 per cent of salmonellosis cases reported in infants could be traced to the handling of pet terrapins.

Another excellent reason for controlling the importation of exotic animals and plants is that when escapes occur, a species might well become established and once that happens there can be all sorts of unforeseen results. Twenty-five different kinds of exotic birds have now become established in the USA and some are beginning to be a real problem. Once animals are released deliberately or accidentally they might do very well. I can't do better than quote Greta Nilsson, who explains that an exotic species may undergo a population explosion due to an absence of factors that held it in check in its native country. Then two things can happen: the first is that the newcomer takes over the ecological niche occupied by a native animal to the detriment of that animal, and secondly the exotic might do so well that in time populations of suitable native food plants can start to decline and agricultural crops suffer. So much so that there is legislation in the States that prohibits the entry of some birds which are classed as injurious, and the movement of others from one state to another.

Public Enemy Number One throughout Africa is the Red Billed Quelea. It is a seed-eating bird about the size of a House Sparrow. In the natural way of things queleas feed on wild grass seeds but when thoughtful people started to plant acre after acre with tasty corn and millet crops the birds would be less than human if they didn't take advantage of the feast. Nowadays there are quite a lot of queleas and a flight of 2 million or 3 million is not uncommon. One of the largest flocks covered 40 square miles and contained an estimated 25 million birds. Throughout their range they are attacked fiercely by every device available to man and large numbers are killed. In West Africa, 80 million birds were destroyed in a few months but it made no difference at all to the overall numbers. Just think what would occur if they discovered the corn-growing prairies of the USA. It could happen—just look at the rabbits in Australia, nowadays present in such numbers that fences have been erected which stretch for hundreds of miles, just to keep them out of certain parts of the country.

South American Quaker Parakeets are regularly imported in large quantities into Florida, New York and California as pets and they are beginning to become established. In Argentina there is a bounty on Quaker Parakeets where they are regarded like the Red Billed Quelea, as an agricultural pest. A quarter of a million of the birds are killed a year but the Quakers continue to thrive.

Over the last 25 years consignments of birds have been arriving with such regularity at most large airports that in the surrounding areas you can always find exotics if you look hard enough. Miami Airport has a very healthy population of foreign birds, and so does London and Singapore and Brussels. Next time you have time to kill at an airport, forget the duty free shops and do a bit of bird spotting instead.

Not too many mammals appear to enter the USA illegally these days although some of the South American primates certainly do for the pet trade, and from some broad hints that were dropped in my direction I suspect that the odd South American cat such as the Ocelot and the Margay occasionally turn up as well. Certainly one dealer that I spoke to in Indonesia said that there was a very small but regular demand from Miami for young Leopard Cats from South Eastern Asia, and all the Asian dealers had stocks of these delightful kittens. One of the problems with smuggling mammals is that an awful lot of them are big, active and noisy just when you don't want them to be. For the reptile smuggler these are problems about which he doesn't have to worry. Herpetology flourishes in the USA and though I know that small numbers of reptiles and amphibians (conveniently known as herptiles as a collective noun in the USA) are exported illegally, I'm not sure how much of a trade there is in the other direction, although I did come upon a case in 1985 when a student in Michigan was driving back from Mexico to his home. Customs officials at the border had been tipped off that he was bringing in some herptiles illegally, but though the men went through his luggage carefully they found nothing and let him go. One of the inspectors felt uneasy and had a hunch that there was something wrong so he telephoned the Highway Patrol at one of the State borders and the car was again stopped, and this time it was discovered that small containers full of animals had been carefully inserted into tubes and jars containing haircream and toothpaste.

The reason for the small numbers of herptiles that leave the USA illegally is due to the considerable demand for these animals within the country, which has meant that dealers have been able to get high enough prices for their stock without having to go through all the palaver of exporting them. A friend of mine in Essex received a letter from Customs and Excise some time ago which told him that they had intercepted and opened a parcel from Florida addressed to him. The contents were stated to be chocolates. On opening the box it became apparent that the contents were not sweeties but two Indigo Snakes which they confiscated.

Some years ago someone I know who was particularly interested in parrots decided to go to Tahiti for a holiday. Each year he made a point of parrot watching in a different, exotic part of the world and he invariably came back bubbling with tales of all the goodies he had seen. On his return from the Pacific

I asked him how he had got on.

'Terrible,' he complained. 'All I saw were mynahs and bulbuls, all Asian stuff. I didn't see any native birds at all.'

'No parrots?' I enquired.

'Only bloody Indian Ringnecked Parakeets.'

One of the troubles is that very often the people whose job it is to enforce legislation have no knowledge of nor interest in the subject. As politicians or civil servants they are only doing a job and a nice example of how this happens, even in a Western country such as the USA, is the case of the Grand Cayman Parrot. In 1982 G. Ray Arnett was the Assistant Secretary of the Interior for Fish and Wildlife and he was responsible for the protection of endangered species in the USA. In October that year he was in the Cayman Islands where the last couple of hundred Grand Cayman Parrots are fighting a rearguard action against extinction. An American newspaper reported on 11 October that he shot two of the parrots, and the same report stated that he also has kept the Sea Otter off the endangered species list and wants to convert the world's only winter refuge of the Whooping Crane into a commercial development.

Even with laws and law enforcement agencies tightening up, when it comes to illegal animals it is often more lucrative to deal in the commodity than in, say, drugs. If a consignment of smuggled parrots is caught it is confiscated, and the offender might very well be fined, though it must be said that occasionally someone does end up in jail for a bit. Gordon Cooke was a bird smuggler who lives in Leicestershire, England and is the only person in the British Isles to have been imprisoned for animal smuggling. He got two years. Drug smugglers on the other hand land infinitely longer sentences. In some countries when a drug smuggler ends up in prison they virtually throw away the key, and in Malaysia and Singapore there is the death penalty for drug smugglers who are caught.

This state of affairs has resulted in more than one drug smuggler turning to the animal trade instead, where the profits are nearly as high but the risks are infinitely lower. And another thing that has started to happen is that some drug smugglers are also involved with animal dealerships so that the shipments of the two are occasionally combined. The drugs involved are predominantly heroin and cocaine but I can remember back in the 1960s, consignments of snakes leaving India for the USA as a cover for drugs. In those days the reptiles were shipped loose on a bed of dead leaves inside wooden boxes, and in amongst the leaves were bits of marijuana. The snakes were often cobras to dissuade customs men from prodding about inside the box, but there wasn't much danger of their finding anything in those days. Customs officials like everyone else were much more innocent then.

I feel certain that the practice of smuggling drugs with animals must be wider than anyone knows, though the method can only be used for small consignments. I tried sounding out dealers in Asia on the subject but only one or two made non-committal noises and no one was saying anything definite, but given the proximity of the Golden Triangle to the animal exporting towns of Thailand and Laos and the fuzzy, confusing borders between those countries and Cambodia as well, I would have thought that there must be something happening.

I was speaking, however, to an Argentinian who worked for a company that exported animals from his country and also had similar business interest in Bolivia. Eventually we got onto the subject of drugs and in time he told me that shipments of animals to the USA sometimes contained drugs. He explained how the best animals for the purpose were either parrots or snakes. In either case the technique was the same. Of the number of animals to be packed in a box a small percentage were killed just prior to export and sealed plastic tubes containing heroin were inserted into the mouth and pushed well down in the gut. The dead bodies were then placed in the box and the live animals packed in the normal fashion. Throughout the journey if the contents were examined it would appear only that a few animals had died on the way and this aroused no suspicion. When he had finished telling me, my informant added, 'But for God's sake don't ever mention this to my boss. He is a very dangerous man.' And he illustrated the point graphically enough to make me gulp a time or two. I afterwards mentioned the name of the boss to various people and without exception they all told me to keep well clear of the man who seems to terrify everyone with whom he comes in contact.

The only other connection I came across regarding the drug trade was a dealer in Germany who said that he had a customer in Miami who always asked him to include in each consignment a few dead birds that were delivered to him the day before it was due to go out. This particular dealer didn't actually know why he had to send the corpses but he could add two and two together to make the several thousand extra dollars he was paid to pack each such consignment. No one mentioned drugs coming into Europe which rather surprised me.

I thought that was the end of the matter, and that nothing further was going to come of it, until I heard from someone who was researching the Californian scene for me. I had asked her to see whether she could discover any connection between animals and drugs. She didn't, but instead when she was visiting the many dealers in the area she found a father and son who ran a combined importing business and pet shop that specialised in, guess what, parrots! She described the two men as decidedly unsavoury and after chatting to them for some time she discovered that their hobby was guns and that between them they had quite a collection. In Britain such a person is decidedly rare but apparently in the States it is a pretty common pastime and being American herself she thought no more about it, but later when she was talking about that particular business with the local Fish and Wildlife Service Inspector she was asked if she had been told about the interest in the guns. Nodding, she asked the reason for the question, and discovered that she had stumbled on the edge of a fascinating tale. Apparently the FWS had first suspected and then actually found out that this particular company was illegally importing parrots from Mexico and the inspector assigned to the case started to build up a file on the subject. During the intermittent surveillance on the couple FWS personnel realised that every so often one or another of the men would drive from San Diego to the border at Nogales where, having crossed over, he would meet a senior army officer who supplied him with the birds which he would bring back and drive home to San Diego. A perfectly ordinary, typical bird smuggling exercise thought everyone, and prepared to move in, until somebody noticed that it was nothing of the sort. Certainly on some days the men would simply go to Nogales, pick up parrots and return, but the business was by no means all one way for on occasion a number of firearms were loaded into the car before departure. Suspicion was aroused when one of the team of watchers wondered why they would want to take guns for a trip on which the car didn't stop long enough for any hunting to be done, and a second point was that even if the man did want to take a rifle in case he came across something to shoot, he certainly didn't need a couple of dozen of the things to bag a bit of meat for the pot. This puzzled everyone until one day it occurred to a particular officer that the guns never came back again across the border. Undercover enquiries on the Mexican side revealed that the guns were smuggled into that country and exchanged for parrots which were then smuggled back. What a profitable enterprise that must have been while it lasted!

Guns and wildlife are alas a common combination. Hunters after trophies tend to fall into three groups—those who have an understanding of conservation and a conscience, and only shoot weak, old or dying specimens of abundant species; those who always want the biggest zebra or the leading bull in the herd—that is the animals that should be left to pass on their genes; and thirdly the hunter that must have an animal that is different to anything that has been killed by their friends—in other words rarities, or if you like, endangered animals. This hunt for rarities leads to bizarre consequences on occasion. There was a case reported in a paper in New Jersey a few years ago where a hunter shot a very special Peregrine Falcon. Cornell University had a captive breeding programme for Peregrines and over the years they had considerable success so that by the time the story broke they had released over 200 birds into the wild. A particular hunter shot one of these birds and had it mounted by a taxidermist complete with leg ring and even the radio transmitter that had been fitted to the bird to enable scientists to trace its movements after release. What a nut! Would you believe such people exist? In the end he was caught and fined $2,000 which quite correctly went to the Peregrine Breeding Fund at Cornell University.

I understand perfectly if someone needs food and goes out to shoot an animal for the pot but to shoot for sport seems daft, and to import and establish a totally alien animal in a country and then artificially rear quantities of the things and then shoot them, as is done with Mongolian Pheasants in Britain, is surely even dafter, but infinitely more reprehensible is the practice of destroying rare animals in the wild for sport. Mind you, even if you are that way inclined you really do not have to bother to go to all the trouble, danger, expense and quite considerable discomfort to get hold of your specimen as there are now businesses that will supply you with a frozen, freshly-killed specimen that you can take to a taxidermist to be mounted to display to your friends. Such firms in Germany are happy to fill the many orders that they receive, particularly they tell me from the USA, the Middle Eastern countries, and Japan. One firm said that they had recently sent Lammergeiers that they had imported from China, to Japan. The great difficulty with obtaining birds for trophies is that if you shoot them you are quite likely to do a fair bit of damage so the Lammergeiers supplied by this firm are guaranteed to be caught live and are then killed by inserting a nail into the back of the skull—voilà, a perfect specimen!

With the enormous legal trade around the world in animals and animal products it is clear that customs officials have difficulty in policing the problem since most of them are not zoologists. There is also an illegal world of plant smugglers, but that is another story. It is to their credit that the customs officials detect as much as they do. One of the advantages that they have is that live animals wriggle and squawk and smugglers need to overcome these inconsiderate habits of their charges. For years bird smugglers had used miles of bandage and surgical tape to immobilise and silence their illicit charges and then someone had the bright idea of trying to smuggle eggs. Eggs are fragile, as you've probably discovered, but otherwise they have a lot going for them. Not only are they silent and motionless but they are small, so provided you can get them through undetected and without finishing up with a pocket full of omelette, you can stick them in an incubator and sit back and wait. Of course it is not really as simple as that but it is being done more and more. In 1985, two men, William Robinson and Jonathan Wood, tried to enter the USA at Los Angeles airport with 27 eggs of rare Australian birds about their clothing. The Americans are great on what they call 'Creative Sentencing' and the technique was used on this occasion when, apart from being put on probation for five years, Robinson and Wood were sentenced to pay for the making of a documentary film on the importance of birds of prey.

The eggs themselves were given to the Los Angeles Zoo. Two hatched into hawk chicks a few weeks later, and this highlights one of the disadvantages of obtaining birds this way—the low rate of hatching success. Still, eggs are cheap and as long as some hatch you've made a profit.

In July 1985, an Australian couple were trying to smuggle birds and eggs into their homeland and were frightened by an in-flight film about quarantine laws so they destroyed the 40 eggs and six young birds that they were carrying. I think it's really enterprising of the airline to show such a film on the plane and it seems a shame that it isn't done more often. A short documentary before the James Bond would be a great idea.

7. The Exotic Food Trade

Previous page: The brains of live monkeys are eaten at secret banquets throughout South East Asia (D. Whiting)

When I was at school we used to laugh ourselves silly at a joke that went like this:

There was a restaurant that boasted that it could serve any dish that a customer could possibly ask for, so one clever-clogs demanded fried elephant steak on toast and the waiter went to fetch it only to return moments later to apologise for the fact that this particular dish could not be supplied.

'Ha ha,' scoffed the diner, 'I suppose you've run out of elephant steak.'

'Oh no, sir,' the waiter responded. 'We have plenty, but the baker hasn't delivered the bread yet to make the toast.'

What was so funny all those years ago was the idea of a restaurant actually selling elephant meat. I've now found that around the world there are restaurants willing to supply enough different varieties of wildlife to stock a zoo. These vary from simple, country restaurants in Third World countries that sell the meat, whether from endangered species or not, quite openly and no one gives it a second thought, to opulent establishments that supply the very rich with the most extraordinary foods, but keep very quiet about it.

The wildlife food trade is an odd one since everyone that eats meat eats wild animals of some sort without even thinking about it. Most of the fish consumed daily are wild animals, as are the prawns and crabs, venison, game and shellfish, and what about frogs' legs that all come from wild animals, mainly from Asia. I mentioned earlier the enormous numbers of frogs that are killed annually to supply the gourmets of the world. It is an appalling trade and fraught with risks for the consumer as the legs, once removed from their owner, are thrown into a bucket of bloody water. By the time it is full, the water is a nice, biological soup, rich in micro-organisms and the legs are frequently packed for freezing directly from this liquid. A year or two ago California banned their importation for a while due to a cholera scare which was traced to them, and sooner or later someone is going to import frogs' legs which are going to cause an awful lot of illness in the diners who eat them; and I will have no sympathy.

Frogs' legs for export are kept in germ soup until frozen (D. Whiting)

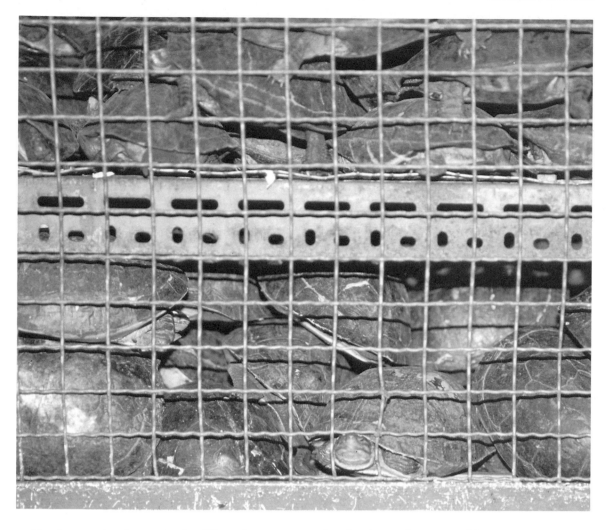

Turtle soup is a luxury in the West that most people who do not know would probably find acceptable, yet all marine turtles are protected and their meat arrives in regular quantities from countries that are both signatories to CITES as well as from those that are not. In 1981 Germany alone imported the meat from about 28,000 turtles (though it must be added that the Republic's figures have gone down appreciably since then), but what is often not realised is that figures like this do not reveal the entire trade as a lot of animals are sold in markets around the world for local consumption and they do not, therefore, enter the trade statistics. In the markets of the West Indies, South America and Africa and the bazaars of Asia one can often find these unfortunate reptiles lying upside down and helpless, awaiting slaughter. In countries which have Chinese populations, marine turtles are to be found side by side with freshwater species, and cages in Hong Kong, Thailand and Singapore are packed with great heaps of small, dehydrated terrapins while larger, more aggressive animals live in plastic bowls covered with wire grids.

Many of the animals for sale in food markets are being traded despite legislation which is supposed to prevent their sale, and usually neither stallholder nor customer realises this, but such ignorance is not always the case.

Terrapins in a Singapore market destined to become turtle soup (W. Newing)

Some years ago a visit to the fish market at Cayenne, the capital of French Guiana in South America, revealed caiman meat for sale. There were two species available, the Spectacled Caiman and the Black Caiman. At the time the Black Caiman was strictly protected whilst the other was not, and the stall holders knew this perfectly well, so whenever a complete carcass was to be sold the head was always removed, as without it identification was almost imposs-ible. The Spectacled Caimans had their heads, and if you asked what they were you were told that they were Spectacled Caiman. When you asked the identification of the adjacent, headless crocodile, you were told, 'Oh, that's a Spectacled Caiman too, but I've sold the head.' Good zoologists, those market men—anywhere else they would have simply said, 'Caiman.'

Common Iguanas are sold throughout South America as food (W. Newing)

The food markets of the Far East sell the usual chickens and so on in addition to the turtles, and depending on the season and the time of day one also finds bunches of small 'rice birds', plucked and tied together by the feet. They are finches of various species and are sold alongside similar bunches of waders, though without feathers the birds are not easy to identify. At Thonburi market in Thailand, when the trains arrive early in the morning from the south, they sometimes bring with them baskets of frozen plucked parrots. Fried or roast squirrels are for sale everywhere and great heaps of half-skinned frogs lie on glistening banana leaves in markets throughout the region. Sometimes there are lizards, and occasionally the eggs of sea turtles or snakes. In the small, distant towns in Indonesia may still be found monitor lizards tied to a length of bamboo, seeming to embrace it with all four feet until one sees the string, biting into the limbs to hold them in place, and on the other side of the world Common Iguanas, like the monitors, are sold as food with their legs tied tightly together behind their backs. And everywhere are to be found crabs of all species, again tied up so that they can neither escape nor inflict a painful nip on a potential customer.

In Thailand the crabs are a creamy white and brilliant purple, in South America they are green with red claws and legs and in most other parts of the world they are a muddy brown. The amount of crabs eaten annually must be enormous, far more than the few Horseshoe Crabs that are to be found occa-sionally in the bazaars. Pigeons of all species are eaten regularly, and the markets in the Chinatowns of Asia are positively zoological. There are egrets and snakes and monkeys though sometimes one needs to hunt to find them on display.

One of the best bits of meat I have ever tasted came from a Paca in Surinam. A Paca is a sort of giant, spotty Guinea Pig from South America. Most available rodents are eaten in that continent (and in Africa) and tapir is readily eaten when it is available throughout South America, though I've never found it on a menu in the only other place in which it occurs, South East Asia. Venison is eaten just about everywhere though I've not seen it in markets, only in restaurants.

You would think that with all the mammals and birds and so on available for food, there wouldn't be much call for insects—but you'd be wrong. In some places one can find heaps of Great Diving Beetles, ants in chocolate, fried bumble bees, and mountains of crispy, fried locusts. The last are sold as a snack by roadside vendors in Thailand though eating them is not recommended. There has been a locust eradication programme in that country and whole swarms have been killed by pesticide. With an eye to a quick buck the locust vendors have been picking up the dead insects by the basketful and frying them for sale, but the toxic chemicals that the locusts have ingested caused illness in some people who have eaten them, and if I remember correctly, even death on more than one occasion.

Village people over the world have always eaten the local flora and fauna and usually that scale of destruction isn't sufficient to cause problems to the populations of plants and animals. It is when someone decides to build a dirty great highway through the area, like the Trans Amazonian Highway, or when there is a local war that the trouble starts. Someone once calculated that the Amazonian rain forest contained about 8 million spiders to an acre. Now, when you start to carve a road through the forest for thousands of miles, just think how many spiders are destroyed, and if you then add that figure to those of the other animals killed in the same way—the moths, the morpho butterflies, the beetles, the antbirds, the tanagers, the frogs, the snakes, the monkeys, the rodents, the cats, and on and on, one can suddenly visualise the appalling scale of the destruction, which is not limited to the width of the road. A good many of the workers on the project have guns which they use within a mile or two of either side of the highway to obtain food. Some of this they eat themselves, some they sell to their fellow workers and their families, and with the new access to the towns that were unreachable until recently, they suddenly have a huge new market for meat and pelts. At one time—not many years ago—the Amazon basin was regarded as a huge reservoir of all sorts of attractive, interesting and potentially useful plants and animals but the plug has now been pulled out.

On the other side of the world the unstable situation and guerrilla war in Cambodia, Thailand, Laos and Vietnam have resulted in whole armies, consisting of groups of sometimes several dozen soldiers, living entirely off the land. Any animal from insects to the biggest mammals are killed for food. Perhaps the largest animal before all the fighting began was the Kouprey, a huge buffalo-like beast that was already close to extinction and whether any exist today is doubtful. When the Wildlife Fund Thailand wanted an emblem about three years ago they chose the Kouprey, and started collecting funds to save it. The group has come in for considerable flak locally as other conservationists maintain that it is a complete waste of time accumulating funds to save an animal that is already extinct. Komain Nukulphanitwipat, the proprietor of the largest firm of animal exporters in the country, insists that there are no more Kouprey in Thailand, and I would give his opinion a lot of credence for not only is he a superb field naturalist with 30-odd years experience, but additionally he has 700 trappers all over the country collecting stock for him and I feel they would certainly know if there were Koupreys within the kingdom or within spitting distance of its borders. Komain has the skin and skull of what I like to think is the last Kouprey of all on his office floor.

The Kouprey is not the only animal under threat. All deer are hunted, and Fea's Muntjac in the same area is severely threatened. Some years ago the dealer referred to above was in Burma when he came across a group of villagers sitting down to their evening meal which they had just cooked over an open fire. He was invited to join them, and as he ate he recognised the meat as venison and asked from what animal it had come. The villagers shrugged and replied, 'Deer'. Upon being questioned further one of them stood up and walked away across the village to return moments later with the head of the animal. Komain did not recognise it but immediately knew it to be rare—something that his fellow diners acknowledged. He told them that he would pay handsomely for live specimens in perfect condition, and said that if they phoned him when they caught them he would collect the animals and pay for them. In due course he obtained five of the deer and set about breeding them. He now has a sizeable herd which he keeps in a secret location miles from anywhere. He gets very angry with officialdom over his deer. Officially he is not permitted to keep them, but because no one knows where they are and he's not rocking any boats nobody says anything. But, as Komain says, what happens if disease occurs in the herd? The whole lot could be wiped out and if they were rare when he got them they are almost certainly even rarer now, if not extinct. However, the law insists that he cannot sell, export or do anything else with them so he continues to breed his deer because he fiercely believes that it should be done. He still doesn't know what they are, and because of the legal position he cannot send them anywhere to get them identified, nor even invite a scientist to see them as that would involve all sorts of hassle with the authorities.

Some years ago I was offered live Dugongs by fishermen off the coast of Ceylon, as it was then, for £25. They are not infrequently caught accidentally in fishing nets, and when that happens the locals kill them and sell the meat in the bazaars. Sea Cows, to give them their common name, occur in warm, shallow coastal waters in many parts of the world, and though protected they are still killed regularly from Sri Lanka to South America, which is one of those places where just about everything that moves is shot. It seems that all human males over the age of 14 have a gun and each weekend they go out to blast out of existence every animal within reach, even the Puna Rhea, an endangered, ostrich-like bird that is hunted from dune buggies by people from the nearby mines.

The trouble is that apart from just being meat, as soon as an animal becomes unobtainable enough it is considered ever more desirable as a gourmet food. About two years ago I was sent some newspaper cuttings by Ilsa Sharp, a journalist in Singapore with an interest in matters biological. These particular stories referred to restaurants on the island that served 'Mandarin Banquets' to clients rich enough to afford them. These meals were very expensive and designed to celebrate special events. They included a variety of dishes, of which the centrepiece was a complete bird of paradise garnished with its plumage.

When the press picked up the story the managers of the restaurants flung up their collective hands in horror and denied all knowledge of the dish, one of them adding cryptically, 'Anyhow, it would be very expensive and no one could afford it today.' And if you believe that I bet you still believe in Santa Claus!

I would be most surprised, however, if you really cannot find a restaurant in Singapore that would not be prepared to serve you roast bird of paradise as they can be obtained with no trouble from the markets of Indonesia, and I asked one of the Jakarta dealers if he knew anything about Mandarin Banquets in Singapore. He said no but added that occasionally they sent live birds of paradise to Hong Kong where they certainly did eat them as a special dish, and then he added, 'We also send them young monkeys for the table.'

I only know of this particular practice from Hong Kong and Macao where, provided one goes to the right restaurants and is affluent enough, one can order monkey brain as the highlight of a meal to impress the guests. It is not just the serving of monkey brain, you understand, there is a whole ritual to accompany the dish. During the course of the day of the banquet the poor monkey who is to be the star of the evening is fed considerable quantities of booze so that by the time the meal is served he is pretty intoxicated. When it is time for the monkey brain course, he is tied so that he is completely immobilised and inserted into a small cage that is just big enough to contain his body but leaves his head sticking out through a hole in the top. From underneath the table the monkey's head is poked through an opening so that he is completely invisible to the diners except for the head, whose chin rests in suitably attractive garnish. When the host is ready, the chef delicately and carefully cuts round the skull just above the eyes and ears so that the whole top can be lifted off like a lid to reveal the brain. All the diners clap in delight at the thought of the treat to come, and tell their host what a super chap he is, and they then all dig in. Each diner dips a bread stick or something similar into the soft, creamy brain tissue and munches it with suitably appreciative noises while the monkey blinks solemnly at them until the eyes close for the last time—and all the brain disappears down the throats of these sophisticated, civilised people.

The restaurants that cater to customers like these will also supply many other dishes. Bear Paw Stew is a favourite dish in the restaurants of Macao when they are visited by diners who arrive via the fast hydrofoil from nearby Hong Kong, and Tiger meat is popular throughout the Indo-Chinese region; and if the Tiger can be slaughtered while you watch the experience adds a certain piquancy to the meal. Only the other day an Asian newspaper reported that a Bengal Tiger that had been imported from India or Bangladesh into Taipei in Taiwan to be served at a banquet in a Chinese restaurant had been rescued by a certain Su Nan Cheng who bought it from the butchers for $420,000 and donated it to a local zoo.

Let it not be thought that it is only in the Far East that such practices take place. Some American supermarkets sell tinned rattlesnake meat, and in a small town in West Germany there is a wildlife restaurant which offers elephant, Tiger, bear and Puma as available, all quite openly, even though some of the animals on the menu are protected. Or should you be in the country, and do not fancy going out for a meal, there are butchers shops in Munich and Frankfurt which will supply any of the above together with python steaks, crocodile meat or joints of tapir which a customer can take home to prepare as the Sunday roast.

It is well known that small birds on migration between Britain and Africa are killed in enormous numbers in Europe, despite legislation in many cases, and larks and tits, robins and blackbirds are consumed with relish, and a careful hunt round the up-market food counters in the West End of London will reveal tins of small songbirds that are imported from Mediterranean countries. The difficulty in such countries is that so many of the population possess guns that the hunting lobby is powerful enough to inhibit politicians when it comes to discussing protective legislation. The result is that as many as 90 per cent of the birds that visit Britain each year do not get back to Africa again through some countries, and the same occurs on the return journey. In Malta all the old wartime pillboxes along the coastline are done up to serve as shooting hides wherein wait the brave hunters, fortified by hampers of goodies and wine, for the migrants to appear each spring and autumn so that virtually nothing arrives on the island. A report in 1985 mentioned Malta's one wildlife reserve whose trustees were having an awful job trying to maintain its boundaries because, tiny though it was, the sight of live birds actually walking about on the island was such an affront to the inhabitants that the government was reducing the size of the reserve from small to microscopic.

If it wasn't so frustrating one would have to laugh. The Maltese like songbirds to keep in cages which they hang on the outside wall of the house, but since the creatures are as rare as hens' teeth on the island, the pet shops import European songbirds from overseas.

Cyprus seems to be one of the countries that is trying to stop all this. In 1985 Jaap Taapken reported that shooting of every bird species continued together with trapping with nets and birdlime, but 'Police control is frequent and those caught receive severe punishment.'

Small birds suffer from hunters everywhere and in 1984 two Brazilians were jailed for a year and fined the equivalent of £300 for holding a wild bird barbeque which included a main course consisting of 2,400 small birds. That was hailed by Brazilian conservationists as being the first time that someone had been jailed for killing wild birds. As far as I can discover it was also the last time, and although it was the highest available penalty for the offence it appears to have had no effect, since when he knew I was researching this book a contact of mine in Rio de Janeiro wrote me an impassioned letter explaining that these barbecues together with a host of other abuses to the birdlife of the area took place frequently and perfectly openly.

8. The Market Place

Twenty years ago most large towns in many countries had a bird market. They were nearly always known as bird markets even though they sold all sorts of other animals as well, and not just animals but all the bits and pieces which were necessary to their well-being such as cages, utensils and foodstuff.

Times have changed and the locations of markets have often been developed into office blocks, and as people acquired more money they wanted birds that were exotic in the true sense of the word, so they went for them to the premises of importers who were often nowhere near the old part of the town where markets were usually found, but instead were somewhere handy for the airport. As housing patterns changed and people moved to smaller flats because of the rising cost of land, they were unable to keep animals as before and had to be content with one or two pet birds. The decline has undoubtedly also been accelerated, at least in some places, by conservation, not to mention local bye-laws on hygiene, pollution and control of business premises. Today you have to hunt a bit harder to find the bird markets and an obvious place to start is those countries that have a rich fauna combined with a 'So what?' attitude about wildlife.

In a way it is a shame they are disappearing because although they were and are awful places for the animals that suffered and died in their millions, the markets were fascinating communities of people with a lifestyle all their own.

London once had a bird market known to everyone as Club Row though I don't know why since the thoroughfare was a miserable little road which was actually named Sclater Street. There used to be a few shops selling scruffy birds by the thousand but most of the punters came along to see if they could pick up a bargain from one of the many stalls that lined the pavement. The market was only open on a Sunday morning, and by nine o'clock it was packed with a shouting, jostling horde stroking the bunnies in their kerb edge tea chests, and cuddling the terrified, shivering puppies or letting the skinny kittens with diarrhoea lick their hands.

The oldest firm in Club Row was Palmer's, a shop with a history in the East End that goes back a long way. The Dickensian shop sold a wide variety of animals from West African finches, through mynahs from India to Guinea Pigs and hamsters to Grass Snakes, Slow Worms and newts that had been brought in by small boys looking to supplement their pocket money.

I can't say that I remember much that was exotic on the stalls—the nearest to that were the unfortunate, immobilised Squirrel Monkeys used as street photographers' props in nearby Petticoat Lane Market, but many of the stalls were full of cages containing what to the experienced eye were freshly caught wild birds such as Goldfinches and Linnets, and all aviary-bred, or so the stallholder would tell you.

On the other side of London, Shepherd's Bush Market underneath the railway arches used to have quite a few animal shops when I was a boy. Now they have been replaced with stalls selling brightly coloured cotton prints interlaced with lurex threads, and 'fallen-off-the-back-of-a-lorry' electronic bargains, and piles of exotic West Indian vegetables and fruit. There is one squalid little hole in the wall that still sells animals but it doesn't stock very much today.

Paris used to have quite a lot of bird stalls at one time, as did Brussels, and I am told that the market in Moscow is still very popular, selling not only birds in quantity but live fish as well and though I don't know it, Gerald Durrell talks of the Corfu bird market when he was a boy. There never seemed to be many bird markets in Africa and that might be because African people tend not to be interested in pet keeping to the same extent as many other races, so pets in Africa seemed to be kept mainly by white expatriates. There used to be heaps of bird markets in Central and South America but they are declining fast. In Georgetown in Guyana there is now only the odd stall where there used to be plenty, Colombia has hardly any, and I haven't found a single one in the West Indies for years. Rio de Janeiro can still boast plenty of places for buying animls, and Manaus, whilst not having a formal market, does have a lot of people with small stocks for sale.

But one of the best places has always been Asia and no Indian town of any size was without a bazaar full of mynahs and parakeets. In the centre of Bombay is the splendidly awful Victorian building that houses Crawford Market and under the cast-iron and glass roof are to be found stalls selling aromatic Alphonso mangoes and chickoos piled high in attractive displays, and vendors of household effects sit side by side with butchers selling shiny, freshly skinned chickens. At one end can be found the fish market whose counters are covered in beautiful silver Pomfret, anonymous catfish and chunks of unsavoury looking dried fillets of God knows what species, as well as the odd looking Hammerhead Sharks. And in one corner, across the rubbish filled yard, is a small, outward-facing circle of stalls that is the bird market. Crawford Market never did sell huge numbers of animals, nor many species, but at one time you could be sure of finding four or five kinds of finches, some bulbuls and Ringnecked Parakeets together with a few odds and ends, and tiny cages full of pathetic little unweaned Palm Squirrels, animals similar to the North American Chipmunks, which were sold as pets, and which died slowly and readily since they were just too young. And always there was someone who would come up and mutter, 'You want to see cobra mongoose fight, Sahib?'

The home of a family of bird catchers in northern India (W. Newing)

The real place in Bombay to buy animals was a nondescript little shop a short distance from Crawford Market along Doctor Dadabhoy Naoroji Road. There wasn't actually much stock in the shop which supplied all sorts of biological material to local students. I remember sitting and talking to the portly proprietor, Mr R. D. Sane, when a young woman came in to buy two worms for dissection which were extracted from a jar where they resided in formalin, stiff and straight, and looking for all the world like twiglets. Apart from the worms there were certainly a few samples of live animals to be seen but the majority of the stock lived in cages on the flat roof of a tower block to the north of the town where Mr Sane had a flat. Though I've not seen him for years I am told that he is still exporting animals, and is the only person in India who handles anything other than the very common species. Crawford Market itself seems to sell little these days apart from pigeons and live chickens.

Delhi used to have an active bird market opposite the Red Fort but this is now dead. There were plenty of pigeons for sale there too, and about a dozen Plumheaded Parakeets, but that was about all. The signboard above a stall, proclaiming that the business was an international exporter of 'zoological' and other animals, hung from one corner and was flaking badly to reveal across the rooftops the famous bird hospital run by Jains, who are members of a particular Hindu sect that do not believe in killing anything. I visited the hospital and the orderly in charge explained that virtually all his patients were pigeons because the Jains would not look after carnivorous species.

'Because of our religion,' I was told, 'we only care for vegetarian birds.' I asked what happened if a bird of prey was brought in. 'Oh, we do get them sometimes, usually with a broken wing. In that case we amputate the wing and release the bird to look after itself. We would not harm it, you understand, but it definitely cannot stay.' He looked at me for a moment before adding firmly, 'Only vegetarian birds here!'

It could only happen in India.

During my recent travels to the 'Jewel in the Crown', and that's a misnomer if ever there was, I paid a visit to Bareilly, a somewhat Godforsaken place known by most people only as a railway town—a sort of Clapham Junction. But in the bird-exporting world it used to be important. The birds that India once exported in large quantities can be conveniently divided into two categories. There are the parrots, mynahs, bulbuls and finches that are gregarious and common, being found throughout peninsular India. They were trapped and flown out of the country during the summer. Their price was always low, as living in flocks they were easy to catch in bulk, and because they were cheap they always had to be shipped within four days of being trapped or they would have cancelled their profit in the food they ate. When winter came the picture changed. It became so cold up in the Himalayas that the largely solitary insectivorous birds that lived at higher altitudes during the summer moved down into the foothills where they were more accessible. When this had happened the trappers from the villages around Kumaon dug out their trapping equipment and set off to see what they could find. Throughout the trade in India, Himalayan species were known as Bareilly birds and comprised for the most part flycatchers, niltavas, sunbirds and rubythroats.

They were all very delicate and as soon as he could the trapper would take his catch to the middleman in Bareilly. I have no idea how the town became the centre for the trade but it was almost the only place to which the trappers brought their stock. Twenty years ago there were three dealers who would buy the catches from the strings of trappers that turned up each day.

The dealers' walled compounds were packed with banks of bamboo cages, each divided into individual compartments as the birds are far too aggressive to keep together. People think robins are sweet little things, but keep them together and they'll fight savagely, although I've never come across birds as fierce as the minuscule Red Headed Tits. Before long a cage of these pugnacious little creatures will contain several corpses and one Victor Ludorum singing out his challenge to any others of his kind within earshot.

Maintaining these birds was labour-intensive as each had to be fed indvidually. First thing each morning someone would make the rounds and throw out the birds that had died overnight until the yard was littered with great piles of multi-coloured bodies. The losses were quite astounding. Surveys of the bird trade from India quote all sorts of mortality figures, which though undoubtedly true must inevitably be incomplete and can be misleading. Tim Inskipp of the Wildlife Trade Monitoring Unit in Cambridge talks of a mortality rate of 2.1 per cent at the exporter's premises in Calcutta which sounds about right, and looking at his breakdown of species most figures seem reasonable. I would guess that individual trappers do not lose more than around the same if only because they do not hang onto the stock long enough. But I have seen Mohammed Khan at Bareilly lose every one of a consignment received from a trapper and 60 per cent was not at all uncommon. He told me once that he reckoned on selling between 15 and 25 per cent of his Himalayan softbills. He would also handle other birds such as birds of prey, and his losses were infinitely lower with these. Provided they arrived quickly and in good condition he rarely lost an owl or a falcon.

Nowadays there is only one dealer in Bareilly and 1985 she shipped out eight partridges. That was her total business. The other middlemen in places like Lucknow and Patna used to handle some Himalayan species but these only represented part of their stock—the remainder was made up of other, hardier birds. I went to the dealers and bird market of Lucknow. The dealers had ceased trading and the market stocked little other than Common Quail and the ubiquitous pigeons.

There used to be one big middleman in Benares. The trade was run by a whole family of Khans who were amongst the nicest people I've ever known, but that business has also closed down, as have the ones in Agra and Patna. The last town was never a great supplier of birds. In the West it is best known for Patna rice, but in India it is where each year in September is held an elephant fair which is famed throughout the country. A huge loop of the river encloses three sides of a flat peninsula and it is here that the 'mela' or fair is held. It is a quite splendid affair that cannot have changed much since the Moghul princes ruled India centuries ago.

Last time I went I was accompanied by a Calcutta dealer who was a good friend. The mela continues today and is as popular as ever. Round the edges of the site myriad stalls appear overnight selling just about everything a local person might (or for that matter, certainly won't) want, from batteries that are completely dead even though the vendor assures his customers that they are the brightest, longest lasting batteries the world has ever seen, to the most exquisite earthenware pots and brass food containers, and printed fabrics for saris. Here one can wander and buy bunches of twigs to use as a toothbrush if you know how

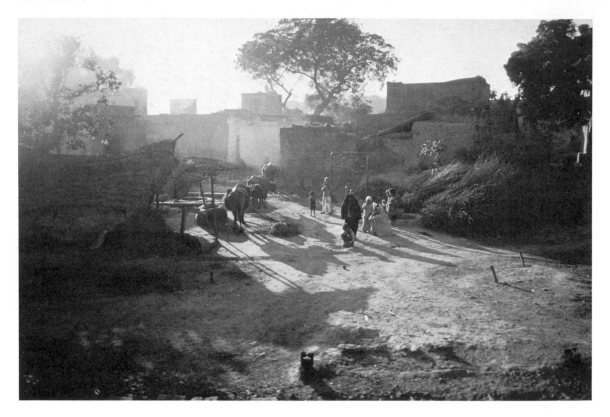

Many of India's bird catchers live in this village near Bareilly (W. Newing)

they operate. I have no idea what species of tree they come from but the trick is to munch on one end of a stick until it becomes shredded and fibrous. You then hold the other end and use the hairy bit as bristles. It sounds dreadfully primitive but it works, and to finish off your course of oral hygiene you can buy a metal tongue scraper like a fine, blunt spokeshave.

Inevitably the mela attracts many food stalls selling all sorts of goodies from softboiled bantam eggs—dropped into boiling water just long enough for the white to become slightly cloudy, to the best tasting stuffed parathas in the world. Or one can pay a visit to a sweety stall for a couple of barfis covered in silver foil so fine that a breath would blow a hole in it. The sweets vary between perfectly acceptable jelabis that look like tangles of bright orange earthworms, to chunks of white, fudge-like confections that are so sweet that they set the teeth on edge, and having made the mistake of biting into one, one then cannot get rid of the wretched stuff which sticks to the teeth and pallet in a sticky paste for what seems to be hours. Indians make some very nice sweets but they also make what must be the world's worst.

The elephant mela at Patna is a lovely place, full of noise and colour and movement, and particularly at night, of smells as well, for after dark each stall lights up one or more smelly lanterns from which the pungent smoke drifts into the still air to mingle with the fumes from mustard oil used by the food vendors. The fair is an occasion for local people, and visitors travel for considerable distances to visit it. There is so much to do and so much to see. There are animal stalls where in the past I have admired Shahin Falcons and Slender Lorises and baby monkeys so small that most of them would certainly not survive very long. I saw once a man squatting beside his boxes and baskets with a whole row of tame juvenile Black Naped Orioles perched along his left arm. There are occasionally snake charmers trying to goad a dehydrated cobra into putting on some sort of show for the wide-eyed audience, who, when bored with snakes, might turn to watch a monkey man and his performing Rhesus Monkey dressed in dirty, miniature versions of human clothes.

Finally, when you've squeezed every last bit of enjoyment that you can from this human kaleidoscope and bought a few real spearheads from an itinerant blacksmith who sells them to those people who carry real spears, and in India there are some, you make your way to the elephant lines which are the reason for the existence of the whole affair. If you really want to buy an elephant you need to know what to look for or you can end up with the animal equivalent of a rusty old banger with no logbook and only a month to run on the M.O.T.

The elephants—lots of them—stand in rows, each tethered by one foot. There are teenage elephants and youngsters, good strong females and more mature models, and what can only be described as dignified old ladies who have seen it all before, and perhaps even remember standing in this same mela many years earlier. Over at one side are the powerful males that are known to be dangerous at times. These animals have a chain around each ankle and the two front legs are pulled forwards and outwards before being tied to pegs and the back legs are similarly splayed behind so that the elephant is immobile. The strain on the poor thing must be agonising and I used to wonder whether the abuse or the bad temper came first. The elephant can remain like that for days until the fair ends, and just to remind him not to even think about thumping a visitor on the head with his trunk, a spear is stuck hilt down in the soil so that the blade is near the eye of the elephant, always there just to make a point. As you look at these males they either return your appraisal with a hard, calculating stare, or they look into the middle distance with glazed eyes deliberately not seeing what is going on around them, and if anyone feels that I am being anthropomorphic they don't understand elephants. They have brains and personalities quite unlike any other animals. I had a very young male once that was perfectly tame but which used to get considerable pleasure from standing on people's feet. He would wait until someone was standing alongside stroking him and exclaiming what a pretty boy he was, when unobtrusively he would shift his weight and quite gently place a forefoot on top of that of his admirer, and then lean towards him. As soon as the sufferer let out a yell and thumped him, the elephant would immediately lift his foot as though it was an accident and with a very knowing look in his eye he would reach up his trunk and put it round your shoulders in a gentle caress as much as to say, 'Sorry, old chap, I didn't realise.' But I was caught more often than I should have been and knew perfectly well that he did it deliberately.

The animals on sale are nowadays nearly all captive-bred; it is just far too expensive today to mount a huge expedition to catch wild ones. Of course it was never cheap, so your average elephant man who wanted to make himself some money on his next visit to the fair used to turn to a bit of freelance elephant catching on the side. To do this he would put foot-long bits of plank with a six-inch nail sticking out of them here and there on well-used elephant trails and sooner or later an animal would bring a foot down onto the rusty point of one of these primitive traps. With luck (from the catcher's point of view) the foot would become infected and then the leg, and eventually the animal would be hobbling around feeling like death warmed up and in no fit state to object to being noosed and tied alongside the catcher's own elephant. The captive was led back home and the infection treated. With luck it healed and the newcomer could then be broken and trained in the usual way.

I discovered all this when I noticed with puzzlement the way that prospective buyers at the fair used to give a fair slap to each leg of the animal under scrutiny. My companion explained that it was to see if the animal winced. If it did it had probably been caught in the way I have described and the infection still had not healed completely, in which case you needed to lift up the foot to examine it very carefully before negotiating a price.

Interestingly enough some years ago there used to be a circus elephant in Britain—I think her name was Burma—and whenever the regulation visit to the circus was shown on television each Christmas this particular elephant had a trick that you might have seen, of stepping over a supine performer in the ring. To vary the shot occasionally a brave cameraman would lie on the sawdust, shooting upwards as the huge beast stepped over him and when he did this you could clearly see the scar on the bottom of one foot that revealed how that particular elephant had been caught.

The biggest Indian market by far for the export of animals was always Calcutta. Massive numbers used to leave India from this city though it is wrong to think that it was all centred in one place. The main market in Calcutta where one can buy all manner of things is New Market, and the well-known bird market used to be part of that, but in addition there were several exporters elsewhere in and around the town. It was such a huge business that it spawned a whole lot of subsidiaries to service it. There were, for instance, cage makers who would make you a wire mesh cage in no time at all, or if you preferred you could have exquisite bamboo cages made by a chap who would go off and buy a single bamboo—not a four foot cane such as we buy from a garden centre but a 30 foot green thing about three inches in diameter. The carpenter would squat on the road, and using the most primitive tools he would soon chop his bamboo down to manageable lengths and split it and shave it until he had a complete cage kit lying beside him. Then with gnarled, scarred fingers, he would construct one of the loveliest cages you could wish for. Being Indian he did not do this on his own for he would soon be surrounded by small boys and watchers, and other cage makers and parrot pluckers.

Parrot pluckers were freelances who would buy all the dead birds from the dealers and pluck them. The bodies would be thrown on a nearby pile of refuse and the feathers would be sold to novelty stationery emporiums which would employ people to glue tiny scraps of trimmed feather onto cards and sheets of writing paper to make the shapes of birds. They were very clever and frequently most attractive. When employees from the Bareilly bird merchants used to bring consignments up to the Calcutta dealers, they would also bring paper bags full of feathers that they had saved from their losses, to sell in New Market.

Near the bird market were stalls selling seed, and the maggot man was a daily visitor. He had standing orders from all the dealers for live food for the animals and he would salaam the proprietor and squat down on the floor of the shop. He was very old and couldn't see out of one eye and was a lovely old chap that I came to know well. He always arrived carrying several anonymous cloth bundles and one of these bags, about the size of a pillowcase, used to be full of maggots. When he opened it if you were foolish enough to be bending with your face over it, a blast of hot air would suddenly hit you, generated by the mass of maggots.

Crocodiles are not farmed in India to provide leather as in some countries (D. Whiting)

The maggot man would sell his stock by the measure, an old tin that he would rummage for in the wriggling heap, and tip 20 measures or 50 or whatever was required into a big cooking oil tin on the floor of his customer's shop. He never tried to cheat and one paid him weekly. Often you didn't see him between paydays but you had only to look in your maggot tin each day to see if he had been. He didn't just sell maggots, he had quite a stock of different insect species and would obtain anything for which he was asked. He would carry wasp grubs in chunks of comb, and ants eggs still swarming with millions of red ants that would come roaring up his arm when he opened the bag, and which bit viciously. Grasshoppers were another of his regular lines and he would sell these individually, carefully counting them out for you and giving a discount for any that had lost a leg. He also sold geckoes which, on the other hand, were priced by the hundred for some reason.

The market was also visited daily by the trappers. Some would come in each evening with their catch and after being paid they would depart with an order for the next day. Others would do what they could to earn a meagre living, trapping on some days, alternating with days of cage cleaning for the dealers or collecting baskets of birds from Howrah station and bringing them by rickshaw to New Market. Some of these men would supplement their income by taking some of what they caught to Sealdah market on the other side of town. This too was a general market with a bird section and it was quite odd because although the stock sold there was entirely for locals, so one would expect the usual run of mynahs and parrots, quite often one could find much more exotic, interesting animals. Some of the animals from Bangladesh would end up here. That was a bit of smuggling that I loved to watch. Quite a few species that the Calcutta dealers wanted for export occurred in East Pakistan as it was then, so a trapper would be despatched to get hold of them. On his return he would travel by train to the Indian border where it would stop for an eternity for immigration and customs formalities. It was forbidden to import live animals from East Pakistan so when the train wheezed to a halt the trapper would climb down with his basket of stock, hoist it onto his head and step across the border into India.

Naturally he was not the only passenger to do this. Carriagefuls of his fellows would accompany him to squat 50 yards along the line to wait for the train to catch them up. Eventually the officials would climb down and shout to all the illegals to get back in as the train was leaving and they would miss it. Everything was done quite openly and the border police seemed not to find anything bizarre in the situation.

New Market also attracted other hangers-on like the makers of export crates and lorry drivers, each waiting for an order for a dozen crates, or to take a consignment up to Dum Dum airport from the airline offices in Chowringhee. Not many years ago the going price of Ringneck Parakeets from the trappers was 1.75 rupees per pair in the days when there were about 20 rupees to the pound sterling, and the birds were exported at about 5 rupees. Nowadays the whole Indian trade in animals has collapsed and prices for those few birds that are exported are a lot higher. Below are the current prices being asked for stock by an Indian dealer, compared with retail prices for the same birds in England. All prices are for a pair.

	Calcutta	Retail UK
Ringnecked Parakeets	18 rupees	£65.00
Alexandrine Parakeets	80 rupees	£65.00
Moustached Parakeets	40 rupees	£125.00
Silverbills	12 rupees	£9.00
Blackheaded Nuns	12 rupees	£12.00
Spicebirds	12 rupees	£12.00

The home of a family of parrot pluckers in Calcutta (D. Whiting)

Today there are about eighteen rupees to the pound.

A couple of hours by air to the east of Calcutta is the lovely town of Bangkok, the capital of Thailand, which has an enormous and thriving market. Known to

everyone as Suan Chatuchak, or the weekend market, it exists in fact throughout the week on a very small scale. Early on Saturday it grows suddenly and throughout the weekend it is packed with goodies of all sorts, and thronged with Thais on the lookout for a bargain. The market sells everything they could possibly want from musical instruments made by the hill tribes in the north to some fascinating Ming pottery that was made for the use of the poor people of the period, so although it hasn't the sophistication and delicacy of what most people think of as Ming, it is pleasing stuff and can be bought for a fraction of the price that conventional Ming pottery fetches.

Although Chatuchak is not a covered market as such, each stall has an awning or roof that overlaps those of its neighbours so that the browser can wander from one aisle to the next without ever coming out into the blazing sun. One fascinating chunk of the market contains plant stalls—a riot of colour, and totally fascinating if you like orchids for they are everywhere. Bougainvilleas, hibiscus and crotons also abound, usually sold in beautiful ceramic pots with raised dragon motifs around the outside. Most of the plants for sale are cultivated, but nowadays there are quite a few wild specimens as well, some of which are decidedly uncommon. They are generally displayed with just a chunk of earth around the roots and by Sunday night they are often looking decidedly the worse for wear. The dealers in these wild plants, and the sellers of wild caught animals, regard their stock as disposable and do not consider that it will necessarily last after the weekend until the following Saturday. Losses amongst the animals particularly are colossal—the wastage in bird markets generally is very, very high. What is very interesting is that the average punter will rarely if ever see corpses in cages. Consequently reports by conservation researchers often underestimate the numbers of deaths since the reports often rely on information supplied by dealers, and which of them is going to tell a Western

The weekend market in Bangkok sells live and dead wildlife, and much else besides (W. Newing)

researcher the true facts? But if you can speak the language—and I don't mean Thai or whatever, but the language of the bird market so that the dealers accept you—then the real picture begins to become clear. Oddly enough in most bird markets moribund specimens are also usually hidden but this is not the case in Bangkok and if dealers really do sometimes sell the half-dead monkeys that can be seen on display there must be more idiots about than I would have thought.

The bird market is extensive and clearly sells a lot of animals. An average weekend sees about a hundred species of birds for sale of which most are native, and of those 90 per cent or so are protected so it is illegal to sell them. And although most of the trading is done quite openly there are occasions when a vendor resorts to subterfuge to avoid any possible comeback; this occurs when the sale of an animal is particularly sensitive. What typically happens in a case like this is that a purchaser will be asked to leave his money in a certain place, well away from the stall which is selling the animal. The buyer will be followed and the money will be extracted from its hiding place by a person who is not apparently connected with the vendor and only afterwards is the small anonymous box that contains the purchase left in another innocuous place for the new owner to collect. There is a large part of the bird market that sells fish for aquarists, and though most of these are captive-bred there are usually a few wild-caught specimens on show including Arawanas, fish that may not be legally traded anywhere throughout their range, but they are apparently regarded as lucky by Oriental people and tanks of one or occasionally two are to be seen all over the place.

While there are more birds than any other form of livestock, other animals may also be readily found. However, so many investigators have been round the market from conservation and animal welfare agencies that the dealers are really twitchy about photography and most of the photographs that were shot had to be obtained surreptitiously. And bird markets being what they are, everyone is either related to everyone else or extremely close friends and it doesn't take long before they all close ranks if they suspect a foreigner so that before long there is nothing suspicious to be found anywhere. Even when things appear to be open and above board there are anonymous bags and boxes lying about that occasionally twitch or emit squawks. I heard a Frenchman ask what was in a writhing sack, to be told with a mocking smile that it contained birdseed.

If you know which stalls to visit you can commonly find baby gibbons, tiny, frightened balls of coarse fur that cling tightly to the arm and shoulder of anyone who handles them. They will rarely survive and are most frequently bought by Japanese who take them back to their own country illegally in their luggage, or by well-to-do Thais who buy them as status symbol pets. They don't need to live for any length of time, only long enough for the owner's friends to have got used to seeing them around, after which they can be replaced by a new and even more impressive animal.

The same stalls that sell the gibbons tend to be those with other species of primates. These are invariably very young monkeys and they often look in a terrible state. There's also usually the odd loris around and if the season is right and you are lucky you might even come across some tiny otters being bottle-fed. All of them are kept in the most inadequate conditions, though by far the worst that I came across was a young Malayan Tapir that lived in a cage just large enough to contain it, but in order that it should not be seen by anybody who might have caused trouble the top of the cage was covered by a board on which rested cages of birds while more boxes and cages surrounded three sides. The fourth was draped with a piece of sacking that was only lifted when the tapir was to be inspected by a potential purchaser. The temperature in the market in the day was in the nineties and in the unventilated cage it must have been far higher. By Sunday night the tapir was dead.

The animal was on the same stall that sells gibbons. I watched as an army officer in civilian clothes, as I later discovered he was, bought a young gibbon. All the participants in the transaction became decidedly difficult when they discovered that photographs were being taken.

The other mammal which can be found every weekend during the season is the kitten of the Leopard Cat. These sweet little animals are really appealing and can be bought for 500 baht which is about £15. They almost invariably die within a few days as they need a lot of experience and the right facilities if they are to survive. I can well understand someone wanting to buy one of these small cats, just as I can understand their wanting to buy a baby monkey although the latter make the most terrible household pets, but what does surprise me is that anyone at all should want a young Tupaia or Tree Shrew. Like the monkeys these are primates though you would never guess it by looking at them. They look just like squirrels so it is not surprising that they are to be found on the squirrel stalls, together with several species of real squirrel including the delightful Flying Squirrel, which the vendors toss in the air to display their gliding technique to anyone looking for a pet that is different.

I can well believe that people leave Chatuchak market with a newly bought squirrel but I do find it hard to accept that they actually buy lizards from the dealers as pets, which is what they say they sell them for. Don't get me wrong, lizards are lovely animals and I know lots of people who keep and breed them, but somehow it does not seem to be a Thai thing, and this market is almost entirely to supply local people. I can only assume that nearly all the dehydrated, skinny lizards that lie crammed into tiny cages, one on top of each other in their hundreds, die during the two days of the weekend, and the same must surely

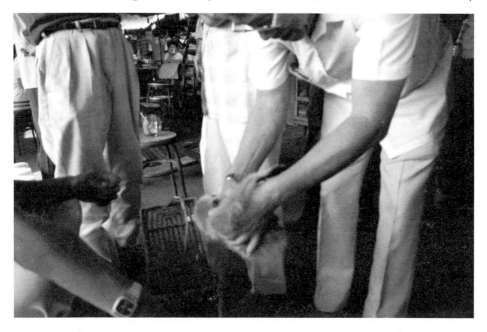

Baby gibbons are sold illegally as status symbol pets (W. Newing)

apply to most of the Long Nosed Tree Snakes which are not only notoriously difficult to keep in captivity, but insist on only eating geckoes into the bargain. Yet there they are in green, constantly-moving knots, waiting to be bought for 5 bahts each—about 15p.

But while there are always some mammals and reptiles on sale, by far the greatest number of animals available are fish, and the birds which come in all shapes and sizes. There are not many domestic birds apart from the baskets full of brightly coloured day-old chicks that have been dyed every hue of the rainbow (and intriguingly some fish, although goodness knows how that's done), and a few fighting cocks, each kept out of range of his fellows in individual baskets.

The commonest birds are the parakeets and the mynahs, the bulbuls and the finches which are packed into cages by the hundreds. In fact these birds probably survive the conditions better than most since they are gregarious and to an extent not too fussy about what they eat and most of the species on display are born survivors. It is the odds and ends that are there in small numbers that must find it hardest to adjust, and there really are the most peculiar birds to be found. In March for instance, during their breeding season, one can walk past rows of cages containing mobs of baby Hoopoes. They are great and I like Hoopoes a lot but everyone I spoke to in Thailand said that they had never heard of anyone keeping a Hoopoe as a pet. March is a good time for babies of other species as well and some stalls have open topped cardboard boxes full of fluffy grey parrot chicks with bright red beaks which all open wide whenever anyone passes. On occasion there are even similar boxes full of baby falcons and owls. Apparently it is the parents of all these baby parrots that are sold frozen at Thonburi market, as I mentioned earlier.

A Thai friend of mine who knows and cares about animals, and is a great believer in making life difficult for animal dealers, one day objected strenuously in the weekend market when she came across a cage full of sunbirds—delicate things which require a highly specialised diet of nectar and small insects. She complained vociferously to the stallholder. 'These birds won't survive!'

'Oh yes they will,' he replied. 'If you feed them on a sugar solution.'

'Nonsense,' said Katy, firmly. 'They'll all be dead in a week.'

'Don't be silly,' responded the dealer crossly. 'If you feed them like that they'll last a good fortnight.' And that is the way they think of their stock.

The Thais are Buddhists, and although many of them very clearly do not follow the religious tenets on the sanctity of life, lots of them clearly do and the shrines and temples are visited by many of the faithful each day, and in the vicinity of each are always to be found a number of itinerant street vendors selling offerings to the Lord Buddha. Little, perfectly exquisite garlands of orchids are the commonest such offering, to be followed by small wooden elephants, and incense sticks. One can also buy stamp size pieces of gold leaf to stick onto the statue of the god or onto his stone attendant elephants, and lastly, one can buy live birds. The sellers of these are usually women, and Buddhists believe that if someone releases captive birds, that person earns credit in the next incarnation. To cater to people who feel in need of a spiritual leg up, the women sell Spice Birds—they always seem to be Spice Birds—for a few pennies each. The birds are transferred from the flock in the holding cage to a very small cage which is taken by the worshipper to the statue. At the appropriate point in the prayers the door of the cage is opened and the birds are allowed to fly free after which the cage is returned to the seller.

A cynical Thai friend asked with a chuckle, 'You realise that these birds are recycled?' And I am sure they are. I imagine that many of them are caught again and again.

Despite that, depredations on populations of wild animals are very large. In addition to all the live animals about which I have been talking, the country exports a vast amount of dead birds to Japan for food. The only guide to quantities that I have is that in 1982 licences were granted to export 45,000 kilos of the things, and most of these are said to have been Yellow Breasted Buntings. When you realise that each such bird is just a bit bigger than a House Sparrow, and then try and estimate how many are necessary to make up a consignment of that weight, you begin to understand the numbers involved.

Implementation of the legislation that covers most of the animals in the country is almost non-existent. There are sufficient laws to ensure that 90 per cent of the animals at the weekend market would disappear from the stalls tomorrow if they were enforced, but they are not because the situation is intolerable for the enforcing authorities even if they felt inclined to do anything. One of the reasons they don't is because of the number of problems with which they could land themselves. Consequently, on the rare occasions when any action is taken, it is at the instigation of a caring member of the public. What happens then goes like this, and if it wasn't so silly it would sound like pure comic opera: someone sees something happening which is wrong—say, a cage full of gibbons that should not be sold—so they approach a policeman and demand that he does something. He certainly won't want to, but if he does accompany the complainant to the relevant stall he should then investigate the matter and if it seems to him that an offence is being committed he has to arrest the alleged criminal and confiscate the evidence—in this case the gibbons. The evidence will be required in court so he carts his prisoner and a large boxful of apes to the nearest taxi and all pile in to be driven to the police station where the prisoner is either released on bail or (less likely) held in custody.

The policeman has to pay the taxi himself. Then he has to hunt for someone to look after the gibbons until the court case. Not many people are willing to do this, and in any case are not likely to have the time and the facilities. Besides which it is not cheap to keep the animals in food for perhaps several months—and who is going to be blamed if they die? Eventually the poor old policeman discovers that no one wants to look after his evidence and he reluctantly realises that he will have to take the crate home himself, so he grabs another taxi and goes home to his wife ('Do you have to bring your work home with you, dear?') with his gibbons to share his home with them till the trial. If then the defendant wins, the gibbons are returned to him and the arresting officer is out of pocket. If the crown wins the policeman is awarded all his costs. His only remaining problem is to return the animals to the wild in the area from whence they came.

Not surprising, I think you will agree, that in the circumstances not more is done.

Most of the animals that end up at Bangkok's weekend market come either from the north around Chiang Mai, or from two places south of the capital: Surat Thani, a small town where the one middleman collects animals from all the trappers for sending to Bangkok each Thursday by road, or from Hat Yai in Songkhla Province right down in the south near the Malaysian border where there are two such dealers.

There is a national newspaper in Thailand that is known by all, and said by everybody to be all powerful, to such an extent that the readers of the same paper really are afraid of saying anything detrimental about it for fear of reprisals. They say that it has made and broken many well-known figures in the country. Copies of this paper are delivered throughout the land by a fleet of lorries that belong to a contractor. When I said to various concerns that I was going to write this they were really unhappy, and asked me to stress that the delivery vehicles and their drivers were not part of the newspaper organisation itself. I was told that the lorries went to outlying parts of the country with their cargoes of newspapers and, having unloaded, they filled the empty space with illegal animals which they bought from trappers who supplied them regularly. Then they drove back to the capital and delivered those animals either to the exporters or the stallholders at the weekend market.

Hat Yai particularly is known in the South East Asian animal trade as an important centre for illegal stock, for two reasons. The first of these is that nowadays it is pretty difficult to get protected animals out of Bangkok onto an international flight—there are just too many checks, so what happens is that consignments of such animals for export are loaded onto internal flights at Hat Yai airport, bound for Bangkok. They are not checked by customs because it is an internal flight. At Don Muang airport in Bangkok they are transferred to an international flight, and since this is an internal transfer on a journey which started somewhere else they are not checked at this stage either, so off they go!

Another fascinating thing about Bangkok airport, the like of which I've never come across anywhere else, is that the customs officials who check livestock consignments are not customs officials at all. They are in fact employees of Thai International Airways. Customs and Excise say that they themselves do not know anything about animals and that if the airline is to carry them it must check what it is carrying. This oddity is not publicised, but I was told this by a senior customs officer and when I subsequently mentioned this to a top official he denied it. Yet in the cargo terminal at the airport, if one manages to penetrate the secrecy and overcome the paranoia, it can be observed.

Hat Yai's other claim to fame relies on its proximity to the Malaysian border. From Hat Yai many lorries leave for Kuala Lumpur and other Malaysian towns, and for Singapore right at the southernmost tip of the peninsula. These wagons contain (so far as I know), perfectly legal cargoes, but some of them at least take a few secret boxes of birds to Singapore. The exporters in that country obtain their Thai stock by air, but in Singapore there is a huge interest in singing birds. Most people do not keep Budgerigars for their ability to talk or other birds for their appearance or to breed, but purely for song. It is illegal to trap any bird on the island except for the House Crow which is regarded as a pest. Yet is has been calculated that about 50,000 inhabitants keep at least one caged bird and almost always more than one. These birds are nearly all of the same five species: the Red Whiskered Bulbul, the White Rumped Shama, the oriental White Eye, the Necklaced Laughing Thrush and a small dove known locally as a Merbok. They occur throughout tropical Asia, and virtually every one must of necessity be imported. To supply the local songbird market most specimens are trapped in Thailand and Malaysia. An awful lot of them travel overland from Hat Yai. In Thailand the Red Whiskered Bulbul and the White Eye are protected whilst the Shama may be exported under a quota licence. However the numbers available in Singapore alone exceed the quota a hundredfold.

There is no bird market as such in Singapore but there are several birdshops to

This hornbill in Hat Yai is known to have come from Indonesia where it is protected (W. Newing)

supply the local demand for songbirds, which are big business locally with the champion singers changing hands for Singapore $50,000 (about £16,000).

The same shops supply all the needs of the fancier from beautiful bamboo cages to a whole range of accessories. These can be little plastic water pots or ivory food containers, carved wooden panels to decorate the cages and beautiful perches fashioned to simulate dragons, and intricate little cricket cages to enable the fancier to provide the birds with live food. You can also buy the crickets themselves at eight cents each or small skinks if your birds fancy something larger than a cricket.

The cages themselves are by no means cheap, and the really ornate ones at the top of the range can fetch £1,000 while one of the ivory food bowls, which are tiny things, can cost as much as another £1,400. The whole business is taken very seriously and competitions are constantly being held at which judges spend an eternity calculating each bird's marks. The whole business is quite fascinating as it apparently dates only from after the Second World War. Nowadays birdsong is to be heard coming from blocks of flats everywhere, and each morning from the crack of dawn till about eleven o'clock fanciers come with their birds from all over the town to a coffee shop at the junction of Seng Poh and Tiong Bahru roads to share their hobby. While they sip their drinks the cages hang above their heads from a grid around a central tree. On Sunday, which is the busiest day of all, you can sometimes hardly hear yourself think for the noise of the birdsong. It is not to be thought that the love of birdsong is the only reason for the contests. The Chinese people like nothing more than a bet, no matter on what, and quite large sums of money change hands at the various

Songbird fanciers in Singapore listen to their pets (J. Nichol)

competitions where the prizes can reach a couple of hundred pounds, and that certainly does not happen at bird shows in Britain. An annual national competition is held each year, promoted by Jurong Bird Park, The People's Association and the Singapore Tourist Promotion Board. This is the highspot of the year for the birdmen and a chance to see about a thousand entries in one place—most of them birds that have been smuggled somewhere along the way.

I have not come across any bird markets in Malaysia though I realise that that does not mean there isn't one somewhere. The nearest one that I know is in the small Sumatran town of Medan which is not too far across the Straits of Malacca from Penang, very convenient for smuggled consignments of Indonesian birds bound for the exporters of Malaysia.

Medan is a funny little place which seems not to possess a taxi, nor for that matter any local buses so that when the visitor wants to travel around the town he needs to hail a motorised cycle-rickshaw that must be the slowest, most bone-shaking means of transport ever invented. The seats are narrow and at just the right level so that exhaust from every vehicle on the road blows petrol and diesel fumes into the passenger's face. This primitive form of torture seems to have inefficient brakes and totally bald tyres which induce a horrifying sense of insecurity, as Indonesian traffic is quite frightening. One particular such vehicle in which I travelled was driven by an elderly relative of Biggles, or at any rate he wore what appeared to be an authentic Biggles outfit—a worn-out old leather overcoat that nearly reached the ankles, holey woollen gloves and a Second World War vintage flying helmet with a scarf over the mouth and nose to protect the driver from the traffic fumes.

The bird shops in Singapore carry huge stocks to meet local demand (W. Newing)

Travelling like this to the bird market in Medan is an experience that does not really appeal, especially as the road in which it is situated is mostly unmade, with potholes deep enough to trap an elephant. Mind you, the whole place is not designed to inspire confidence—as the plane touches down at the airport the first thing to be seen is a crashed and burnt out passenger aircraft nose down in the grass beside the runway.

The bird market is a little one, consisting of only about ten or a dozen open fronted shops, most of which are small and pretty dark. Most of the bird cages are piled in heaps on the pavement outside. There are a few macho-looking fighting cocks, of which the Indonesians are inordinately fond. The rest of the birds are a mixture of all sorts, including the usual mynahs and parakeets and Sumatran softbills such as flycatchers and flowerpeckers and woodpeckers. There seemed not to be any mammals at all except for a single Slow Loris and although I asked if anybody had any gibbons no one made a definite answer and I got the impression that there was never any call for anything as exotic as that out here in the middle of nowhere, though I am sure they could easily have been obtained had I pressed the matter.

The market at Pontianak in Borneo is rather similar—it too has a depressed, hopeless air about it, though in this instance I was offered a pair of baby Orang Utangs, which were brought out for me from the back of somewhere when it became obvious that I was looking for animals and that I knew what I was talking about. The man who tried to sell me the orangs was a Dayak who said that whenever he came into town from his jungle village, he always brought with him some sort of animal that he felt he might be able to sell. As he spoke the two bright red babies sat on his hips, looking at me solemnly. Finally one of them felt brave enough to reach across to me and when I put a hand out to him he climbed across and began to investigate my beard which greatly amused the watching populace. I can't speak Indonesian but it was perfectly clear that they were making remarks along the lines that here was one orang talking to another. A nice joke since orang means man, so Orang Utan is man of the forest, and orang puteh is white man.

The real bird market in Indonesia is in Jakarta. It is enormous and has a huge stock, quite the biggest that I have seen in a bird market anywhere in the world for years. The market itself is surrounded by a whole warren of tiny hovels which are inhabited by the birdmen and their families and once one has established a trust and rapport with these blokes, it is in and around their homes that one finds the really interesting animals. They are well aware of what is illegal and they keep it well out of sight, so it was with a considerable sense of excitement and anticipation that I accompanied my Indonesian friend, and Woody, one of the dealers, into the narrow alleys between the tiny shanty-type bungalows. Watching all the time that I did not put a foot into the open drain that ran down the centre of each of these little alleys, I had to squeeze past the cages piled outside most of the houses. Before long we were being followed by a gang of small children, who, unable to speak any English, gleefully parroted everything I said to them. This led after a while to a faintly farcical situation.

It happened like this: I turned round at one moment to face a solemn group of small followers.

'Hallo,' I grinned.

A chorus of 'Hallo' and broad smiles was returned.

'You O.K.?' I asked.

'You O.K.' replied everyone.

'Don't you speak English, anyone?'

'Don't you speak English, anyone?'

This was getting ridiculous, so to liven things up I asked 'Anyone for tennis' to have it echoed back at me.

The taxis in Sumatra have no tyre-treads and almost non-existent brakes (W. Newing)

A Slow Loris in Medan market, Sumatra (W. Newing)

An advertisement for a singing contest for bulbuls and White Eyes (J. Nichol)

A dying eagle at the back of Jakarta's bird market (W. Newing)

'Hippopotamus milkshake.' This one caused some problems with the many syllables but they had a crack at it. Later on as I was leaving I heard them all conversing with one another in their newly-acquired English, 'Hallo,' said one, 'Hippopotamus milkshake?' 'O.K.,' lisped a little tot, 'Anyone for tennis?' They are all probably doing it today; try it when you go there!

It was in this little secret community round the back of the bird market, or to use the Indonesian name, Pasar Burung, that I was offered the real goodies, and as we wandered about from one house to another cage after cage of rarities were brought out for my inspection.

Gibbons and other primates were commonplace, each of them a baby, kept individually in small wire cages which prevented the social intercourse that is essential to monkeys and apes. They were all under quite a bit of stress and immediately showed signs of tension whenever they realised that someone was going to pick up their cage. You can see worry on the face of a primate just as you can on a human, and all of them in the Pasar Burung bore this expression. After a while in captivity, once an animal has had a chance to adapt to the new circumstances (and provided that all its physical and psychological needs are catered for) it will generally relax, but when badly kept it cannot ever feel secure. This is particularly so in Third World countries where most people seem to lack a sensitivity towards animals, regarding them either as something to eat or as something to provide them with entertainment which is often provoked with the aid of a pointed stick. In these conditions the captives become stir crazy and a sort of mad resignation can be seen on their faces. I am not at all against properly kept zoos and I do not have a lot of time for people who want to ban them all, but I do dislike seeing animals kept like this. I would guess that once an animal has reached this sort of stage, it would find it almost impossible to establish any normal relationship with another animal. In Pata Zoo in Bangkok there is a splendid adult male Mountain Gorilla that lives in solitary state in a concrete jungle. The wretched thing has been there for years ever since it was

Polar Bears in a temperature of over 100°F in the rooftop zoo at Pata department store in Bangkok (W. Newing)

little. Having nothing to do, the animal lies immobile on its back for most of the day. The keepers said that he was most aggressive and extremely difficult to handle nowadays. So much so they added, that when it was necessary to move him from one compartment of his cage to another, they had to use hot water from a jet nozzle on the end of a hosepipe to get him to shift. They wondered what had made him fierce.

All the primates at Jakarta's Pasar Burung had not yet reached either of these states of relaxation or resignation—they were still extremely anxious and frightened and tried to make themselves as small as they could in the furthest corner of their cages, even though this was only ten inches further away than they had been previously.

There were also a few Leopard Cat kittens available but they were far too young to be really aware of their predicament although they certainly hissed at anyone who stuck a hand too close. This particular species is exploited heavily—Leopard Cats are to be found everywhere on sale as kittens and the skins of the adults may be seen adorning many a shop window or the wall of a room in a private house. The surprising thing about these animals is that they continue to survive; like most animals at the top of the food chain they do not reproduce in nearly the numbers that many animals do, and like so many species that are captured as babies the adults are shot at the same time. Baby cats do look so appealing. So too do the lorises, and as a result they are on sale all over the place and Jakarta had its quota, but what did surprise me was the number of Fruit Bats in cages. I love Fruit Bats, but no one can pretend that they are an ideal pet for a layman. Of course it might have been that they were being sold for food though the chaps in the Pasar Burung said not.

This particular market sells only animals and the things necessary for keeping them in captivity, and some of the stalls sell just cages, or food of all sorts from black rice and millet to ants' eggs and beetle larvae. And everywhere there are birds. Around the outside of the market can be found those sellers who do not have an actual stall. They sit surrounded by their stock which usually includes several large, beautifully self-confident fighting cocks. Inside the market is pretty dark as the whole place is covered over, resulting in many of the stalls being so gloomy that it is difficult to see the stock, especially those birds in the cages that are hung way above your head. It does not seem to deter the birds though, who continue to sing away noisily. The Indonesians also seem to like singing birds as do the Singaporeans, though not to the same extent. There is a wide variety of birds here that have been collected throughout the 13,000 odd islands of the archipelago including New Guinea, and Irian Jaya which is the other half of the same island. Here and there if you hunt assiduously can also be found birds from Australia and the dealers will happily admit that they came from there, though everybody is well aware that the practice of trapping birds in Australia and exporting them from the country and then importing them into Indonesia is against the laws of both countries. Amongst the stock in the Pasar Burung are quite a few rarities. Black Palm Cockatoos can be found on many stalls and Eclectus Parrots and Leadbetter's Cockatoos are easily seen. There is even a scattering of Bali Mynahs and birds of paradise of various species, but it was while I was gleefully hunting through this Aladdin's cave full of treasure that I came upon two or three birds of a species that I could not identify at all. The birds were about the size of a large sparrow, pitch black all over with the exception of a bright red rump and a large banana yellow bill shaped like that of a grosbeak. They were super birds and I would have loved to have known what they were. The dealers said that they came from Irian Jaya and they were pretty rare since they only appeared occasionally. The price being asked for these little jewels was £45.00, though I am certain that with a little negotiating I could have obtained them for a third of that figure. The prices asked for birds varied from a few coppers for common things such as Pied Mynahs to £1,500 for birds of paradise. Being the world's worst mathematician I found it pretty difficult to work out the prices since the rate of exchange in Indonesia is 1,500 odd rupiah to the £ and it really made my head reel when somebody told me that a bird was 91,450 rupiah, only to discover after a lengthy session with my fingers that we were only talking about £60!

Another aspect of the market that interested me was the number of imported birds that were available. It seemed ironic that here was a country rich in avian life and people were wanting to buy Budgerigars from Belgium, but that is what was happening, though to be honest the consignment from the wholesalers in Europe also included a lot of other birds as well. African finches seemed to be popular, and Pekin Robins, and there was even a cage full of Waxwings. I took a birdy friend to the Pasar Burung one day, and I stood to one side watching while he started to negotiate with the vendors and before many minutes were over he was surrounded by a ring of cages full of Rufous Bellied Niltavas and Blue Flycatchers and sunbirds. As I waited, Black Robins fluttered at the bars of their cages watched by a couple of phlegmatic kingfishers while vivid azure Fairy Bluebirds sat shoulder to shoulder with almost fluorescent yellow Black Naped Orioles in cages that were far too small for them. Before long, my friend, who suffers from asthma, was having puff after puff of his Ventolin spray as his excitement aggravated the condition. After our visit he stood beside me wheezing like a steam engine while I watched for a taxi, but with a happy smile on his face and his arms full of paper bags filled with birds.

There is no doubt at all that bird markets use up great numbers of wild animals, nor is there any doubt that many of these die a long drawn out agonising death, usually, if indeed it matters, an undignified death, and I would be delighted if this could all be stopped; yet in some ways I think it would be a shame if bird markets did disappear. They are very exciting places, with always the possibility of coming across something new or particularly interesting. The people who work in bird markets are usually most knowledgeable and frequently are highly competent field naturalists. They are often likeable, and these locations are invariably well populated with a sprinkling of real characters.

Furthermore many of the animal accessories such as cages are truly beautiful and when the markets disappear the cages will too, being replaced by plastic and chromed wire monstrosities as is already happening. In the Jakarta market I found two half-weaned bear cubs, each sitting in a fibreglass dog-carrying box. It must have been sweltering in there. At any rate they were delighted to be released and rushed to grab my ankles as I squatted before them. They both stood upright and sucked eagerly on my thumbs, and given the chance, would have done so forever. Each time I extracted a soggy digit from their little mouths they would set up a plaintive bleating. Finally their owners stuffed them back in their boxes but their wails followed me around the market for quite some time. Nice people, bears, but fancy selling them as pets. They grow huge and even a friendly bear has great long claws that dig into you during a friendly cuddle.

9. Cruelty in the Trade

Previous page: Live
turtles at Orissa await
the bus to Calcutta
(D. Whiting)

Man was keeping livestock long before the first animal welfare organisation was formed and he always will, and whenever an animal is kept in captivity there will be cruelty involved along the way. Nowadays there are organisations whose aims cover every sort of cruelty that you could imagine, and the daft thing is that they just will not join together to work for a common end. Ask an official in any of them if this would not be the best system and they all solemnly agree that of course it would, and then after a pause they add, 'But you must realise that our organisation is rather different to all the others,' and then promptly tell you why they should not join such a union. The truth is that each organisation is administered by folk who are far more interested in empire building than in their cause. This is another charge to which they will all agree and then point out that it does not apply in their case. The poor old punters in the street who donate their pennies to a good cause don't ever understand that the money could go so much further if it was pooled. And such movements do for some reason attract odd folk so that the whole scene is surrounded by a loony fringe which is thought by the public to represent the rest. This is an erroneous picture but newspapers being what they are, they would far rather print a photo of a chap in wayout gear and long hair hanging over his mad eyes, especially if he is accompanied by a solemn bra-less girl cuddling a small puppy than a boring mugshot of a tidy middle-aged man in a collar and tie.

The whole problem is exacerbated by the fact that such organisations are often very poor at PR, feeling that because they care so strongly about their subject everybody else must too. One result of this is that the layman confuses each group with the others which is hardly surprising when one considers that there are probably hundreds in the UK alone from Chickens' Lib (Chickens' Lib, for Pete's sake) with a few hundred supporters to the RSPCA with thousands and thousands. Animals the world over would be even worse off if it was not for such groups, but for goodness sake, isn't it time they got their act together?

Members of such societies will sit down to a steak pie and complain about animals in captivity, while others with an aviary in the garden will object to the brutality of a cattle market. In the end each person must accept his own level of cruelty. Having said all that, there are many cruel practices throughout the animal trading world that most people in Western societies would find unacceptable and one in particular that made me cringe recently was in the weekend market in Bangkok. The squirrel stalls do a steady trade each week selling both adults and youngsters to a gullible public. Hand-reared baby squirrels can make delightful pets but I could not understand how a wild-caught adult could be handled because not only are they fierce but they have BIG TEETH. By watching carefully I discovered how the taming was achieved. It was not easy to observe as the process was carefully carried out so that no one could see. The squirrels arrived at the market crammed into a cage about two feet long which was divided into four compartments, each of which held a dozen or so squirrels. The dealer would open one compartment and extract a squirrel in one hand, gripped in such a way that it could not bite. Held like this each claw and sometimes the end joint of a toe was then removed with a pair of nail clippers and when this operation was completed the same clippers were used to chop off the two upper and lower incisor teeth against the gums. A styptic pencil was applied to any bloody bits and a string noose was placed round the squirrel's neck. The cord was cut off leaving a six inch tail and this was tied to one of the bars of the top of the cage, so that the animal could not run away. Voilà, a tame squirrel! It was unable to bite and because it had no claws to get a grip, when it was placed on the clothing of a purchaser it clung on tightly so that it wouldn't fall off, but to someone who didn't know it really seemed as though it was cuddling the new owner. The treated rodents cannot have lived long because they were unable to eat. Can you imagine what the jolt must feel like when you crunch a bit of food after your teeth have been cut off at the gum. It gives me goose pimples just to think of it. As I watched the whole business one day an untreated squirrel escaped, and as he flickered across the ground towards the nearest tree I wished him well.

Escapes from such places must be fairly frequent, but it must be rare for a monkey to escape. It happened once though at Crawford Market in Bombay. As I entered one day two men were squatting in the entrance. Between them was a large adult male Rhesus Monkey with a collar round his neck. Attached to the collar were two chains, one at either side, and the other end of the chains were held by the men in such a way that they were tight, thus preventing the monkey from biting either. The monkey was remarkably quiet though it barked briefly at anyone who approached too close. The sight was an unusual one and I squatted down to ask the men what was happening. The story they told me was this: some years ago this particular monkey was brought in as a baby with a group of other youngsters. It had escaped and promptly shot up into the rafters of the covered market and there it had lived ever since. Whenever it was hungry the monkey would make a sudden lightning dive onto one of the fruit stalls to grab a mango or an orange, demolishing carefully prepared displays and scattering terrified customers in all directions. As it grew bolder the stallholders would try and beat it off, so that in due course, it became ever more savage and would readily bite anyone who tried to foil one of its raids. It lived in this fashion for years until one

Squirrels, their teeth and claws cut off, are sold as tame. The bags contain a variety of animals (W. Newing)

particular day when, during the heat of the afternoon the market was quiet and the stallholders were all dozing. One of them was covered in a cloth to keep off the flies and for some reason the monkey did not realise that there was a man beneath this covering. He carefully scanned the row of fruit stalls below, and noting that all was quiet he dropped onto the nearest stall, straight on top of the sleeping man. The sudden thump of a heavy Rhesus Monkey landing on him caused the man to awake and he leapt up with such a roar that the monkey scrabbled up the nearest pile of custard apples which terrified it even further as the heap collapsed beneath it and leapt from there to the next pile of fruit on the stall. The resulting din had woken everyone who joined in the fray while the poor monkey galloped the length of the row of fruit stalls while ever more irate greengrocers swiped at him with anything that was available. The monkey emerged at the other end unscathed where he shot up the nearest pillar to the relative safety of the roof, leaving chaos beneath.

Some of the fruit sellers had large lumps growing on their heads where they had inadvertently been whacked by their fellows, and though there was now not much fruit on the stalls, the floor of the aisle was knee deep in pineapples, sweetlimes and bananas. Nobody knew which bit of fruit belonged to whom and as they argued noisily about it they continued to thump one another and inevitably some of them fell in the slippery mess of damaged fruit until in the end the whole area looked like hell on earth.

Eventually order was restored and the place cleaned up. Abrasions were tended and apologies grudgingly given were grudgingly received. Enough was enough. Everyone agreed on that and a mass meeting was held. The result was that a considerable reward was offered to anyone who would rid the place of this turbulent beast. In time the monkey was captured by the two men holding his chains, and in due course they were going to kill him. The captors were now comparatively rich men but they were not going to lose an opportunity to increase their capital, so they were displaying the monkey and telling the story in the hope that the audience would DROP A FEW COPPERS INTO THE PLATE. I got the message and did just that as I stood up and then something occurred to me, so that as I was turning to leave, I stopped and asked, 'But if the monkey is as fierce as you say, why is he sitting so placidly?' Certainly he was savage, I was told, and he would make life most difficult for passers-by if they had not taken steps to curb him and that was why they had carefully broken his back before the display so that he could not rush out and attack people.

I came across this broken back technique in Delhi as well. Perhaps the best-known shopping area in New Delhi is Connaught Circus. Along the edge of the pavement small stallholders with fruit or magazines, and shoeshine boys call out in the hope of a bit of trade. Amongst all the other commodities being offered, one used to be able to find native cures and medicines. The men who sold these potions would make them on the spot, cooking the ingredients in a pot over a small fire. An essential ingredient for one of these mixtures was essence of gecko. Geckoes are soft-skinned lizards that are found throughout the tropics where they commonly live inside buildings, hence the usual name of House Lizard. Geckoes are active creatures and don't much like sitting around, preferring to dash off and do things. Therefore, if you are a medicine man with a basketful of geckoes on the pavement alongside, you have to take steps to ensure that they stay put. A lid costs money, and besides which, each time it is opened there is a chance that some of the stock will escape, so these medicine men

Facing page: Out of sight, round the back of animal markets, is where the rare stuff is to be found (W. Newing)

would snap the spine of each lizard between the thumb and first finger of each hand, as you might break a twiglet, before dropping them into the basket. It certainly was an effective way of ensuring that the stock did not escape. When the broth was ready to receive the geckoes they were dropped into the bubbling mixture alive.

When I was recently in Delhi I looked for the gecko men in Connaught Circus but found none and assumed that they no longer existed, and then one day after visiting the bird hospital opposite the Red Fort I turned the corner and went for a wander down Chandni Chowk, which is an Indian bazaar that must have changed little over a great many years. The place is absolute pandemonium and packed with human beings from end to end. One can buy anything in Chandni Chowk or in the warren of tiny medieval streets that surrounds it, and there amidst all the din, the smell and the flies, outside a roadside foodstall I found a medicine man complete with stock of geckoes. He was very old and blind in one eye. I stopped to talk to him for a while which was not easy as, squatting on the edge of the pavement, one was forever surrounded by a sea of legs. What a way to earn a living! I asked him if modern medicines had made any difference to his trade and he admitted that it is not what it was, though, he added, there were still quite a few people who came to him. I asked if he still used the eyes of the Slender Loris in his medicines and he told me that he did and asked how I knew about that. Years ago I had accompanied some hunters into a forest in Orissa on a nocturnal expedition. I was looking for owls but they were after lorises. When they discovered one in a tree a man would shine a torch in the animal's face while another scuttled up the tree to catch it. Usually the loris remained motionless but sometimes it tried to flee at speed. A loris in top gear is a contradiction since they move astonishingly slowly, rather like a mammalian chameleon. So even an escape attempt made no difference in the end.

When a loris was caught, each eyeball was quickly cut out of its head with a single circular stroke of a very sharp knife and the blinded animal was returned to a branch where it stood, rocking slowly. I asked the hunters why they did not kill the loris before removing the eyes. It was against their religious beliefs one of them told me with a smile, to kill any animal, so they only took what was necessary for their business and let the animal go on its way.

Surely one of the most cruel parts of the animal trade these days must be the business of the frogs' legs. At one time only the French ate frogs' legs, but over the last 20 years or so the trade has caught on to such an extent that nowadays they can be bought everywhere and some fish and chip shops sell frogs' legs and french fries. Though some frogs are taken in the Americas, most of those in trade are found in India and further East. Nowadays there are not many decent-sized frogs left in Europe to meet the huge demand, although more than 300,000 are caught each year in the Belgian province of Luxembourg. Most of the frogs used in the trade are Tiger Frogs because they are large amphibians with good, meaty legs.

The animals are caught and placed in hessian sacks in their hundreds. These sacks are then sent to the processing centres. It is calculated that India, Indonesia and Bangladesh catch over 250 million frogs a year. Quite a lot of these are not exported as they die before they can be processed but when they do arrive at their destination the slaughterer holds the body of the frog in one hand and the outstretched legs in the other and slices their legs off with an upright fixed blade. The legless frog is then tossed aside to die slowly. Amphibians can put up with considerable abuse before they die so these frogs can last quite a time before they finally expire. I was talking about this to a Frenchwoman some time ago, who said that 10 or 15 years ago she and her family would periodically go out into the country around her home to collect frogs to eat. Once in the kitchen these were always skinned alive before being jointed for the pot.

I would never eat frogs' legs as I find the business quite horrific, and another dish that I would not take is turtle soup. I have always refused it because of the status of turtles—there just are not enough turtles around, but for some reason I had not given any thought to the way the reptiles are killed. I discovered recently how it was done. I was walking around a large, bustling market a stone's throw from the expensive hotels of Bangkok looking to see what wildlife was being sold as food and I came across two men hauling a marine turtle onto the top of the stall from where it had been lying face up on the floor. Then while one man held the turtle by the front flippers, the other approached with a small electrical circular saw. He only took a few seconds to cut the side of the shell from hind leg to foreleg before spinning the turtle on its back to do the other side. The saw was switched off and an ordinary knife joined up the two saw cuts across the abdomen and the throat, and the base plate was lifted clear. As it was freed one man sliced away at retaining tissue and in a fairly short time the turtle was dead and in bits. But the whole process had been commenced while it was still alive and conscious and a fair bit of hacking and chopping was done before it died.

I did not see any marine turtles for sale in Singapore but there were plenty of large freshwater terrapins. These also were killed the same way though a small handsaw was used rather than an electrical device.

The legs are cut from live frogs for Western gourmets (D. Whiting)

99

One of the most stomach churning of all cruelty stories however is one that I witnessed in Delhi and though it is about domestic rather than wild animals I feel it should be related. Many of the Domestic Cattle and buffaloes that are slaughtered for meat in Delhi start their life in Rajasthan whence they are frequently transported by lorry. The people who are responsible for the actual journey are concerned to pack as many animals as possible into each vehicle as this saves money. The easiest thing to do would be to slaughter the animals at the beginning of the journey as they could then be closely packed. But refrigerated vehicles are expensive and, therefore, the animals must arrive in Delhi alive or the meat will have spoilt so the open lorries on this run are fitted with stout metal grids like a framework for a roof above the animals' heads. When the beast is to be loaded a metal rod is pushed through the nose from one nostril to the other and a rope is tied round both ends of this rod and taken up to the grid and tied, thereby keeping the animal's head up. Another line is tied tightly to the tail and that also is hauled up tight and tied to the framework above. The animal cannot now move about, flick flies off or shake its head. When all have been loaded in this fashion the calves have all four ankles tied together and they are heaved up onto the floor of the lorry and slid between the feet of the adults so that they fit beneath their bellies. It must be exceedingly hot down there and before long they are being defaecated upon by the adults. And there they all have to stay while they are driven along an Indian road (and Indian country roads are like tank tracks) to Delhi which is many long, hot, painful hours away. In time some of the standing animals are suffering so much they slump so that they are left hanging by their nose and tail and it happens not infrequently that the bar in the nose tears free so that the buffalo drops to the floor snapping the tail under the strain. The sudden weight on the calf underneath causes an immediate prolapse of the rectum. None of the animals can take any sort of action to avoid any of this torment, and in this fashion the consignment of suffering finally arrives in Delhi to be made into steaks and curries.

I had always considered the owners of buffalo carts to be exceptionally silly when they prodded the rump of the animal to make a lesion which easily became infected, as this lowers the value of their animal, but for cattle dealers to actually ship animals in this fashion seems unforgivable to me.

But as I said earlier, people in such countries view animals in a totally different way to Westerners and in bird markets in many Third World countries I have seen parrots and mynahs and crows being sold to be trained as talking birds. For some reason the myth persists that the bird will learn to talk better if the tongue is split from end to end and the bird dealer will do this for the customer at the time of purchase. Either a sharp penknife can be used or, even a thumbnail for the mynahs. It is quite ridiculous because a bird does not use its tongue to mimic speech anyway.

The funny thing is that it is easy enough to generate enthusiasm in animal welfare if the cruelty in question is practised on mammals or birds, but far fewer folk are willing to do something for the lesser animals.

I told a friend of mine that I had recently seen some Pekin Robins for sale in a pet shop in Singapore, and that one of the birds had somehow been completely scalped, by which I don't mean that it had lost the feathers on its head but that the whole top of the skull was visible. My friend, who spends much of his time and energy promoting animal welfare causes, became excited and commenced a long tirade about the captive animal trade in general, but when I interrupted him to point out that in the same shop there were for sale great numbers of tiny froglets which anglers buy to use as bait, which is not much fun for the frogs as the hook is inserted into them after which they are allowed to swim about until taken by a fish, he dismissed the subject in less than twenty words before continuing to talk about the Pekin Robins.

The whole question of cruelty can only be answered by education, as there is absolutely no use trying to impose Western ideas onto peoples with entirely different cultures. Some years ago someone I know was collecting animals in West Africa for a number of different zoos and amongst his orders he had requests for several Crowned Cranes, so one day, finding himself in a Crowned Crane area, he asked the local trappers to collect some for him and told them that he had to move on but would be back some days hence to pick up and pay for the birds. But the best laid plans of mice and animal collectors gang invariably astray and it was nearly a month before he arrived once more in that particular village where he was delighted to find that in the interim his trappers had done well, as there were dozens and dozens of Crowned Cranes standing about in an enclosure. His pleasure did not last long for when he examined the birds he discovered that one wing of each of them was broken. Furiously he asked why.

'To stop them flying away, naturally,' he was told by the men who were puzzled at his anger.

The same chap used to specialise in nectar-feeding birds and on the same expedition he collected a great number of African sunbirds, the males of which are frequently brightly coloured and highly iridescent, and among his birds he came across a single specimen that he could not identify. He was better than anyone I have ever known at identifying African sunbirds. This one had him stumped, but happy with his catch he placed the bird in an aviary he had erected at his holding camp together with the other sunbirds that he had collected, until the day came when he was to return home. As the sun rose he and his African helpers were already packing animals for the journey as fast as they could manage, and by late afternoon everyone was hot and tired, leaving only the sunbirds to catch and pack. As the men were boxing these delicate little animals the unidentified bird either scratched or bit the handler, neither of which can have done him any damage at all since these birds are completely harmless. Nevertheless it was the last straw at the end of a hard day, and spinning round he whacked its head on a post to kill it. That the animal was a rarity did not occur to him. On his return to this country the collector searched through every book on sunbirds that he could find but he never did identify it.

Elsewhere in the same country—Sierra Leone—I was out one day looking for snakes when I heard excited childish voices coming from the other side of a clump of trees. I made for the sounds, thinking that perhaps the children had found something interesting, only to discover that they were throwing small stones at a row of naked, cheeping chicks which they had suspended by their necks from a horizontal piece of string that was stretched between two branches while the mother bird scolded frantically from a twig above their heads.

The world is full of the oddest attitudes towards animals in an age when we are probably more sensitive to their needs than ever before. When one comes across cruelty as in the case of the little West African boys and the birds it is easy to think, 'Yuk, that's awful but these people see animals in a different light,' and one can forget that even in Western society many are quite uncaring about wanton cruelty to animals. Only yesterday I watched an American movie on television during which a young boy was telling his uncle that his ambition was to keep salamanders, '. . . which are like lizards but more brightly coloured and if you snap all their tails off they grow new ones.' I would have thought that the uncle could have pointed out that it is not a good thing to go around breaking tails off salamanders, but instead he merely laughed. But if you think that is crass, what about the aristocratic old lady I saw in Whipsnade Zoo. She was affectionately watching her grandchildren chasing the free-living peafowl all over the place, causing considerable panic with chicks and peahens cheeping and honking to such an extent that a member of the public went up to the old dear and complained about the behaviour of the little oiks to which she responded that they were only enjoying themselves. At that moment a keeper who had been summoned by another irate visitor, approached and seeing him the grandmother raised her chin and enquired 'Is it all right for my grandchildren to chase the peacocks, keeper?' His blistering reply, delivered in a broad Bedforshire accent is a gem that I will always remember with pleasure.

I would have thought that there might be some animals that are regarded with affection around the world and thus treated with care, but none comes to mind—even harmless old fish constantly have nasty things inflicted upon them. I have watched them being scaled alive in Guyana when they are still alive and kicking vigorously, or whatever fish do.

One of the commonest criticisms aimed at the wild animals trade is that they are cruelly packed for transportation. It is true that sometimes the crates in which animals are shipped are quite disgusting but usually nowadays the worst cases occur when an animal is to be smuggled, so that it needs to be placed in the tiniest possible space so that it won't be detected. There is today a code which specifies many of the packing conditions, and exporters go to considerable trouble and expense to provide the best possible crates. One of the great problems of making export crates is that there are so very many different sizes, numbers and shapes of animals in each consignment that it is only possible to standardise crate design to a certain extent.

There are features of many export cages that appear cruel to the layman when in reality the features that he objects to most are designed for the animals' welfare. A common objection to crates for large animals is that they are not wide enough for the animal to turn around. The person who is doing the complaining seems not to ask why the box is designed like that. It certainly does not save money, nor is it made that way because the shipper thinks to himself, 'Ha ha, if I make a narrow crate it will be nice and cruel for the antelope that will travel in it.' The reason for a narrow crate is that, unable to turn around or lie down, the occupant will of necessity remain quiet and therefore will not come to any harm before it arrives at the other end. A crate that was large enough to allow movement would result in the animal wandering about the whole time in an enclosed space and making constant attempts to escape. After a few hours it would have any number of abrasions and cuts and broken horns or teeth. And the same thing would happen if it could lie down—in a panic to stand up in a dark, enclosed place an animal could easily snap a leg, so although it seems cruel to prevent a large animal from lying down, it should be remembered that in the wild many animals spend a great deal of their rest periods dozing on their feet. After all, when all is said and done, most flights nowadays last only a matter of hours.

Flamingoes and other birds with long, thin legs are packed into sacks with only the head and neck sticking out so that they have to remain in a sitting position. They are then placed side by side in a large box. Whenever the animal welfare organisations report this fact they do so with tight-lipped anger and many photographs, but again it is the least cruel way. Flamingoes' legs are so very fragile that if they were packed standing up the chances of the legs of every single bird being broken by the time they were unpacked is pretty high. Packed in a sack no legs get broken and when the sack is removed some birds clearly have cramp, at any rate pins and needles, but in a few minutes they are fine. And if you have flown halfway around the world in a Boeing 747 you will know that when you step off the plane at Heathrow your own legs feel cramped and your ankles are swollen but by the time you arrive in the middle of London you feel normal once more.

I watched a whole pile of crates being constructed at the Wing Loon premises of Terence Loh in Singapore. Those being made to house a number of birds were fitted with wire mesh floors which must be uncomfortable to stand about on during the journey but they served two purposes. Firstly all the faeces dropped through so that the birds did not have to paddle about in them, and the food would not be contaminated, and secondly the mesh provided the birds with something to hang onto so that each time the crate was tilted they did not all end up in a great heap in one corner which was a common occurrence at one time, causing the death of many, for although such crates are clearly labelled 'THIS WAY UP' and 'LIVE ANIMALS WITH CARE', I have seen airport staff in many parts of the world handle the boxes as though they contained plimsolls.

Where Terence's men were making crates that were to hold a number of birds that could not be housed together because of aggression, each box was fitted with carefully made partitions and every compartment was fitted with food and water receptacles. Mortality does occur on consignments of animals but when they are shipped properly the numbers that arrive dead are very low. The major exporters who have been in business a long time take care that the whole business of packing and feeding the animals, transporting them to the airport and getting them onto the appropriate plane is done as efficiently as possible.

10. The Trapping of Live Animals

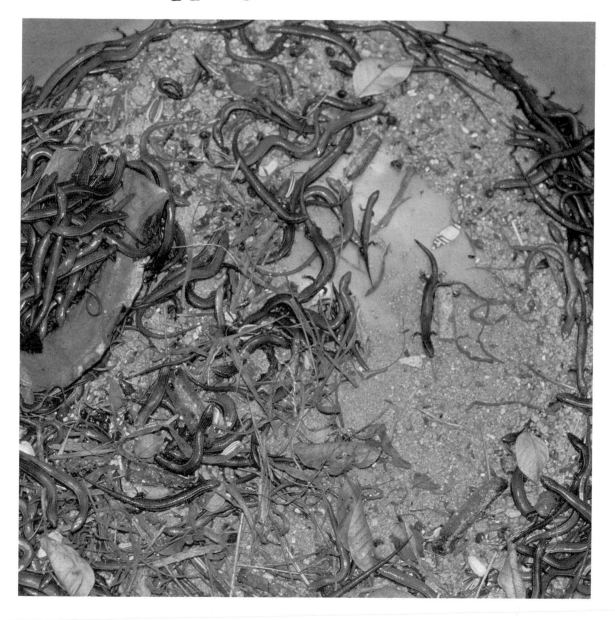

*Previous page: These
skinks are noosed and
kept live in a bucket to
feed songbirds
(W. Newing)*

There must be nearly as many ways of trapping animals as there are trappers and it would take a far fatter book than this one to describe them all. However, certain techniques are found with variations all over the world and it is these and the most commonly used methods that I shall describe.

Animals that are ultimately exported are obtained in one of two ways. Either they turn up 'accidentally', by which I mean that someone in a country area who is not a trapper manages to obtain an animal when perhaps it has fallen from the nest, or when a tree is cut down, or even when young animals are picked up after the mother has been killed for food. In this sort of case the villager will usually offer his catch to the local animal man, and in due course these animals can end up in a mixed consignment at the premises of an exporter.

Or, and this is by far the more common, professional trappers collect the animals as the first link in the complicated chain between the jungle and the living room. Although a few trappers get into the profession by mistake, most of them come from a long line of animal collectors who are part of a whole community, so one finds villages whose inhabitants have traditionally existed by catching wild animals, and though such people will collect any species to order, they are usually fairly specific in their expertise, so in India for example, most of the snake men are Rajasthanis while the bird trappers are found in the Himalayan foothills and Orissa.

The trappers are highly skilled men who are without exception very good field naturalists. Since there is no point catching what cannot be sold they need to be able to identify the species they come across and be able to differentiate between the sexes where they are not alike and also identify the juveniles which often look totally different from their parents. These men need to know the calls of the animals, the trees which they feed on and the seasons in which they may be found or during which they breed. What they fall down on is maintaining their catches in captivity which I initially found most surprising. Catching an animal is one thing, but getting it over the next couple of weeks is another headache altogether. Often the difference between persuading a newly caught animal to accept food in captivity and losing it altogether is a fairly simple process, but if a trapper gets it into his head that a particular animal eats a certain kind of food he will continue to feed that food to that species year after year even if most of them die.

Sunbirds have always been regarded as delicate in captivity and a good deal of this reputation is because they arrive emaciated and barely alive so that they need constant coddling for weeks if they are to survive. Importers had always insisted that if the birds could arrive healthy they would not be too much of a problem. This is quite true, they are not nearly as delicate as once was thought and I have seen Bronzy Sunbirds bathing in freezing water in an English aviary when there was a good layer of snow on the ground. Bronzy Sunbirds are African, and were never regarded as being as delicate as Asian Sunbirds which are tiny little mites. I watched trappers catching these minute nectar feeders using birdlime. After capture the birds were transferred to bags till the trapper got home when he put them in cages with a dish containing a sugar solution as a substitute for the nectar which forms a large part of a sunbird's diet. The birds soon deteriorated and many died, and by watching them I discovered that the reason for this decline was that the birds did not recognise the dish of nectar as food. I wanted to try something so I went out with the sunbird catchers on their expeditions taking with me a small bottle of the nectar substitute and as soon as a freshly caught bird was unglued from the birdlime I would insert its beak into the liquid. Usually it fed instantly. If it didn't I inserted the beak a bit further until a drop of nectar dripped into a nostril whereupon the bird opened its beak to breathe and some liquid would trickle down its throat. Only a split second was needed before pulling the head back a bit after which it too would feed readily. Then, when it had finished, if it was put into a cage with a nectar pot on the floor it would feed quite happily and after this hardly any sunbirds died. As a result any sunbirds that are exported today and arrive in good condition have been treated like this, because having discovered the technique I have shown trappers and exporters all over the place how to keep their sunbirds alive. When I returned to India recently one of my old trapper friends in Naini Tal told his teenaged son that it was I who had taught him this technique that he had now passed on to the boy. I first went trapping with him nearly 20 years ago.

Waders were one of the other problem groups of animals and many zoos wanted Redshanks and Golden Plovers but they too were difficult to ship in good condition until I discovered in Guyana that if newly caught waders were fed on beansprouts for the first few weeks there were no problems with them, and nowadays that technique is used also. There are lots of such tricks of the trade that are only learnt by experience but which, alas, trappers usually seem not to learn, while at the actual trapping they are quite superb.

Birdlime must be one of the oldest of all trapping devices. Why it is called 'lime' I have no idea since what it really is is a sticky substance to prevent birds from flying away. There are two ways of using it. Either it is stuck onto twigs so that when a bird lands it cannot escape, or it is applied to some sort of device with which the bird is touched to catch it. There are umpteen recipes for birdlime and some of them are very complicated. Nearly all involve a messy, prolonged cooking period, and I can recall watching people making birdlime in Britain years ago. One way was to boil up chips of holly bark which took forever—where do you find large quantities of holly bark chips, and great handfuls of the stuff was required to make very little birdlime, but an even worse technique was to boil pounds and pounds of linseed for hours on end. This process certainly resulted in quantities of extremely sticky goo that got everywhere, in your hair and clothes, and gummed up anything you touched. The whole business stunk like hell, and trying to strain out the husks of the linseed was an impossible task.

The Indians make birdlime from the sap of the peepul tree which works well but they tend to use mustard oil to remove the residue from feathers which is a practice of which I don't approve, for though it works well some of the oil remains which the bird must ingest when it preens. Have you tried mustard oil? It would certainly win one of the runners-up prizes for the most revolting foodstuff of the year and cannot possibly help the bird (already under considerable stress) to adjust to life in captivity.

It was in Trinidad that I finally discovered the most civilised birdlime of all. It was first prepared for me by a taxi driver with the unlikely name of Harry Clark. I also thought that it was odd that a taxi driver in Port of Spain should know how to make birdlime until Harry pointed out that all Trinidadian boys go out catching birds. The practice is illegal in Trinidad but once you know what to look for the scars on the trees from which the ingredients are obtained are so common that it is obvious that boys will always be boys.

A long time before I met Harry I had been in Gujerat in Western India staying with a man who maintained a large and interesting collection of birds. I told him that I would like to watch the bird catchers of the area at work and he immediately offered me the use of his car and his driver the following day with instructions to the man to show me the bird catchers. The next morning we set off early for a long drive. My companion spoke fairly well the language that the Indians call English, and during the course of our conversation I expressed an interest in birdlime. He did not understand the term and I had to translate it in various ways, none of which worked, until I finally referred to it as 'sticky stuff to catch birds'. That elicited immediate comprehension. 'No problem', I was told, one could buy the stuff in the bazaars and he would get me some. A while later we pulled up in a small town and my friend wandered off. When he returned he handed me a small bag of fruit for the journey which I munched happily as we drove on. Feeling refreshed I dropped the bag on the floor and asked once more about birdlime since none had appeared at our last stop.

'I will get you some in the next bazaar,' I was assured. 'There is no problem, it is available at all places.'

At the next village we again stopped and again I was given some fruit and again we drove on. Oh no, I thought, like many people in the country my friend had promised me what I wanted rather than say no, and he was obviously finding it difficult to get hold of birdlime after all. The pattern repeated itself until in the end I was up to here with fresh fruit. All was revealed when I was halfway through a pineapple and I enquired once more for birdlime. My companion exploded. 'Vat do you mean? At each stop I have been buying you sticky things the birds are liking—look, you are eating it even now—and still you are asking me for more!'

So it was with surprise that when I asked for birdlime in Trinidad, Harry Clark (you thought I had forgotten Harry Clark, didn't you) told me firmly that we must go to a baker's shop to buy some stale rolls. I said nothing but watched with interest. Harry conned a dozen free stale rolls out of the baker, and wielding a machete he led me to a rubber tree in the waste ground behind the shop. The trunk at about head height was covered in scars, but Harry carefully found what he thought was a suitable place and gave it a few mighty whacks with his machete. Within seconds a few drops of white latex began to seep from the wounds, and as the stuff trickled down Harry broke open a roll and using it as a sponge he started to mop up the sap. As he worked he explained that the best time of the year to do this was just after the rainy season when the sap was abundant. In a quarter of an hour Harry has saturated quite a few rolls which he dropped into a polythene bag. He rubbed a bit of soil into each cut to seal it and he then led me to a nearby breadfruit tree where we repeated the whole process.

Eventually we returned to the bakery where there was a tap in the yard. Harry got hold of a large tin bath from somewhere and filled it with water and then he and I sat on the ground on either side of the bath and he lobbed all the latex filled rolls into the water. He explained that you always had to work the stuff under water, and indeed keep it in water, as out in the air it was exceptionally sticky. The two of us worried and worked at the rolls under the surface, gradually separating the bread, which fell to pieces in the water, from the latex. Harry insisted that every last crumb was removed from the latex, and as we worked we moulded the stuff into a ball in which the two different types of sap were well amalgamated. In the end we had a ball of lahgli as the Trinidadians call birdlime, which we carted off in a plastic bottle filled with water.

Harry completed the demonstration by showing me how to use the lahgli. A small piece was removed from the ball and teased out into a long thin string in constantly wetted fingers. This was then wrapped round and round one twig after another so that in time all the uppermost twigs of a small tree were very sticky perches. In a quarter of an hour we had caught one hummingbird, one Bananaquit, two Blue Tanagers and a ten-inch-long iguanid lizard that came scuttling up from below. The lahgli was carefully removed from each with a little lighter fuel on a paper hanky and the captives were released. Then wetting our fingers once more we unwound the birdlime from the tree and returned it to the bottle for use next time. Harry instructed me to remove each scrap of bark and debris scrupulously when I got home or the stuff would not be any use in the future. I did, and I still have part of that original ball in a plastic jar of water. That particular type of birdlime I have made many times since. It is superb in the tropics but is no use in cooler climes since it temporarily loses its stickiness as the temperature drops.

Birdlime is used in various countries actually applied to traps. For ground-feeding birds, such as lapwings, two lengths of pliable cane are tied together at right angles and the four points are bent downwards to form a domed, umbrella-like framework. It can be tied like this or the four points stuck in the ground until the sticks dry out in this position. The device is then tied to a stone or similar weight with a short length of string and a large insect such as a cricket is tied to the end of a fine thread whose other end is tied to the junction of the twigs. The cricket stands on the ground in the middle of the dome and the bottom couple of inches of each bamboo is covered with bird lime. Several such domes are dotted about in a likely area. When a bird tries to take the insect and fly off, the pull of the thread surprises the bird so that it loses its balance and instinctively it throws its wings forwards. If the dome has been made correctly the wingtips should contact two of the sticky legs of the dome and the bird is held fast until the trapper runs forward to release it.

A trap which works on much the same principle exists both in India and West Africa for eagles. A length of cane is again bent into a bow and a small crosspiece is tied at the centre of the bow so that the device can rest on the ground with the horns pointing up. A lump of meat is tied to the cross and again the ends of the stick are limed.

Several of these are placed in good eagle country and the trapper disappears into a handy bush. This time when a bird flies down for the meat the wingtips stick to the horns of the trap if the length has been properly calculated for the particular eagle that you want to catch.

It should not be thought that birdlime is only suitable for catching birds. In Brazil I have seen it used to obtain Ocelots, of all things. On that occasion the trapper placed a live young Agouti, which is a largish, tailless rodent, in a cage on a path which he knew was regularly used by an Ocelot. He then applied dollops of birdlime to many of the fallen leaves that littered the path for some yards on either side of the bait. This particular birdlime was not as solid as the chewing gum-like lahgli, but more like the linseed I referred to earlier. Then we hid. In time a splendid male Ocelot appeared, silently padding along the little path. It saw the Agouti and paused before lowering itself into a crouch just like a domestic cat after a bird. It waited motionless for several minutes watching the Agouti in the cage. I opened my mouth to breathe, so that the Ocelot would not hear me, and I looked away briefly every few seconds and unfocused my brain. I am convinced that it is the unremitting concentration of an inexperienced hunter that transmits itself to an animal, so that in the blink of an eye it vanishes, or in some cases it will fade slowly into the background and disappear without making any movement at all. This is the sort of sensitivity that cannot be taught, and many will not believe, but anyone who has collected wild animals or filmed them will know what I am talking about.

On that particular day the Ocelot slowly shifted its weight so that it moved forwards an inch, and then again, and once more until it put a foot on some birdlime. It was far too professional to try and shake it off but you could see the animal register the fact. It moved again and another leaf stuck to it, and this time it glanced briefly down at the sticky leaf. One more movement and one more leaf, and I swear you could see the Ocelot think to itself, 'Blow this for a lark, I can't creep up on an Agouti with half the Amazon forest glued to me.' So he gave up the hunt and tried to remove a leaf from his foot which stuck instead to his face. Each move he made stuck more debris to him and when he lay down to pull some off he got himself well covered. In a few minutes he was completely absorbed in his task, swearing away as he worked. The hunter quietly stepped up to him and before the Ocelot could register a presence he had been scooped into a sack.

We gathered up all the other sticky leaves so that nothing else could get caught, rescued the Agouti and set off home with our sack of Ocelot. An hour later in the village the leaves were all peeled off the angry cat and he was dumped in a cage to lick himself clean.

Trapping animals of any sort requires two things; a device of some sort, possibly employing bait or a decoy, and a knowledge of the beast together with an understanding of animal psychology. A trapper can set any number of traps but unless they are put in suitable locations and he understands why they are set there he won't catch anything. This is why so many people who set mousetraps complain that they do not work and worry that they are not using the correct bait. Bait recipes for mouse-catching are legion, but it doesn't matter what you use for the House Mouse. What is important is the location of the traps. Equally there is no point buying one trap, for to be sure of success the householder should buy a dozen.

Most traps that are commercially available for catching animals alive are basically of a single type, consisting of a wire mesh box with a door through which animals can enter but not leave. Occasionally trappers use Brailsford type traps which have a door at either end so that the trap appears as a perfectly open tunnel, but when the bait is taken or a treadle is stepped upon, both ends close at the same time. I have only found these being used where trappers have come into contact with Europeans or Americans—they do not seem to have evolved in other parts of the world. What is very common, however, is a trap with a balanced self-closing door. The advantage of this type is that it can catch a number of animals whereas the previous trap will catch only one until it is reset. These multicatch traps are simple devices that can be made of any material. In India I have seen them constructed from half inch wide metal strapping as is used round large packages and crates. In that country they are used to trap Palm Squirrels which enter them so readily that one has to check them frequently, otherwise you find the thing jammed full of little striped faces peering out at you and with as little freedom of movement as commuters in the Underground in the rush hour.

One of the cleverest traps that I have ever seen was being used in West Africa to trap weavers and small finches and interestingly the only other place where I have seen the same device used was in Bedfordshire (where it was known as a crow trap) by the local gamekeepers who used it for trapping corvids of all sorts such as Magpies and Jackdaws, though it was most efficient at catching smaller birds as well. The pleasing thing about crow traps is that there are no moving parts. The trap consists of a six-foot cuboid framework covered in mesh and with a small door at one corner so that the trapper may enter. In the middle of the roof is a hole with a diameter of twelve inches and from this hangs a foot-long cylinder of mesh. The trapper puts a whole pile of bait on the floor directly under the funnel and goes away. What happens is that birds come along, see the bait and climb about over the wire neeting until they come to the edge of the hole. Looking down, they can finally see the food with no intervening barrier, so they drop down through the funnel. When they have finished feeding they try to fly outwards whereupon they meet the walls of the trap. None thinks of flying directly upwards which is an extraordinarily difficult thing anyway for most birds to do, apart from quail which are like avian helicopters and need special terylene topped traps as they fly up so fast that they scalp themselves on wire. Periodically the trapper empties the trap, leaving only a few birds each time as decoys. These crow traps are astonishingly effective.

Another trap, and again without moving parts, that seems to be particularly African, is one designed to catch skinks, which are ground-living lizards that look as though they have been enamelled and then polished to a high gloss. The trap is a chunk of solid wood about the size and shape of an ordinary house brick through which have been drilled a number of lizard-diameter holes. These bricks are then put in suitable locations where skinks congregate, and I have found that rubbish dumps and leaf litter at the bottom of trees are good places. They do take a while to be accepted by lizards but eventually the skinks regard the tunnels in the wood as good hidey holes so that when the surroundings are disturbed by the approaching trapper they all dive for these tunnels. The brick is picked up and placed in a plastic bucket but persuading the lizards to come out needs a bit of patience. Sometimes blowing sharply through a hole causes the occupant to shoot out of the other side into the leaf litter at the bottom of the bucket, but frequently a bit of gentle prodding with a twig is required to empty the brick so that it can be replaced.

Bigger lizards, like the monitors in Africa and the Tegu Lizards in South America, are caught in an entirely different type of trap that looks like a long, loosely woven cone of wicker which the lizard enters and then cannot back out from without assistance. Do you remember those funny toys you played with when you were small that were called Chinese Handcuffs? They worked on exactly the same principle for they were a cylinder of woven palm leaf or something similar. If you stuck a finger in each end you soon discovered that it was impossible to pull it out. The only way to extricate yourself was to push the two fingers together so that the Chinese Handcuff became short and fat rather than long and thin, and somehow holding it like that it was easy to extract a finger.

By far the commonest way of catching lizards is with the hands but that does involve the trappers in considerable dashing about and many lizards escaping. The best way of all is to attach a small nylon monofilament noose directly to the end of a long stick. Then if you are patient you can gently slide it over the lizard's head and round his neck, and you've got him. The only point to note is that the noose must be tight up to the stick, not drifting about several inches from it or you will never catch anything. The snag about the technique is that you have to compromise between how close you can get to your lizard and how long a pole you can conveniently carry and I once got unstuck in just such a situation.

There was a large patch of waste ground in French Guiana out of the middle of which stuck a pole. It wasn't really a pole, it was a palm tree without a top that had died. Halfway up was a magnificent iguana and as I looked at it I realised that it was undoubtedly the biggest, most beautiful specimen that I had ever seen in my life. I scuttled back to the house and grabbed my lizard-catching stick, a heap of bamboos like garden canes and a ball of string, and back I hurried to see if the iguana was still where I had left him. Surprisingly he was, so holding my sticks and string above my head I started to force my way through the undergrowth towards the dead palm tree. The whole area was covered in a chest-high tangle of bramble-like mimosa with savage thorns which leapt at me from all sides so that before I was halfway I was covered in myriad scratches and my T-shirt was patterned with little right angle tears, but through all this I kept my eyes on the iguana who took no notice of my crashing approach, even though it was punctuated by muttered curses. The lizard remained glued vertically to his tree with his head facing the sun, his eyes closed and a slight smile on his face. When I got to within 20 feet he opened his eyes and cocked his head to one side to look at me. Five feet further on he was looking decidedly nervous so I decided that I had better stand still. The iguana was about 12 feet from the ground and I had brought plenty of sticks with me so that I should be able, by tying them together, to reach him without any trouble. It wouldn't be easy as each movement I made resulted in further lacerations, and by now I was covered in sweat and trickles of blood which every flying insect between the Amazon and the Rio Grande had decided was just what they needed for lunch.

Moving very slowly I tied the end of the noose stick to my next length of bamboo and cut off the string with my penknife. I stuck these up in the air and tied on the next stick while the iguana shuffled a bit and glanced from me to the noose. I was sure that I had a long enough pole by now so I gently propped all the other canes against the undergrowth and accidentally dropped the ball of string on the ground. Then I carefully inched the noose towards my lizard. He didn't think much of this idea, all he wanted to do was sunbathe, so judging distances perfectly he edged up the tree just sufficiently so that the noose was impotently waving about a foot below his tail. I carefully fed my stick back into the hole in which I was standing and took up another cane and then remembered that the string was by my feet. I started to (Ouch) bend my knees keeping my (Ooh) elbows to my (Eek) sides until I was (Ow, my neck) squatting on my heels at the bottom of a vegetarian barbed wire entanglement. I couldn't see the string so I had to feel for it, not quite knowing what I was going to put my hand on, until with the ball firmly in my hand I straightened up once more (Aieeh!). When I wiped the sweat from my eyes and put my glasses on again I discovered that while I had been away the iguana had climbed a good ten feet higher up the tree. I was sure he was still within range, but only just, so I frantically started to tie more bamboos together before he moved any further. Eventually I had a device that looked as tall as a television transmitter mast, and when I lowered it towards the reptile on the tree I discovered that not only was it heavy but the far end of it was waving about all over the place. The iguana found this interesting and watched carefully. The noose approached within a few inches; ahh, I was almost there, but the strain was making my arms ache and the noose was wobbling about all over the place. This is really great, thought the iguana—I could see him think it—let's see what he does next, and he turned 180° so that he was head down. He watched the quivering noose with as much interest as my daughter watches *Top of the Pops* and thoughtfully licked the noose to see if it was tasty. The time ticked away for several minutes until the largest iguana in the world got bored and started to edge down the tree. I tried to lower the noose with him, only to discover that my pole was now too long and was getting snagged in the mimosa behind me. The only thing to do was to cut off one stick. I moved the whole thing upright and the iguana stopped moving. I cut the string at the bottom joint and tried again, only to find the same thing happened, and this went on and on until the lizard was back where he had started. I made yet another desperate attempt to get the little nylon circle around his neck because I realised that as soon as he disappeared into the undergrowth I would never find him, but the iguana had had enough, and with a final glance in my direction he launched himself into space.

I didn't think, or I would not have done it, but as he flew through the air I dived at him and we met several feet from both the ground and from where we had started. I clutched the madly scrabbling thing to my chest so that as I landed it would not be hurt, and crashed into the undergrowth. I was so delighted with my capture that I didn't even feel the pain as I struggled to my feet, collected my gear and fought my way back to the road. It was only a short distance to the house and we both made it without further incident. The iguana really was very beautiful, but just as I was putting him into a cage he gave me an almighty swipe across the face with his tail. Iguana tails have little saw teeth along the top and such an experience is not much fun but I was well pleased with my catch even though it took a long time to pull out all my thorns and disinfect the multitude of punctures.

But despite this story these lizard nooses work very well. Iguanas are odd animals anyway; in another part of South America I was staying in a house which had a huge tree in the garden, at the top of which lived a pair of iguanas. Four or five times a week there would be a tremendous crash and one of them would fall out of the tree. This strange behaviour never seemed to do them any harm for on landing they would look around for a few moments before strolling back to commence the climb up to the top once more.

A most excellent trap for monkeys is used in Asia. I was first told about this method as a child and didn't believe it but I have seen it used often and it really does work. Earthenware pots with narrow necks are baited with food and tied down in areas where monkeys feed. This system seems to work best with langurs who investigate the pots, peering into them to examine the contents. After an initial period of suspicion a monkey will insert its hand into the pot and grab a handful of the bait. When it tries to withdraw it finds that a clenched fist is wider than an open hand and cannot be extracted from the neck of the pot. If the monkey released the food it could easily escape but this does not at first occur to it so if the trapper rushes out of hiding quickly he can grab the monkey and bundle it into a sack. Given time a monkey will lose interest in the food it can no longer see and let it drop and extract the hand from the pot because something else of interest has been spotted, but provided the trapper rushes out each time the method works.

A way of catching Brahminy Kites exists which also relies on the animals' reluctance to let go of food. Pariah Kites are abundant all over India and they are a plain, dull brown all over, but in some locations they are found only in small numbers, their place being taken by the much more handsome Brahminy Kite with its rich chestnut body and white head. In the Sunderbahn delta at the mouth of the River Ganges Brahminies occur in fair numbers and the method of catching them is simplicity itself. The trapper ties a lump of meat to the end of a very long line and walks to a congregation of these kites, swinging the meat round his head just like a falconer with a lure. He lets out more line and sooner or later one of the birds grabs the bait. It will not let go of the meat and is easily caught.

Funnily enough Pariah Kites will readily relinquish the meat when they realise that they will be caught, so trappers sew loops of horsehair onto the bait so that it is completely covered. This time when the bird wants to let go it finds that often it cannot as its toes are entangled in the hair.

One of the cleverest bits of bird-catching I ever saw was in Gujerat in the North West of India. A good chunk of this state is covered by miles of hot nothing marked on the maps as the Thar Desert, and right in the middle, miles from anywhere, is a large lake called Nal Sarovar. The lake is completely hidden from even a short distance away as there are dunes of sand around it. Nowadays it is a recognised centre on the birdwatching tours but when I knew it no foreigner had discovered the place. It is totally absorbing because the whole surface of the water is covered in birds—you could not visualise the numbers unless you have seen them. Most of them are ducks but there are also many hundred Coots and some pelicans swimming around while in the rushes along the banks and on the beaches are innumerable waders of many species, even Avocets by the hundred which in England we think of as rare. And as if all this was not enough there are flamingoes, not a hundred or two but great pink wodges of the things wandering about the far side of the lake (they are always on the far side of the lake) filtering small food particles from the nutrient-rich water with their serrated beaks. The water itself is like pea soup with many wondrous things in suspension throughout, and rich in large, tasty fish which are caught in considerable quantities by the little communities of fishermen that live along the shore. These villagers dry the fish which they take to market to sell, and they also earn themselves additional income by catching and selling ducks.

The duck catchers have primed the lake by allowing to float on it all the time a number of small rafts to which are tied bunches of green coconuts and glazed earthenware pots. The birds are so used to these that they take no notice of them. When a man is setting off to catch some ducks he carries one of these rafts down to his boat. This one has 20 or 30, six-foot lengths of string hanging from it. The boats that the men use are some of the most primitive that I have encountered—they are much like kingsize shoeboxes—without pointed bows or other features that are generally associated with boats. The trapper and his colleagues tie the raft behind the boat and tow it out onto the water. Nowhere is the lake very deep so it is simple enough to punt the boat slowly along until it is quite close to the quarry and at this point the trapper slips over the end of his shoebox into the water and swims under the raft. His head comes up through a gap in the middle so that he looks out through a hole in the side of a pot that fits over him like a diver's helmet. He loops strings under his arms and ties them off so that the buoyancy of the raft supports him and then the whole thing is cast off and the trapper slowly dog paddles over to the ducks, looking for all the world like just another drifting heap of rubbish.

When the duck catcher has drifted into the centre of a suitable group of birds he reaches up and grips one by the feet and pulls it underwater where he ties one of his dangling pieces of cord to an ankle. The bird pops back up to the top. It gives no sign that anything untoward has happened so none of the other ducks panics and they all continue behaving as before. Another duck is caught in the same fashion, and then another until all the lengths of string have been used up. The trapper then drifts his raft and his catch back to the boat so slowly that the captives do not try to escape. At the boat they are untied and caged and the episode can be repeated as often as necessary. It is an impressively efficient operation.

I love all those stupid 'Bring 'em Back Alive' books that were written in the first half of this century which purport to describe animal collecting expeditions during which animals walk out of the jungle and surrender to captivity. No animal trapper has that sort of luck, or at any rate not unless he is in South America catching trumpeters. I am not really sure how to describe a trumpeter unless I say it is like a spherical black chicken on long legs, which does it no justice at all. If you don't know them go to your nearest zoo and make their acquaintance, for they are lovely animals with great personalities, and they are tame. There never has been in the history of the world an untame trumpeter. So much so that when I watched for the first time an Amerindian birdman catching trumpeters I had to laugh, but even that did not prevent the operation from succeeding. It is so silly that I must tell you how it is done!

You go out into an area in which trumpeters are commonly found and you sit on the ground with some empty bags and you say, 'Boom-boom-boom-boom-boom'. Don't laugh, that is really what you do. Keep repeating the phrase and ere long a trumpeter will appear and wander up to you. Put it in a bag.

Repeat as required.

Then go home.

Of course nothing is really as easy as that, and what I have described in a few words may take a couple of days while you find an area replete with trumpeters, but the one thing animal collectors must always have is patience. None the less that is how trappers obtain trumpeters. It is much harder to photograph trumpeters than to catch them and I think that I must have the world's largest collection of out-of-focus photographs of trumpeters. They are so uncooperative. They confidently stride up and peer into the lens from half-an-inch away or clamber about your legs while you are sitting on the ground, and even if you tell them that no one wants fuzzy pictures of trumpeters standing on trousers they do not seem to understand that they would look far more natural against a background of foliage.

A most common way of catching a variety of animals is to get them intoxicated. Naturally if a trapper goes up to an animal and offers it a Guinness it will probably take to the hills (unless it is a trumpeter), so it is necessary to accustom an animal to the taste of alcohol. I have watched teams of catchers trapping quantities of monkeys in this way in Brazil and Colombia. Enormous numbers of indigenous primates, particularly the delightful little Squirrel Monkeys, have been exported over the last 30 years for use in medical research. Squirrel Monkeys have been a particularly easy animal to obtain as they live in large groups and they are easy to trap when intoxicated.

Great mobs of Squirrel Monkeys follow the same paths through the tree tops each day of their lives so trappers hang an enormous hand of bananas at some suitable point on one of these routes. The rope from which the fruit is suspended goes down to the ground so that the bunch can easily be raised and lowered. The troupe of monkeys comes along and eats the bananas and after their departure the stem is lowered to the ground and replaced with a new one. This is done for some days until there are no reservations among the animals about this extraordinary supply of free food. When this stage is reached small amounts of alcohol are injected into the bananas, and local rum or whatever is available is used for this. The next day the quantity of alcohol is increased, and over the next several days while the process continues, the bunch of bananas is hung at a rather lower level so that when in due course the level of alcohol in the fruit is enough to make the monkeys intoxicated they are near enough the ground to be manageable, and then, depending on the terrain, they can either be caught by hand while they are unable to think straight, or else a net is thrown over them.

An identical system is used in Assam and Malaysia to catch ground-living birds such as fowl and pheasants using alcohol-soaked grain as a bait, but the most spectacularly simple way of catching pheasants that I have seen is practised along the southern Nepal border. Small wicker cones about the size of a cupped hand are inserted into holes in the ground so that the rim is flush with the surface. A ring of birdlime is applied an inch or so up from the bottom and some grain is dropped in. When the pheasants get used to the presence of these traps they stick their heads in to eat the grain and the birdlime glues the cone over their beaks. The poor old pheasants cannot see where they are going and lumber about until picked up moments later by the trapper.

There is a pretty big trade in butterflies, to such an extent that some species have become endangered because of it. Two of the main areas for collecting these insects are Malaysia and Taiwan, where in the capital, Taipei, the wings are removed to adorn all sorts of rubbishy tourist souvenirs that are exported in large consignments.

Such quantities of butterfly bodies remain that bins full of them are taken away each day for feeding to pigs. Butterflies are very fragile animals, and once they have become adults they are not traded live. Instead they are killed immediately on being trapped and are sold to be mounted in display cases or for collections. For people who are more interested in studying, breeding and conserving live butterflies they are exported as pupae.

Adult butterflies are trapped in Malaysia and also Central America by making small nylon net cages without floors but with the bottom couple of inches of all four walls missing. These are stood about over heaps of bait which varies according to the species of butterfly being collected. Many butterflies readily come to bait, and when they do and have fed, they take off at a fairly steep angle so that they fly up into the cage and can easily be removed even though they could in theory walk out of the bottom again.

It is well known that lamps are commonly used to obtain night-flying insects and the most efficient light of all is a mercury vapour lamp, but I have watched considerable numbers of moths being caught in Venezuela by using Tilley lamps resting on the bottom quarter of a white sheet which then hangs vertically behind them. The moths, attracted by the lights, settle on the sheet and can be picked off.

In the north of Trinidad is a Texaco oil refinery surrounded by a long

John Walsh inspects the stock in the bird market at Barranquila, Colombia (WSPA)

white-painted wall, which for security reasons is brightly lit throughout the hours of darkness. This attracts insects and on occasion I have found all sorts of goodies from huge, brightly-coloured long-horned beetles to moths in abundance. The local amphibians know all about this light trap for insects as well, and when conditions are right one can find a long line of Marine Toads, crapauds as they are called locally, studying the insect life every bit as avidly as the dedicated entomologist. The crapauds make a good living along that wall.

Traps of every sort, as well as birdlime, have been used throughout history and so have nets, but what completely changed the netting scene was the arrival of the mist net. Generally nets are visible to the acute eyesight of most animals, and in the past if nets were to be made fine enough not to be seen they were not sufficiently strong until the discovery of Terylene, and not long after that the Japanese and then the Taiwanese commenced making very fine nets from black Terylene that are known the world over as mist nets.

Due to their superefficiency they are illegal in many countries including Britain unless one has an appropriate licence, and in many countries that trap and export birds in numbers the trappers cannot afford them, but where they are used they have made life infinitely easier for the bird catchers.

Fine though they are, mist nets are by no means invisible and considerable skill is needed to set them so that they work efficiently. I have even known bats caught in mist nets so they are clearly fine enough not to register with the bats' sonar apparatus.

It is said that in South America some Indians use nooses made from spider's web filament to catch hummingbirds. Though I have not seen this some webs could certainly be strong enough. In Surinam I came across a horizontal thread of a spider's web that for some reason had not been built upon by the animal that spun it. It was about six feet long and four feet from the ground. To test its strength I placed my finger on the centre of it and started to press downwards. It stretched until I was touching the ground and still didn't break.

The advent of the mist net has not eliminated more old-fashioned netting methods, and clap nets of one sort or another are to be found in India and West Africa to trap flocks of finches. Their mechanism is almost impossible to describe but what happens is that two rectangular nets are laid parallel on the ground with a space between them on which is scattered a quantity of millet or rice and sometimes a decoy is used as well, either in a tiny cage or with a tether tied to the ground and stitched through the abdominal skin of the bird. The nets have a long line attached whose other end is held by the hidden trapper. When there are a good number of birds on the open space between the nets a smart tug on the line causes both nets to fly over and cover the flock. A very similar system uses a large single rectangular net which is fixed to the ground along two sides, and a heave on the string carries it over any feeding birds as before. The nets catch a lot of birds but can kill odd specimens that get hit by flying sticks or the net itself.

Clap netting would never work if the site was not made attractive to the birds by placing bait and a decoy where they can be seen from some distance. Traps and nets of all sorts can be made more efficient by using bait, and the simpler it is the better, despite the fact that trappers around the world have complicated formulae that sound as though they were filched from the three witches in *Macbeth*. Fruit and grains, together with meat and fish, are used in every country where animals are trapped but it would be a mistake to assume that plonking a handful of rice on the ground automatically makes a trap more attractive to animals. Once again one needs to apply psychology for frequently a decoy will work much better than any sort of bait. The decoy is nearly always a live animal and we have already talked about some of them. I mentioned earlier how trappers in the East use an owl as a decoy when catching birds, but I have also seen them use a snake which small birds come to mob as well. The snakes that are used do not last long and are regarded by the trappers as disposable. The reptile decoy is tied to a convenient branch or pole but because all snakes are Houdinis which can escape through the unlikeliest hole they have to be tied very tightly, so once in place, though they wriggle magnificently (from the trapper's point of view) the constriction of their tether causes their death fairly quickly. On the other side of the world, I have watched Amerindians use snakes as decoys when trapping hummingbirds. I am not at all convinced that hummingbirds mob snakes or anything else but the unfortunate reptile is soon surrounded by small passerine birds of all sorts that kick up an astonishing din in an attempt to drive the snake away, and my impression is that the hummers come along to see what is going on. They seem to hang about on the edges of the mob, trying to look over their shoulders. Whatever the reason, they do appear, but as well as catching them with birdlime the Indians use tiny blowdarts with a small knob of solid latex as a head to stun them. The expertise required to do this without killing the birds is astonishing. I was sure there would be a fairly high number of mortalities but I never saw a bird killed—they always recovered consciousness after a short while though my heart was in my mouth as I waited. I thought it was incredible that the men could even hit the birds which are pretty tiny, but they assured me that that part was simple and suggested I try. I did, aiming at a hummingbird sized piece of paper stuck to a tree by a thorn. I didn't

1. One of the exquisite Golden Pythons bred in Bangkok (W. Newing)

2. Many birds including these Eclectus Parrots are sold in Singapore bird shops (W. Newing)

3. *Every souvenir shop in Thailand sells ivory (W. Newing)*

4. *This Tiger had the bones removed from its paws to render it harmless (D. Whiting)*

5. *Day geckoes can be bred in captivity but they are still traded illegally (W. Newing)*

6. Even well-chewed seconds can be made into wallets (W. Newing)

7. This mother had been caught with the aid of a rusty nail through her foot (W. Newing)

8. *Baby parrots are sold as pets. Their parents end up as food (D. Whiting)*

9. *A big male monkey caused chaos in Crawford Market in Bombay (D. Whiting)*

10. *Brahminy Kites are handsome and easy to catch (W. Newing)*

11. *Turtles travel on the tops of buses in the hot sun (D. Whiting)*

12. *A Leopard Gecko. Many species are an ingredient of folk medicines (W. Newing)*

13. Handbag kits at a Thai crocodile farm (W. Newing)

14. Marine Toads, common amphibians throughout South America (J. Nichol)

manage to hit it once though I think I managed to stun every tree and shrub in the Amazon basin.

Even the most simple part of this operation was astonishing. When a bird had been hit it would fall to the ground. Sometimes it would flutter slowly down and it was easy to see where it landed, but more often the bird would rock for a moment and then drop fast onto the soft litter of the forest floor, and though it was rarely more than a few feet away I could hardly ever spot it in among the multicoloured bits and pieces which form a carpet below the trees. The hunters on the other hand would walk straight up to the little mite, pick it up and hand it to me. They were amazing.

Birds are the most commonly used of all decoys and virtually all commercially made trap cages contain one compartment for a decoy and one for the newly trapped bird.

Many years ago I watched an old trapper in Pakistan preparing for an expedition to catch birds of prey. I imagine that this particular technique has fallen into disuse if only because there is almost no trade in wild caught raptors today compared with years ago. The trapper, Abdul, was patiently sewing loops of horsehair into a small piece of thin leather, and as he worked he explained what he was doing. The leather, he told me, was a saddle to be tied firmly onto the back of a pigeon before it was released with a long line attached to it. If all went well a bird of prey would spot the decoy and fancy it for lunch, but when it closed its claws on the pigeon's back it would get them entangled in the horsehair loops so that Abdul could bring the pair of birds back to earth by pulling on the leash and disentangle the bird of prey. I could not watch him catch birds like this but he assured me that it was a good system.

I bet he got through some pigeons!

The thinking behind using most decoys is easy enough to understand. One either chooses an animal that would be good to eat, or an animal of the same species as those to be caught so that they come to join it, or as in the case of the snakes and owls, an animal that is regarded as a danger to the species that the trapper wants to catch, but occasionally one comes across the oddest decoys. In the South of France I have watched a man catching Edible Frogs to sell in the market. He used a method that I have not seen anywhere else. This wonderfully gnarled old frog catcher would row out onto the middle of a suitable waterway in the most clapped-out boat you have ever seen in your life. He would then slowly and deliberately take a large circular net with a long handle in his left hand and a primitive fishing rod in his right and make his way to the stern of the boat and sit facing the transom. On the end of his fishing line was, of all things, a ping pong ball. When he was settled he would make his cast in such a way that the ball first landed on the water several feet from the boat, then as part of the same movement the rod would be manipulated so that the ball bounced on the water four or five times, each time a foot or two nearer the boat, the last bounce judged nicely to land about three feet from the craft. The peculiar thing was that a frog, on spotting the ball land in front of him would skitter quickly across the surface of the water following the decoy. The last bounce of the ball was placed exactly above the centre of where the net was lying just below the surface, so when the frog arrived at that point the net was brought up from underneath the amphibian and he was transferred to the boat. The whole operation was a delight to watch, and not many casts of the ping pong ball failed to result in a capture. I still haven't figured out why the frogs chased the ball; I don't know whether they thought it was something to eat or another frog which needed chasing for some reason, but whatever the frog thought of it, the ball was effective.

I suppose that the decoy (or is it a bait?) with which we are most familiar is the anglers' fly. I have always thought it odd that a similar technique is not used for catching other animals but without a hook because there is a whole host of beasts that will grab something in their mouth and nothing in the world will induce them to let go until they feel like it. I first pondered on this system in Bombay. I was staying in a grotty room in a grotty hotel not far from Crawford Market and one afternoon there was a knock on the door. I opened it to find three teenagers. One of them thrust a hand forward to show me that he had caught a three-foot-long monitor lizard which was slowly spinning round and round at the end of a piece of string that was tied far too tightly around the waist. Most Indians consider lizards of all sorts to be venomous and the trepidation with which these chaps viewed their monitor implied that the bigger the lizard the more venomous it must be. The monitor was fairly cross and each time it twitched impotently the brave big game hunter, who was holding the string as far as he possibly could from himself, flinched while his two companions peered over his shoulder nervously.

Word soon gets around that you are interested in animals and these three young men wanted to know if I would like to buy their catch. I took hold of the lizard behind the head and at the base of the tail to examine it. The salesmen gasped and edged a bit closer. I guessed that the monitor had only recently been caught as it showed none of the signs of starvation or dehydration that long-term captives exhibit when they have been held by someone who doesn't know how to look after them.

'How much do you want for it?' I asked.

A figure was quoted that would have been exorbitant for all the lizards in Asia, and I pointed this out to the monitor catcher and suggested instead a sum of more reasonable proportions. I knew the going rate for these animals so I was on firm ground in my negotiations, but even so nothing was achieved for quite some time until finally I said, 'O.K., I don't want it. You take it and sell it to someone else.' The man on the other end of the string whimpered audibly, and suddenly decided that my offer was reasonable after all.

That day was pure farce. I had to get some money from my pocket to pay for my acquisition and I had both hands full of lizard, but when I suggested that one of the men held it for me he seemed not at all keen. In the end I put the monitor on the floor and stood on the string. It was content to remain quite motionless but then the guy who was holding the cord discovered that it had become tightly knotted around his wrist so that he couldn't undo it. Therefore when I put my foot on the cord he had perforce to bend double and there he stayed, muttering nervously to himself while I fished in my trouser pocket for some change which I gave to his companions. They were delighted and prepared to leave until I suggested that they pass my penknife so that I could cut their friend free. This was achieved without difficulty and with many mutual salaams they again turned to go. But India being India they discovered that their exit was blocked by about half the population of Bombay who were now crowded noisily in the corridor to watch the fun. My immediate job was to release my newly bought reptile from his string belt, so I left them to it and bent down to pick him up. All this time the monitor had been sitting perfectly still, and I was fooled by his immobility into approaching carelessly. As soon as my hand was near his head the seemingly torpid monitor leapt, closed his jaws round my left thumb and hung on.

Instantly there was silence.

I straightened up slowly with the lizard dangling from my hand to see that my audience was watching me wide eyed, waiting for me to drop dead from the bite of this supposedly venomous animal. The bite didn't actually hurt much but it was bleeding profusely so that within a minute or two my hand and the lizard were covered in blood that dripped onto the widening puddle on the marble floor. Hoping that the jaws would hang on for a moment or two longer, but keeping an eye on them in case they did not, I felt about for my penknife which had been dropped onto the bed, and sliced through the string round the monitor's waist. I then took a firm grip around his neck with my right hand and waited for him to let go. Needless to say nothing happened. By now some minutes had elapsed since I was first bitten and though my left arm must have been fairly empty of blood judging by the state of my trousers and the floor, there was no sign of my dying and the ever growing mob in the corridor began to speculate on the reason. 'Oh he will soon,' declared someone who obviously knew.

'No he won't,' came the response from a little old man who looked exactly like a reincarnation of Gandhi in a black, shiny, baggy suit. 'Europeans have a special immunity against such things.'

These comments started off a fairly heated debate which got noisier and noisier while I wondered how the hell I was going to get rid of my dangling monitor, or whether I was going to have to cart it about for the rest of my life like my own personal albatross. I started to hunt for something to insert between the beast's jaws to lever them apart. I wanted something that was strong enough but at the same time would not do any damage to the lizard. The only thing remotely suitable was a plastic ballpoint pen which I eased into the gap between my thumb and the back of the mouth. The point emerged from the other side and I gingerly pushed down. Nothing happened. I pulled up. Nothing happened. This was ridiculous. I began applying more pressure but it made not the slightest difference. During all this palaver the monitor showed no sign of life at all. The eyes did not move, there was no scrabbling of the claws, the tail hung limply and the dusty black flanks were motionless. Surely the thing hasn't died, I thought briefly, so that I have to wander about with a decomposing lizard attached to my thumb—could be embarrassing shaking hands with someone. This immobility had overcome the fear that most of the watchers had initially felt so that they were edging closer and closer until the bedroom was pretty crowded. I gave everyone a sickly smile to show that there was not really a problem. They looked unconvinced and I decided that the only thing to do was to bring the whole disaster promptly and efficiently to a close. I put extra pressure on my pen, and wouldn't you know it, it snapped. By the time I extricated the splinters of plastic from the monitor's mouth both of us were covered in a psychedelic pattern of royal blue and vivid red. Ballpoint ink gets everywhere.

Suddenly I realised what a fool I had been. If I could stop the thing breathing it would be bound to let go while it gasped for air, so I pushed my way through the mob to the basin and filled it with water and when it was full I immersed hand, lizard and all beneath the surface and waited confidently. I was still waiting confidently some minutes later.

The penny dropped.

I did feel a fool. Monitor lizards are perfectly at home in the water, so he would be quite content to remain there for a long time, even though by now the water was so red that I could only see the bits of him that stuck up above the surface. However, the principle was good, so extracting my hands and attendant appendage I looked round and asked someone if I could borrow a lighted cigarette.

'That is good idea, Sahib, you can burn it off,' was the enthusiastic comment from a corpulent Bengali in a white dhoti with a tasteful pattern of red polka dots, a pattern he had not as yet noticed.

'No, I'm not going to do that,' I corrected him, and added confidently, 'I will blow smoke in his face and he will let go.'

'Ah,' nodded the Bengali turning to those behind him, 'Sahib will blow smoke in the face and it will let go pretty damn quick.'

'Oh yes, most excellent idea,' said someone else, and 'This is bound to be working' commented another with a knowing nod until the whole room full of people were nodding and praising my sagacity. I had no idea what the lizard would think of the plan but I knew I wouldn't enjoy it because I didn't smoke, but I had to give it a try.

There was only one snag. To take the cigarette, put it in my mouth for a suck, and remove it to blow the smoke at the lizard I had to release my grip on the thing with my right hand. I did it without thinking. Have you ever had a day like that?

Anyhow, I sucked mightily at the fag and promptly coughed a mouthful of smoke at my nearest admirers. It took me a couple of minutes of gasping and spluttering before I could apologise, but the whole thing was taken in good part, this lot wouldn't have missed the performance for anything. I tried again, more hesitantly this time, and blew a good faceful of smoke straight in the nostrils of the lizard. Nothing happened except for the first time it looked at me and I'll swear that there was a look of distaste in those eyes. Encouraged I took another mouthful of smoke and puffed again.

BAM! It worked.

It worked so fast that several things happened at once, and with no warning whatsoever the monitor let go, leapt for the fat Bengali's shoulder and leaping from one shoulder to the next, shot faster than thought for the open window which it disappeared through like a bullet. There was instant pandemonium. Every single person in the room screamed and frantically fell to the floor or tried to escape through the packed doorway. I quickly stepped over the prostrate bodies as everyone surged passed me and leaned out of the window. My room was on the third floor so there was a fair drop and I expected to see the lizard lying dead on the rubbish-littered courtyard below, but no, I was just in time to see his tail vanish into a heap of broken pots. Though the courtyard was full of people squatting about chatting or talking or defaecating as people do throughout the sub-continent, none of them appeared to have noticed the entry of a flying three-foot lizard.

Hopefully, I thought, having found a refuge he would stay there for a bit and I might still get him so I turned to ask if I might quickly squeeze through, only to find the room empty. I galloped along the corridor and down the stairs. Before me on the bottom flight I could discern the portly form of the Bengali hurrying after the rest. His white shirt now bore a most attractive row of red and blue lizard foot prints over one shoulder. I squeezed past him through the doorway and turned right to reach the archway into the courtyard. Apparently everyone who had been in my room had the same idea and it was with some difficulty that I squeezed my way to the front. The first arrivals had advised the occupants of the courtyard of the presence of a man-eating dragon in their midst so that when I arrived they were either standing well out of the way or bashing and poking at likely hiding places with sticks. Just as I arrived at where I knew the monitor to be, someone whacked the heap of pottery causing the lizard to rush across the intervening six feet to a large metal tank and dive underneath.

This once more caused mass panic and the whole situation was getting so out of hand that I would have left things as they were, except that I knew that the poor old lizard would be hounded down and killed, so unenthusiastically I lay down on the filthy ground and stuck my head under the tank.

In amongst all the rubble there were more animals under there than in Noah's Ark. I could see the back end of the monitor a few feet in front of me. His front half was hidden in the remains of an old wicker basket and he obviously felt secure as he didn't move, but as I inched my way forward I found all sorts. A Wolf Snake gave me a suspicious look and silently took off. A couple of large, black scorpions wandered away in hurt dignity when I disturbed them and a pair of Musk Shrews scared the daylights out of me when I moved their home and they rushed out fighting and swearing and screaming for all the world like a couple of drunks being thrown out of a Camden Town pub at closing time on a Saturday night. Musk Shrews are like that.

I gulped a couple of times to let my heart stop pounding and then reached for the cause of the chase. I just touched him with one finger and he was off again. I slithered back out, covered in unmentionable gunge and quite ready to throw in the towel but I was grabbed by my well-meaning followers who dragged me towards the archway shouting that the lizard was crossing the main road. I tottered forward in the middle of the mob, straight across in front of all the traffic which noisily and angrily screeched to a halt. Some of my gang stopped long enough to explain to the drivers what all the excitement was, with the result that many leapt from their vehicles to join in the fun.

Of the lizard there was no sign but his progress was being monitored by my many assistants. I had never till that moment realised just how many people there were in India. They were all pointing into the peaceful garden of the police barracks just opposite where a single off-duty copper was quietly flying a yellow kite until he was surrounded by the noisy members of the hunt. In the end the lizard was run to earth under some steps and after much grunting and heaving I got him out, and with no further trouble at all, apologising in all directions, I got back to the hotel and deposited him in a cotton bag and tied the neck very tightly.

My army of helpers, chattering among themselves, reluctantly left the room. The last to go was the fat Bengali. As he went through the door he turned and came back into the room.

'Sahib,' he said, 'Please tell me, are you able to charm all animals or only this one? I was thinking, you see, that it was possible only to charm snakes.'

11. The People

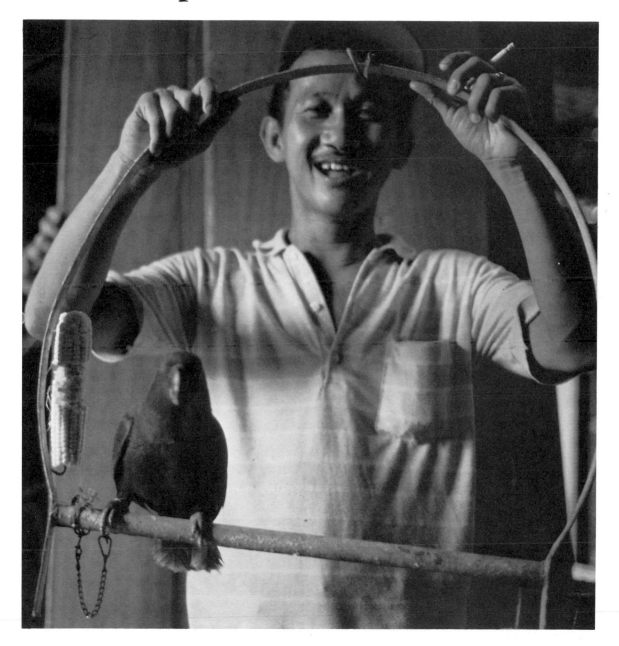

Previous page: Woody the anglophile at the Pasar Burung in Jakarta (W. Newing)

The very nature of the trade in animals attracts people who are characters, and strong personalities abound on both sides of the fence. Many of them care passionately about their own perspective of the trade and will argue for it fiercely. The reality as with most things lies in the middle.

My own feeling is that so many collectors are doing wonderful conservation work, sometimes illegally because the legislation that exists to conserve wild stocks is either counter-productive or ineffective. I do not in the least object to people who know what they are doing from being able to obtain licences so that they can either collect or have collected for them, wild animals to build up a breeding stock. Many species of animals have been saved from extinction by being bred in captivity and today we understand far better the requirements of animals so that these conditions may be created more often in a captive environment so that more breeding is possible.

Most people who are knowledgeable about animals seem to agree with this. Those that disagree are those who feel that a captive animal has lost its freedom, whatever that means. Just because an animal lives in the middle of Africa, say in Cameroun, doesn't mean that it can visit Mombasa for a holiday as you or I can or go for an educational visit to the Pyramids of Giza. Each animal has constraints upon its behaviour and boundaries to its living space which is surprisingly small in a lot of instances. Nor does an animal want to go to the pictures when it has finished eating or to visit a rock concert. Consequently an animal in captivity that is not doing anything should not necessarily be regarded as bored or frustrated.

Certainly it may be, but I always maintain that if an animal is kept properly so that all physical and psychological needs are catered for, then there can be no doubt that it is better off in captivity than in the wild.

One need only see a fledgling bird that has had three or four parasite eggs laid beneath the skin which become caterpillars the size of cocktail sausages to know that it will not live long enough to appreciate freedom; or a snake that is going to become too weak to survive long because it is covered in thousands upon thousands of mites. And a mammal must take very great care not to become injured in any way for the slightest lesion can become infected and result in death. These are not unusual occurrences, and animals have to put up with a multitude of day-to-day stresses in the wild such as the constant threat of being eaten or of there being no food or water.

An animal does not want what an anthropomorphist sees as freedom, it wants to live in its own familiar world in security where it understands each animal's relationship with every other and where it can obtain sufficient nutrient. And should anyone doubt this they need only watch when an animal escapes from captivity. Unless it becomes confused and cannot get back or gets blown or washed away it will almost invariably hang about, often actually re-entering the cage from which it escaped. It knows when it was well off.

No, I do not object to animals kept in captivity by caring, knowledgeable people. What I do object to is mass trade in animals because the cruelty is great and the losses horrific. Some animals can put up with this sort of treatment better than others but for many species you wouldn't believe the number that die.

Many birds suffer badly as do small lizards and I have watched consignments of frogs from capture to retail sale and only about one in 2,000 gets to that point, which even then is not the end of the journey. But taking all that into account there are just too many aspects to consider before one can say that all trade in all animals must be stopped, which is what is recommended by many well-meaning people in the West.

In my recent visit to India I went to the bird market in Calcutta. A once thriving centre of trade, whatever you might have thought of it, it is now the few dejected stalls I described earlier, from which hopelessness hangs together with the great swathes of dusty cobwebs from the roof. There was no activity, no bustle and no noise. I wandered around not recognising any of the people nor the businesses. Finally I stopped by three or four cages of baby Rhesus Monkeys which stared at me from the gloom with big eyes. The floor of one cage was covered with a hump of newspaper from the edge of which hung a sad little hand and foot of a monkey which had died. As I looked, a couple of fat cockroaches bustled out from under the paper and rushed off busily.

'Sahib,' said a voice from the gloom, 'Sahib, what are you wanting? Come, come sit down and tell me what it is you are looking for.' I walked round the block of monkey cages and in the darkness I could see four or five men shuffling along a bench to make room for me. I sat down on the rickety plank, and seconds later a voice beside me murmured quietly, 'Tea, Sahib, I am bringing you tea.' I took the drink, made as only the Indians make it with the water, the tea and the condensed milk all boiled together. The drink was served in a cracked porcelain cup on a saucer that had seen better days but which had originally been of good quality. Now it was just a dirty, cracked cup.

The old man on my right looked at me. 'Sahib, are you not knowing me?' I peered at the dark, leathery face and the white stubble. I looked down at the threadbare shirt and lunghi. Embarrassed I looked into the old eyes and shook my head.

'I know you, John Sahib, I remember you from a long time ago. Have I changed so much that you do not know me?'

'Tell me who you are,' I said. 'It is dark in here, and undoubtedly you have changed.'

The man gave a sad, sardonic smile. 'I am Shahnawaz Khan. Now do you remember?' Instantly it all came back. Of course I knew him. Long ago he had been a friend.

'Shahnawaz, how nice to see you once more, though truly you have changed.' Shahnawaz Khan took my hands in his and lifted them to his forehead in a traditional gesture of affection and respect. 'You do remember me, Johnbhai,' he said and smiled, and in a moment we were as we had been. It was a lovely moment and one of the very few that I treasure from my last visit to India. Shahnawaz and I talked about old times. He told me how the old bird market had been knocked down for redevelopment and they had been housed in this building, incongruously named Charlie Chaplin Square, until a new site could be found for them. 'But the business is dead,' he finished.

'But what has happened to everyone?' I enquired.

'All gone, bhai, all gone.'

'I realise Basheel Cha cha must have died,' I told him, recalling Basheel, a lovely old man that everyone called 'Cha cha'—uncle. He was an old man when I last saw him.

'Basheel is dead.' And after a pause, 'He was my cha cha too.'

'And tell me what happened to the others; where is Hussein and K. C. Sen, and where are Sausman Sahib and Joe Raymunna?'

It took him half an hour just to bring me up to date. Sausman Sahib was an old friend called Vivian Sausman who used to run a big animal export business in Calcutta. He was unusual for an animal dealer because he was Anglo-Indian. He had not been seen for years, he was working in an office, I was told. I asked what had happened to his man Kasim, and to Rocky Ray. Vivian used to have premises not far from Calcutta in the little village of Chandi Tala. He lived in Calcutta itself but all his animals were housed behind a high wall in the village. Kasim lived there with his wife, looking after the stock, but the couple had moved to Pakistan, the old animal dealer told me. He had no idea what had happened to Rocky, but he thought he must have died since he could no longer be a young man.

Rocky was a character straight out of C. S. Forrester. He, like Vivian, was Anglo-Indian but had been born in Burma and had lived there during the early part of his life making a living by hunting and taking hunting parties out into the jungle to look for trophies. Rocky was a large, bald pale-skinned man with freckles who always wore a frayed white shirt and khaki British Raj shorts. He would spend hours talking of the well-known people that he had taken hunting in the first half of this century. But the time had come when there was no longer any money in the business. Europeans could not afford to travel across the world to Burma after the Second World War, and in any case they had all gone soft and only wanted to take photographs of animals instead of hunting them, and for Rocky there was no mileage in that. In the old days he could supplement his fee by selling meat on the side or recommending a taxidermist in Bangalore from whom he got a commission, but nowadays there was no money to be made and he had gone down in the world. In due course he had sold his beloved guns and drifted north to Assam, and from there he had found his way to Calcutta where eventually, owning no more than the clothes he was wearing, he spent his last few rupees on drinks in an hotel. As luck would have it (and it could only happen in C. S. Forrester) he met Vivian Sausman at the bar. Vivian was a good listener and they had a common interest in animals and when Rocky's tale emerged Vivian suggested that perhaps he could do something to help. Rocky was by now so low that he could not afford to turn down anything and accepted gratefully. Vivian suggested that Rocky could stay at his animal compound at Chandi Tala—it wasn't much, only a single room, but at least it was somewhere, and he could do Vivian a favour by helping Kasim act as watchman over the animals for which Vivian could afford to pay him a few rupees a month until Rocky got on his feet. This fiction was maintained by all of them for many years, and as far as I know Rocky continued to live in his room until the end of his life.

Once Rocky's morale and self-respect had recovered somewhat and he had settled into his modest home, he set about making a new life for himself. He soon became friends with Kasim and the people of Chandi Tala who regarded him with affection and did their best to look after him. But Rocky was restless and needed a *raison d'être*, and he found one when he read in a local paper that someone had been killed by a man-eating Tiger in the nearby Sunderbahns. Unable nowadays to go out and hunt down the Tiger himself as he would like to have done, Rocky came up with an idea as eccentric as himself. He would head a nationwide man-eater control programme. Each state would have a centre of operations which would be immediately contacted by informants in every village whenever someone was killed by a man-eating Tiger. Word would be passed along until it finally arrived at headquarters, i.e. Rocky. He would then

Sunset over the lake at
Alipore Zoo, Calcutta,
where thousands of wild
birds come to roost (W.
Newing)

organise and pull together the hunt via radio control, despatching the best hunters from wherever they were, to go and look for the culprit.

Naturally all this would take a considerable sum of money so Rocky set about interesting people around the world with enough fund-raising clout to realise his dream. He bought himself a geriatric typewriter and began writing to heads of state and other eminent personalities and when I last saw him he had dozens of files full of replies. His favourite, which he showed me with pride, was from the Duke of Edinburgh. Like every other single letter, it said in the nicest possible way, 'Don't phone us, we'll phone you.' Yet Rocky did not see the refusals that way. The letters were all full of fuzzy phrases on the lines of 'how interested we are to hear of your scheme, and we hope ...,' which were taken by their recipient to be a positive indication of awareness and help.

Rocky's Tiger Watch came to nothing, but it gave him a reason to live and sustained him for over 20 years. Most of the money that Vivian Sausman gave him went on stamps so Rocky spent quite a bit of time hunting for food bargains amongst the vegetable stalls in the bazaar, and he would cook his meal over an open fire in front of his room in the animal compound. For fuel he would use dried cowdung. In India nothing is wasted and this valuable commodity is collected and slapped onto walls like pancakes to dry in the sun. Rocky's budget would not run to fuel as well as food so after dark he would slip out of the gate to steal an armful of cowdung patties. He would return gleefully giggling over his prize which he would pile onto his fire so that it emitted clouds of pungent smoke. He insisted that it kept the mosquitoes away but I was never convinced. They were the biggest, fattest, healthiest mosquitoes I have ever seen, but with or without their attentions Rocky and Kasim and I would sit round the fire and talk about animals while the bear cubs in the cage behind me coughed and spluttered when the wind blew in their direction and Sweetie, the Hyena, lay draped over my lap so that I could tickle behind his ears.

The two bear cubs were dear little souls that Rocky had brought back for Vivian from one of his trips to Delhi when trying to drum up support for his cause from the politicians in the capital. On the return journey the train had stopped for a considerable time at a one horse station in the middle of nowhere, and as one does at such places, Rocky had climbed down to the platform, and there, squatting on the concrete in the middle of a mass of India's travelling public was a man with two tiny bear cubs. Rocky watched until the man became aware of his presence, whereupon he became acutely embarrassed and ever more reluctant to answer Rocky's friendly questions as to how he had obtained the cubs and what he intended to do with them. Initially the man said that he had accidentally shot the mother, and was now taking the bears to sell to a dealer, but then he changed his story, saying that someone he knew had killed the adult bear and that he himself was only minding the cubs while this other chap had gone off somewhere. He grew more and more uncomfortable and in the end pushed the wicker basket of bears at Rocky, muttering that he was not going to wait any longer, and promptly slipped away into the crowd leaving Rocky the new owner of two bear cubs. He knew that Vivian needed some to fulfil an order so as he carried them off to the guard's van he congratulated himself on this heaven sent opportunity to repay a little of his benefactor's kindness. When he handed his present to a delighted Vivian he expressed his surprise that the man had so willingly abandoned his valuable charges. The animal dealer chuckled drily and explained that it was illegal to kill Himalayan Bears or to keep them in captivity without a licence, so on hearing Rocky's probing questions about the cubs' history the man must have assumed that they were an interrogation prior to some unpleasantness with a representative of law and order.

When Shahnawaz and I finished reminiscing about Rocky he told me what had happened to all the other animal dealers. The Khan family of Benares had gone to Pakistan except for their youngest son Nufis who was a doctor and whom I had helped when he was a student many years before.

With holes through noses and lips, performing bears are not an uncommon sight throughout India wherever tourists gather (D. Whiting)

I enquired after Baidyanath Acooli, a fat old rogue who ran a large concern on the road to the airport. His main claim to fame in Calcutta was that he had once told one of his men to 'borrow' a Leopard cub from another dealer as he could not obtain one fast enough to fulfil an order. The owner of the Leopard discovered where it had gone and mounted a raid in retaliation to retrieve it. He managed to find the cub and put it in a box in the back of his pick-up, but so furious was he over the whole affair that he and his men felt that they really ought to bring Acooli to justice and, finding a length of rope, they tied it tightly around his extensive waist and made the other end fast to the back bumper of their vehicle, and with the portly criminal trotting reluctantly behind, they drove to the nearest police station. The man was disliked by most people so the story was told and retold with much glee back at the bird market.

There was another old crook by the name of Jemil who used to hang about on the edges of the trade in Calcutta. He was quite astonishing. When he was speaking to me I found it difficult to know where to look as his eyes seemed to point in opposite directions so that I was never sure if he was looking at me, but despite this affliction he was a jolly good trapper and to watch him catch a bird in a branch high above him was quite entertaining—one obtained the impression that he was looking in every direction except that of the bird he was trying to catch. Jemil was still about, unlike old Ibrahim who had been killed by a Russell's Viper. Ibrahim was a venerable old Muslin snake catcher whose tiny shack was full of containers filled with snakes and monitor lizards. He would insist that he was immune from the effects of snake venom after a lifetime of bites, and I had seen him bitten on a couple of occasions when we were out trapping together but obviously he was not as immune as he thought.

As I was leaving the Calcutta bird market after our conversation, I asked my old friend what had happened to someone whom I knew well in the old days. Allarakah was a delightful young man full of modern ideas, who when I last saw him was just about to marry his second wife. This wife was his own choice in contrast to his first who had been selected for him by his family. We had talked for ages about the relative merits of the two systems and he had said that he would let me know how things turned out the next time I saw him. Since then, Shahnawaz told me, he had married a third wife, lost all his money and his health through drinking, and was now an extremely sick man, both in body and in mind. I met his son by his first marriage, a toddler when I first saw him and now a shy, intense young man. It was with great sadness that I bid him and the old man, Shahnawaz Khan, farewell, for they are both people I shall think of with affection.

I have described some of the characters in this chapter as rogues, and indeed they are, for the trade is full of rogues, but none was ever so great as an Anglo-Indian dealer who started his professional life in the centre of Calcutta as a perfectly proper purveyor of wild animals, but before many years had passed

Since the banning of the export of most wildlife, many of India's animal dealers are reduced to selling pigeons and tame white rats (D. Whiting)

he was beginning to earn a reputation as someone who would bend rules and obtain the necessary export documents for animals when no one else could, and was more willing than most to smuggle animals out of the country. He did pretty well out of it for a long time until the authorities began to lean on him to such an extent that he could no longer buy his way out of problems, and one day only hours before a visit from the fuzz, he hopped on a plane for Japan.

India's animals are now thriving. This area at Agra is rich in birds and reptiles (W. Newing)

The dealer stayed in Japan for quite a long time, arranging the delivery of Indian animals for Japanese and other overseas customers via his contacts within India. A few years later the Japanese authorities could no longer turn a blind eye to his activities either, and they too started to investigate the deals, and once more at the last moment he slipped out of the country and made his way to the USA where he continued to work in the same fashion. The States were a totally different kettle of fish, however, and it was only a very short time before people started to raise eyebrows.

This time he slipped quietly back into India, apparently without anyone noticing. He lay low for a bit but in due course word got out that if anyone was looking for those special, hard to get hold of Indian animals, the specialist was back in action so long as nobody made any waves. This worked well until rumours started seeping out that a certain person who wished to remain nameless was able to supply very limited numbers of baby Great Indian Rhinoceroses. Nothing was then heard of this tale for ages because first these rhinos are horrendously expensive and secondly no one really wanted them because they were immediately recognisable and, because of their size, difficult to hide. It is much harder to sell an illegal rhino than an illegal python or parrot. Then suddenly the animal world was stirred to excitement (though I don't remember it ever becoming public knowledge) by the news that two baby Indian rhinos had found their way to Japan. The Indian authorities could not ignore this and for a second time our dealer had to depart in haste from Calcutta. Quite where he went no one seemed to know, and for a long time there were odd mentions of his appearing all over the place, but he seemed to have dropped out of the business, until a few years ago he turned up as large as ever in Belgium, where he can be found today, still dealing in animals. I don't think for a moment that we have heard the last of him.

He reminds me very much, though they are not at all alike, of another dealer, this time in Indonesia. Chuck Darsono is a dealer in primates, and as far as I know he does not export anything other than monkeys. To people outside the industry it is frequently impossible to determine whether a particular animal business is absolutely straight or as bent as a nine shilling note and when a dealer is a convincing, likeable person, investigators are fooled so frequently that I now view with suspicion the many reports that come back from researchers in different parts of the world on various aspects of the trade in those countries. Only recently some people I know became totally convinced about the honesty of various animal dealers who are known to deal regularly, and frequently illegally, in a variety of stock, and yesterday I spoke to someone who insisted vehemently that he had seen scientific papers written by academic researchers on some supposed animal breeding project, and at first was reluctant to accept that frequently there is no such thing. Several international dealers pass themselves off as quasi-scientific or breeding establishments to build up credibility for their enterprises, sometimes even setting up a small cosmetic operation for PR purposes. The reason I mention all this is that Chuck Darsono likes the world to think of him as a conservationist. He says he runs a primate breeding centre in Java, and has even had printed a small booklet to show the world what a caring person he is. I find chunks of it being referred to and quoted in learned publications on primate breeding—and that is something that must please Chuck Darsono greatly.

The reality is that he is a buyer and seller of monkeys, and he certainly does not breed them in commercial quantities. At his premises one can see adults and young monkeys, and I am sure that on occasion a pregnant female will give birth while in his care, but that is the extent of his breeding programme. The USA and Japan are the two major consumers of primates for research, and though demand is falling as prices rise, and though numbers of primates of some species are now being bred in captivity, many monkeys are still taken from the wild. At one time most Asian monkeys came from India. Today there are not too many left so that most are exported from the Philippines and from Indonesia, which means from Chuck Darsono.

Given his concern for his reputation, it is hardly surprising that he fiercely resents criticism. Some time ago he was visited by Shirley McGreal, an American zoologist. Initially he was very taken with her appearance and her interest and wrote to her in effusive, affectionate terms. When he read her report on his operations his tone changed completely and his next letter to her started, 'Dear She-Devil, Shirley McGreal,' and he then went on to doubt that she had a doctorate in anything at all, but even if she had, it could certainly not be anything to do with zoology.

One of the long-time characters of the animal trading world must surely be Billy Miller of West Africa. I first met him many years ago at his home in the jungle. He had arrived unobtrusively after the Second World War when there were few restrictions on the trade in live animals, and quickly made his name as a large exporter of Pigmy Hippopotamuses. He certainly dealt in other species but the hippos were his speciality. On his staff he always had one or more attractive young girls that he had bought as slaves. The trade existed then as it exists now, but Billy would buy his girls from a dealer and explain to them that they had cost him a certain amount of money, but what he was willing to do was to employ them at the current rate without pay until they had worked off their purchase price and thereafter they were free to leave, or if they preferred to continue working for him as a normal employee. It always seemed to me to be a practical and humane solution to several problems which, in the light of what is being suggested today about Billy Miller, is interesting. Certainly his girls seemed perfectly content with the situation and generally stayed for long enough to earn sufficient money to make the return journey to their home.

Over the years Billy Miller's trade changed so that he no longer deals in Pigmy Hippos but instead has taken to exporting Chimpanzees, and for a number of years has been one of the best-known suppliers. Until some years ago quite a few chimps were imported into the USA, Japan and Europe and for a while he was making a lot of money by dealing in chimps. Many of his animals went to the beach photographers in Spain who also use Lion cubs as props. Despite considerable protest from concerned organisations and publicity by the more responsible tour companies asking tourists not to pose with these animals for photographs, enough fools continue to do so to make it worth the photographers' while to remain in business. In the meantime their unfortunate animals continue to be abused, hurt and drugged until they are too old to have 'aah-appeal' whereupon they are killed.

As the world became more conservation conscious, Billy Miller's operation came in for investigation. He, like Chuck Darsono, claimed to have a successful breeding programme on the go but of course he has no such thing, and the taking of baby apes from the wild is particularly wasteful as it involves the death of other members of the group. Miller has spent a fair bit of money in West Africa on public relations and, as he is a wealthy man, he has considerable clout with the people who matter in that country.

As his business and history has been researched it has started to emerge that Billy Miller could be a bit of a mystery man. He invariably refused to talk of his life before he appeared in West Africa and recently allegations have been made about his wartime service in Europe and his quiet arrival in Freetown, with quite considerable financial reserves, immediately after the war.

I am friends with a number of animal dealers around the world and know a lot more, and with most of them I feel perfectly comfortable but I would not care to dig too deeply into the background and doings of some of them.

Billy Miller looks exactly as an animal dealer should look—large and white-haired and one legged, and in the same country is another colourful character who exports more birds than anything else. His premises are even more ramshackle than Miller's and he is not as knowledgeable nor as interested in his stock as his competitor. He sends a lot of his United Kingdom consignments to a firm which in turn is associated with an animal dealing company near Bruges in Belgium. The managing director of the London company is fast acquiring for himself a reputation as the person no one wants to know in the animal trade for some of his dubious practices. He very nearly came adrift some time ago by juggling parrots from more than one consignment, so that quite a lot were sold before they had completed their statutory quarantine period. What he failed to realise was that the flock was infected with ornithosis so that when he started to receive complaints from his customers that their parrots were now dying he had to do some rushing about to prevent the law finding out. He was too late.

One of the most amazing animal dealer stories must be that of Mike Tsalickis. Mike is of Greek extraction who went to South America a long time ago to set up an animal dealership. For some time he drifted about discovering that life was difficult, and then found himself with a photographer from National Geographic. He demonstrated the catching of a largish Anaconda and the photos were used in the magazine. The article did not do Mike's business any harm and orders started to come in with more regularity and finally he moved to Leticia in South Colombia. This small town is the capital, if you like, of the Leticia peninsula, a long, skinny bit of Colombia that sticks out into the surrounding countries. It is still very wild and the whole place is a constant hotbed of activity by guerrillas, border guards and bandits, and only the very brave or very foolhardy live there. Despite all this it is advertised as a tourist attraction and safaris from the capital, Bogota, take in the wildlife of the peninsula.

When I was telling a Colombian friend last year that I wanted to go to Leticia, he warned me not to unless I had connections 'with the army, the local mafia or the church—preferably all three, since between them they have the whole place tied up.' He was right and there is considerable tension in the air of Leticia that one feels could explode into violence at any time, but the extraordinary thing about the town is that the real king of Leticia is Mike Tsalickis, for when he settled there he began to build up his business. He paid local men to trap his animals and build his cages and their wives to clean them and feed the stock. His reputation grew and as it did, so did his affection for the place so that when his mountain of dollars became ever higher in the bank he began to plough some of them back into the place that had made him rich and he built a school for the children of the Indians, and a hospital, and staffed both at his own expense. Business continued to expand so that the next priority was an airstrip so that animal consignments could be sent out more efficiently. Today the one hotel is owned by this man, and the local safari and holiday outfits and most of everything else as well. Mike Tsalickis is, as you might imagine, a strong personality and a powerful man. He has been prosecuted again and again for allegedly being involved in various illegal animal deals. He is no angel—he would be the last person to claim that he was—but he is successful and he has done an awful lot for the people of Leticia who are fiercely protective about the man. I can well imagine that when he dies there will be a riot in the place as the army, the local mafia and the church battle it out for superiority.

It is funny how the business is populated with such opposites. On the one hand you have someone like Mike Tsalickis and on the other you find individuals like Dick Jones who is a small time dealer in England. Some years ago he was prosecuted for something shady unrelated to animals so that he gave up in disgust and started up a new project. This venture too landed him in so much trouble that when he had sorted himself out again he figured that he was better off in the animal business so he changed his address and within a few weeks he was openly advertising Radiated Tortoises and other species that he was definitely not supposed to be selling. He seemed not to realise that the Department of the Environment, TRAFFIC, Customs and Excise and just about everybody who has any interest at all in the field read the adverts each week, so to the surprise of Dick Jones but to no one else at all he found himself being prosecuted once more.

One dealer for whom I have affection is Komain Nukulphanitwipat, the proprietor of Siam Farm in Bangkok. He deals in animals quietly and unostentatiously, and he does breed quite a number of species, and particularly colour variants in which he has a special interest. He is known by everyone as Dang—the Thai word for red—because when he was born he was very pink, and the name stuck.

Dang is a delight to talk to, and like all dealers he has no time for do-gooders who do not understand the business. He has arguments which contain holes big enough to drive a bus through but some of his points are very valid. He says, for example, that his trappers are mainly villagers who live for the most part on what they obtain from their immediate environment. If he pays one of these trappers a few baht for a mynah, that man will go off and buy food with the money so that the family can live for the next few days. If on the other hand Dang refuses to buy the mynah and the trapper cannot sell it elsewhere he would eat that mynah, and during the next few days he would kill several more mynahs as food, so by buying one bird Dang claims he is saving several others from ending up in the pot. He has a point. In Thailand, Greater Hill Mynahs may only be exported under a quota system which is extensively flouted. People buy quotas from each other freely and exceed their quotas all the time. Dang, and no doubt his competitors too, have friendly customs inspectors to make life easier.

It is certainly true to say that conservation legislation is affecting many people whose communities have existed throughout history by trapping and hunting animals. I don't refer to the case of someone like Ramratan, a dealer in Paramaribo, the capital of Suriname, who has had to close down his business and go to work in a prawn processing factory, but rather people like the hunters I went to visit in India. Not long ago there were villages around Kumaon and Naini Tal in the Himalayan foothills where most of the men were trappers supplying Bareilly birds to the trade. I went to stay with one a while ago. He is now an old man who can no longer go birdcatching anyway, but just as Shahnawaz had in Calcutta, he told me that many of the trappers and their families that I had previously known had left for the towns. Youngsters nowadays, seeing nothing for themselves locally, were leaving as soon as they could and the whole community was falling apart. Once they were all superb naturalists. Today the young generation could not tell one animal from another and because of this ignorance they can see no reason for conservation. Undoubtedly it is not a good thing for any area to be stripped of a particular species but a certain amount of sensible collecting should not damage the populations of most animals. It all depends on knowledge and education.

There used to be a cantankerous and awkward old hermit who lived in Tanganyika (now Tanzania). Like Mike Tsalickis he was of Greek origin and his name was Bunty Ionides. He was not the easiest man to get on with, though I remember him with amused affection, but he was a quite brilliant herpetologist. When he was collecting snakes he would carefully inspect them when freshly caught and if he felt that a particular specimen should not be removed he would release it again and sit watching with satisfaction as it wandered off to its hole. I have watched him return gravid snakes more than once. Ionides was an educated eccentric man, dead now, who lived in spartan isolation and although he only collected reptiles and sometimes amphibians, he was extraordinarily knowledgeable about his world. He seemed to prefer the company of the animals among which he lived and apart from his various helpers he resented intrusion by people and could be very prickly. I drew a portrait of him once, and he objected because I had not drawn him wearing his hat which was a scruffy, worn-out old thing which was as much part of him as his moustache. He was unusual as a dealer in that he collected the animals, maintained them in captivity until they were ready for export and then sent them off to the customer himself. Today most dealers buy in stuff from the collectors and most collectors have not the knowledge to do the actual exporting particularly as today there are so many regulations to comply with and so many forms to complete. It was much easier in Ionides' day.

I mentioned this to young Woody in the bird market in Jakarta. He works on one of the stalls as a general dogsbody cum salesman. He is a rabid Anglophile who sports a cap with the word Britannia on the front and a Union Flag on the crown. His mother is Indonesian but his father came from America, which accounts for Woody's name. Originally he lived in a small village some 13 bone-shaking hours by bus from Jakarta. He had grown up in the middle of the jungle catching birds, first for fun or the pot and later to make a bit of money for himself by selling them to the agent of one of the dealers from the capital when he made his regular round to collect stock. Woody became pretty good at understanding his environment and found that he was better at keeping alive the delicate softbills with which his companions had no patience. This skill brought him special attention from the agent who suggested that he leave his village and travel up to the metropolis to work for the dealer maintaining the softbills in the shop. To the boy from the jungle it was a step that bridged centuries and he found Jakarta a frightening place for a long time, but he settled down in his new life and slowly forgot what it was like to be a villager. Nowadays, he told me, he hardly ever went home because when he did he felt a total stranger. His family and former friends lived a different life and had a different set of priorities. Today he tended the birds in the bird market and was good at it, but he added that he could no longer go out catching birds in the jungle. He would not want to do it any more and he would not be any good at it these days. His priorities too had changed.

Woody did, however, regard birds as living things and he understood them, unlike Terence Loh in Singapore. He is a great guy and a good businessman, and like all good Chinese businessmen he has a finger in all sorts of pies. In fact his office is in the Golden Wall Auto Centre since some of his pies are filled with spare parts for vehicles. Terence knows his birds well, just as he knows his carburettors and camshafts, because each is worth money, but unlike Woody he sees them as pound notes, which is not to say that he is uncaring about them. His birds are kept in better conditions than in most Third World dealers' premises and a lot better than the cages of many Western dealers. Terence is trying particularly hard to co-operate with the requirements laid down by the governments of the importing countries but was somewhat irate recently when he received a letter from an official of the Animal Health Division of the British Ministry of Agriculture who was insisting that Terence fitted his birdrooms with fans that filtered dust and other undesirable material from the air before blowing it in for the birds to breathe. It was a nonsensical requirement as birdrooms in the tropics just do not have walls—only wire netting. 'If the man wants me to,' Terence told me, 'I will fit the fan, but it will serve no purpose whatsoever.' This is just one example of how silly the bureaucratic system is—the person who should have written such a letter to Terence ought to have travelled extensively around the world talking to dealers and have had experience in keeping animals, to be in that particular post. Terence is getting ready for the day when

*Terence Loh's manager
at the Wing Loon
holding station
(J. Nichol)*

Singapore signs CITES. It has been putting it off for ages, much to the fury of conservation bodies and the delight of the dealers, since the country makes far too much money exporting birds to rock the boat, but under ever-increasing international pressure Lee Kwan Yeuw, the prime minister, has finally told the world that the act is imminent. In the interim Terence and the other reputable dealers are setting up breeding establishments and ensuring that their premises cannot be faulted by the bureaucrats of the world. When that day comes some of the lesser dealers will certainly fall by the wayside.

The Wee brothers have exported animals for a long time from Singapore, including illegal stock. One of David Wee's letters to a customer has been reproduced in books so often it is famous. In the letter Wee tells his customer that he is ready to ship some (illegal) Black Palm Cockatoos but the import documents must refer to them by another name or the export cannot be arranged.

Nowadays the Wees' business is run down. The eldest brother, Christopher, complained to me bitterly that it was all the fault of Mrs Doggett. Marjorie Doggett is an elderly British lady who lives near Changi Airport. She has lost a fair bit of impetus now but she was obviously a force to be reckoned with at one time. I was told repeatedly that it was Marjorie's efforts that had finally stopped the Singapore trade in mammals and her constant nagging at the authorities had made life more difficult for the bird trade. Marjorie has been in Singapore for a considerable number of years. She lives and breathes animal welfare and keeps many cuttings files containing reports of abuse to animals over the last quarter of a century. Her husband collects butterflies and though nothing was said on the subject it is clearly something about which Marjorie would rather not know.

One only has to mention the word 'conservation' in Singapore and everybody says, 'See Majorie Doggett,' and when I did, she was one of the people who insisted that I had a talk to Katherine Buri when I got to Bangkok.

Katy Buri is something else! She is an active, independent lady who is intolerant of people who disagree with her ideas but she is a livewire who is passionately interested in a wide range of subjects. Katy is getting on (but she's younger than you or I) and is married to a lovely retired doctor named Rachit who is one of the very few people I have met that I feel truly merits the title 'Gentleman'.

Katy is up and about at the crack of dawn long before anyone else is feeling

Katy Buri, the author and Katy's husband Rachit, discuss the intricacies of breeding hornbills (W. Newing)

even halfway human. She is a wealthy woman who uses all her money in a positive way. Some time ago she rescued some baby otters from the weekend market, and not to do a thing by halves, she had an otter pen built in the garden. When the otters were put outside they bred and the offspring bred and as the numbers increased Katy had to build more pens which are magnificent structures with waterfalls and forests and rivers contained within. So many offspring are born that Katy refers to them as a crop. Her garden is completely walled and has electronically controlled gates, so when the family come in after a day's work, all the otters are released from their enclosures and Katy feeds them on minced beef and on the fish that Rachit goes to the market early each morning to buy, and after their feed all the otters slink their way around the grounds like great, furry, processionary moth caterpillars.

Another of Katy's passions is her hornbills. She rescued a couple of youngsters, again from the weekend market a year ago and brought them home. At first there was nowhere to keep them so Katy bought a great heap of nylon netting and threw it over a mango tree by her bedroom window. These two birds live in this instant aviary which gives them access to Katy's bedroom through the window whenever they wish to enter. Consequently when she returns from an outing the first thing she has to do is clean the bedroom of a layer of hornbill droppings. Katy is most worried because these birds are decidedly less common than they were in the recent past and she is setting up a hornbill breeding project. She owns a large piece of Thailand at a place called Chanta Buri, and on her land is a patch of forest as large as half-a-dozen football pitches and Katy is contemplating building an aviary around and over this so that her breeding stock can live in it.

Katy Buri talks such a lot about her hornbills that it is a bit of a joke but her caring attitude and her knowledge is not to be questioned. She drives along regularly to the weekend market to spy on what animals are available, and promptly terrifies the life out of all the dealers. Dang almost grits his teeth when he mentions her name.

The Thais love flowers, and orchid stalls are everywhere (W. Newing)

Katy is certainly a force to be reckoned with and the dealers have good reason to be wary of her. Nor is she at all afraid to bring pressure to bear anywhere that she feels might help. When she can get away without her husband finding out she carries a loaded revolver in her handbag as she drives her opulent, air-conditioned, uninsured Mercedes around the country. The only thing that Katy is frightened of is royalty. She is not Thai, coming originally from Malaya, but the Thai people are deeply respectful about their Royal Family and take it very badly if anyone does something that they perceive as being disrespectful. Now it happens that outside Bangkok there is a strange complex of craft centres, reproductions of old Thai buildings and a sort of mini zoo that is supposed to be a breeding centre for a variety of native animals. Some of the birds live in an attractive walk-through aviary but the rest of the animals are kept in dreadful conditions. This so-called breeding complex exists under the auspices of the Queen and really is pretty disgraceful, and Katy is most upset over it but she cannot do anything to improve conditions for the animals, because as she says, any criticism from her will be taken as a reflection on the Queen and would result in Katy finding herself in deep trouble.

'Only you,' she said earnestly to me, 'can do something about it. Next time you see the Duke of Edinburgh, tell him to write to our Queen to tell her that the animals should not be kept in these conditions.'

Katy cares a lot about the animals of Thailand but she has an uphill task in a country where they come just about at the bottom of most people's list of priorities. Pisit Na Patalung, the head of Wildlife Fund Thailand made this very plain when he was telling me about the launch of the fund. The organisers had managed to get Queen this and Princess that to attend and they were flying in the Duke of Edinburgh and goodness knows who else, and the idea was that the well-heeled of Bangkok should shell out a thick wodge of hundred baht notes to dine at the palace and have their photos taken shaking hands with royalty, and by so doing, put a lot of money into nature conservation in their homeland. A few days before the event only about a dozen or so tickets had been sold so a despondent Pisit said to his tame Princess that he was worried since it would look terrible for the visiting dignitaries to turn up and find no one there.

'Don't worry,' said the Princess, 'I shall wave my magic wand', or whatever Princesses say on such occasions. She did too, she went around the palace telling everyone she met that they were all volunteering to go to the Wildlife Fund inauguration and on the night Pisit went along in fear and trembling, only to find that every seat in the place was full, which makes my point nicely; no one will do anything for animals in Thailand, but for royalty, they will do all they can. I find it really strange because it seems that every single inhabitant of the country loves plants. Garden centres abound and orchid sellers are everywhere and almost every house, however humble it might be, had pots of orchids outside and cut flowers indoors.

This contrast is very typical of the Thais. Even Katy, who cares very much about conservation, is most selective in what she chooses to conserve. When I went with her to her property at Chanta Buri she showed her ambivalent feelings towards conservation. At one moment she would be talking about setting up reserves for breeding this or that and at the next moment she would be telling me what a pain the Tokay Geckoes were that entered her house each night. For some reason she felt no animosity towards the common geckoes but the beautiful blue and red tokays she objected to and would knock their eggs off the wall and destroy them whenever she came across a pair that the female had hidden. Snakes she killed too, and when we found a large black scorpion she would have killed it on the spot if I had not leapt to its defence. I mentioned to Katy that I had kept scorpions on many occasions and she immediately told me to take it. When I explained that, much as I should like to, the proposition was impractical as I had to visit other countries before I returned home, 'Kill it then, keep it as a specimen', was the instant response. 'It is very easy, you put it in alcohol to kill it and then you inject it with toothpaste to preserve it.'

One night a pretty little feral tortoiseshell kitten found her way into the house and there was immediate pandemonium. The dog flung it across the room, the son went for his gun and Katy took a heavy length of wood to kill the cat but she was to be disappointed since the dog finally killed the little mite.

'You have to kill these things,' said Katy fiercely as she sat back down to finish her meal.

But for all Katy's aberrations, without her the wildlife of Thailand would be in an even worse state than it is now.

It frequently surprises me that in countries all around the world there are Katys of both sexes beavering away in the name of conservation. I don't know where I first heard of Ulrike von Mengden. I was perfectly willing to believe that she existed, but the more I heard of her, the less likely she sounded; none the less she is quite real.

Ulrike von Mengden is an elderly German lady who arrived in Indonesia when the world was a more civilised place, to work in the Embassy. She was interested in wildlife so it was inevitable that she became a frequent visitor to the Ragunan Zoo in Jakarta. Jakarta Zoological Garden is quite the most depressing collection of animals that I have seen for a long time, so it is hardly surprising that sooner or later Frau von Mengden made herself known to the staff of the zoo who were astonished and then pleased when she offered her services as a volunteer. She became established over the years and eventually was doing so much for the zoo, and especially for their Orang Utans, that she was offered a house within the zoo grounds and a bit of money, and there she lives to this day in a hidden-away bungalow filled with the Batik work for which Indonesia is so famous. The keepers call her Ibu Monyet or monkey mother since today most of her work is with orangs.

She shares her home with these marvellous animals whom she treats as fellow human beings. The number of her friends varies. Sometimes she is brought baby animals that have been confiscated from a market, or perhaps one whose mother cannot or will not feed it and she looks after these lovely apes that Johnny Morris so beautifully describes as being made of liquid mahogany and elastic, until they are able to join the others in the zoo itself. This is not to say that all Ulrike's orangs are small. Some of them are large but whatever their size they are clearly as fond of their human companion as she is of them. I am not sure if she ever wonders if she is an ape but I am sure that some of them must think that they are human. Recently, the star of the household was Judith, a sweet little seven-month Orang Utan dressed grotesquely in a frilly pink party dress.

Ulrike von Mengden generally plays host to about 20 orangs at a time, and as if this were not enough, the occupants of the house also include an armless gibbon called Jope, two owls named Athens and Remus, God knows how many dogs, and a pony. The owls had arrived as chicks and one of them survived despite having been well chewed by rats when in a previous home.

The birds have the run of the house, or rather the fly of the house and spend the night on the end of Frau von Mengden's bed. She has infinite patience with all her friends—one can hardly call them pets or charges, it just isn't that sort of a relationship—and the only time she tends to get a bit cross is when the owls carefully extract the lenses from her spectacles.

Just like Katy Buri, Frau von Mengden cares desperately about the fast-disappearing flora and fauna of our world but she is especially concerned with the plight of the beleaguered Orang Utan which, despite legislation, is exploited throughout its tiny range. Ulrike gets right up the noses of those dealers who refuse to accept that orangs just must not be traded these days.

Yet another person who is disliked by the baddies in the animal world is David Whiting, who has been dubbed 'The Animal Spy' by the press. David lives in the South of England but he has travelled to many parts of the world to expose abuses to animals in trade. Most of his work had been concerned with animal products rather than live animals, and in his time he has found himself in dodgy situations on various occasions. Mind you, David is a real nutter who is not afraid of diving in at the deep end. He is an odd animal in that he is a vegetarian who holds a Slaughterman's Licence which he took the trouble of acquiring so that he could study cruelty to animals in slaughterhouses.

A raid at New Market, Calcutta. The customer is offered an illegal Tiger skin . . . (D. Whiting)

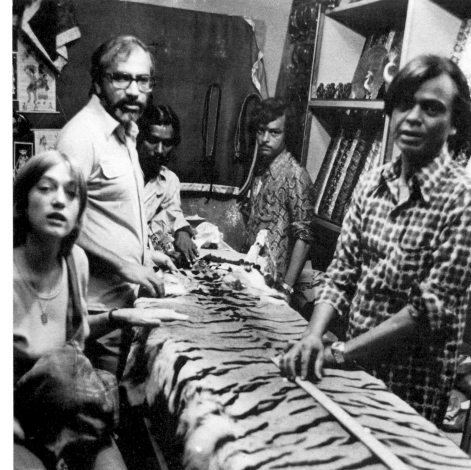

David Whiting got himself arrested in South Africa on one occasion when he was busy filming the processing of whales in Durban, and on another occasion he ended up in the middle of a bunfight in New Market in Calcutta when he posed as a buyer of Tiger skins. He promised to return later with the money, and kept his promise but he also brought with him a few members of the CID and a handful of uniformed constables. The result as far as David was concerned was that he ended up with a contract out on him in Calcutta.

Before he left for India on that occasion he asked me for any useful leads which would be worth following while he was there and one of the things I suggested that he looked at was the Frogs' Legs Story. On his return to the United Kingdom he made public the appalling horrors of the trade and for the first time people asked themselves whether they ought to eat the things in restaurants. Since then others have investigated the story as well and nowadays the information has become widely known. Nevertheless, the demand for frogs' legs continues to increase. The producing countries continue to make noises about curtailing or eliminating the trade but nothing actually happens.

The trouble is that the chap who orders frogs' legs in a restaurant is not in the least bit concerned with the welfare of the frog from which they have been obtained nor about the status of the amphibians in the wild, unlike the collectors who buy live frogs from dealers to add to their precious collections. Today, live wild animals are pretty expensive to buy so that most of them are purchased by those who want them enough to lay out a fair bit of money. Consequently, the animals generally end up in a carefully controlled breeding group. The 'establishment conservationist', if there is such a beast, generally ignores or even denigrates the work done by such people but that really is not at all fair. A lot of careful scientific study is going on in animal rooms all over the country. The enthusiasts who own these collections keep their heads well down so that nobody outside a few close friends are aware of what is happening. There are three reasons for this secrecy. The first is that thefts of exotic animals from private premises are becoming ever more common and such robberies are not random events. Only the most valuable animals are taken by thieves who are obviously used to handling the animals. The second reason is that the animals have often been illegally obtained and are being kept in contravention of the law. The third reason for the security is that there is a constant fear that a collection will be visited by a load of ignorant louts who will release the animals into the wild which will result in the death of the animals themselves and might well cause disruption to the native flora or fauna.

Recently, I have visited dedicated animal people who are breeding humming birds, Papuan Green Tree Pythons, Indigo Snakes and Count Raggi's Birds of Paradise not to mention the many, many people who are propagating a host of less common but none the less protected animals.

A recently formed group of responsible animal keepers points out to me that if some proposed legislation goes through, the Pigmy Marmoset will be considered a Dangerous Animal in British law. A Pigmy Marmoset is a tiny, South American primate that can easily fit into a teacup. There can hardly be a less harmful mammal whilst on the other hand the common or garden moggy can be kept by anybody. Yet any cat that decides it does not want to be handled is a decidedly dangerous animal that not only has a face full or teeth but a handful of razor sharp claws at each corner, and they don't at all mind using all these armaments when they feel like it.

I am all in favour of banning trade in Pigmy Marmosets for a variety of reasons, but to class them as dangerous animals is nothing short of ridiculous.

REAL conservationists tend quietly to get on with what is important. They are all pragmatists and are the people who should be consulted by the law-makers. Instead, it is some of the sentimentalists and the noisy that earn the reputation of conservation spokesmen. These people care very much—to use a dated cliché, their hearts are in the right place—but they go about things the wrong way and without thinking through to the consequences of their actions, which are sometimes contra-conservation. What could be more crazy than deliberately releasing Mink into the English countryside?

The reluctance of bureaucrats to accept private collectors is illustrated nicely by the case of Rosemary Low and the Grand Cayman Parrot. What Rosemary doesn't know about parrots can be written on the back of a stamp and still leave room for three Lord's Prayers and she is well-respected for her success in breeding endangered parrots for a number of years. A few years ago, a sailor was given a Grand Cayman Parrot while he was in the West Indies and knowing nothing about the technicalities of importing such a bird he asked Customs & Excise what to do; they told him to get hold of a licence from the Ministry of Agriculture, and to quarantine the bird when he arrived in the United Kingdom. But what no one mentioned was that he also required an additional licence from the Department of the Environment. Anyway, there were no problems. The bird arrived and was quarantined. The importer then read a copy of one of Rosemary Low's books on parrots and discovered that his bird was a rarity, so thinking only of what was best for the species he offered the bird to Rosemary for breeding and she accepted it with alacrity. At this stage Customs & Excise decided to confiscate the bird as it had been imported without a DoE licence and it was sent back to the Cayman Islands.

Rosemary contacted her Member of Parliament and London Zoo and all sorts of people and the general consensus was that she should have the parrot. The Cayman authorities however insisted that they were going to 'rehabilitate the bird at a special centre' before returning it to the wild. They took no heed of the fact that the bird had been hand-reared and would not manage in the wild, and they chose to ignore the fact that on the island there is total disinterest in the parrots, which are shot as pests by fruit growers although there are only around 50 of that particular sub-species. And the authorities chose to ignore the fact that there was no such thing as a 'special centre' for parrots. Six months after the bird's return to Grand Cayman, it was still sitting alone in a cage and there were no plans to do anything more with it.

Dealers sometimes complain that conservationists object to their making money from animals, whilst conservationists themselves do exactly the same in a different way. The reality is that most conservationists make little or nothing from their work, doing it only because it is important to them. I talked on the telephone the other day to a German lady in the North of England who runs a breeding centre. The organisation is a registered charity that raises money from an endless round of coffee mornings and jumble sales, and specialises in working with birds. As we were talking she bemoaned the fact that funds were really tight, 'In fact we exist all ze time from hand to beak.'

I see nothing reprehensible in the mere fact of earning money from animals either as a dealer or a conservationist and there are one or two of the latter that do make a living from their work. One such is Dr Esmond Bradley Martin whom I have mentioned earlier as the world's rhino and elephant man. He lives in Kenya and is so busy that he is pretty elusive. For several months last year I tried to phone him at his office and in the end I discovered that he would be travelling the Far East at the same time as I was. I jotted down his itinerary and discovered that we would be in Singapore on a particular date and we finally arranged to meet in the bar of the Raffles Hotel. While I was waiting I felt I really had to try a Singapore Sling which originated in that very bar. It was quite disgusting, like all the foul medicines remembered from childhood and I was delighted when Esmond arrived and we could go out for a meal. Over the next two hours, some friends of mine and Esmond and his wife discussed rhinos and elephants and the problems they faced, and we ended the evening making tentative arrangements to meet in Jakarta or Bangkok or Delhi or somewhere but in the event, nothing came of them.

Esmond is a realist and does not say 'Thou shalt not sell rhino horn' because he knows very well that such an approach would not work. He tries to educate people to realise that rhino horn is useless as a medicine and that there are infinitely better substitutes.

A magazine in front of me has a headline on the cover which asks plaintively, 'Will Whaling Ever End?' Of course it won't. While there is somebody who is willing to pay for whale products or rhino horn or live parrots there will be somebody to provide them, and the more illegal these commodities become the higher the profit margins involved. Most livestock dealers who sell animals that they shouldn't, still sell most of their stock quite legally. The smuggling is a small part of the business that puts a considerable helping of jam on their bread, but there are some who exist purely to supply birds to countries which cannot get them on the open market.

In a fairly big town, not far from the industrial centre of Dortmund in West Germany, is a little pet shop with a most grand name. From these premises on an unimposing side street, the proprietor supplies animals of all sorts to a steady string of customers from other countries, including Great Britain. A trip to the continent is something quite special when it involves a visit to the shop for collectors who arrive in cars already fitted with secret compartments, and if a customs man thinks he knows all the tricks of the trade, he ought to see some of these vehicles. The shop reckons it supplies between 100 and 200 animals a week to British people, and looking at the trade from a purely financial point of view he would be a fool not to. It can sell an African Grey Parrot in Germany for £70. In Britain, the same bird could sell for between £250 and £300. Animal collectors who are unwilling to take the risk of doing the actual smuggling themselves can let the dealer handle the problem for them—for a price, naturally.

To anyone in Britain who keeps his ear to the ground it seems likely that the trade is going to change in the near future when commerce in most species is going to be knocked on the head and only accredited dealers and collectors will be able to obtain licences. With this in mind, caring animal people are already going to considerable pains to show that they are just not willing to handle anything remotely suspicious. The newly-formed Association of Responsible Animal Keepers is a sign of this attitude, just as are the remarks of Barry Riley to me a few weeks ago. Barry is a much respected dealer in London who has been campaigning for a responsible approach to animal-keeping for years. Barry is on the committee of the Pet Trades Association and one of the things he does is to vet dealers who wish to become members. There are some dealers whom the Association will never admit to their ranks due to their dubious trading methods. The animal dealing world is a small one and word soon gets around.

12. What Does It Matter Anyway?

*Previous page: Scenes
like this are disappearing
fast. Conservation
comes a poor second to
profit (W. Newing)*

So what effect does trading in animals have on wild populations? What we in
the West should realise is that we have a very limited perception of the
problems. This is because we do have strict conservation legislation which, with
all its flaws, limits the number and species of animals and animal products which
arrive in our countries. A consignment of 500 Red Whiskered Bulbuls or
Paradox Frogs may look a hell of a lot, but without the controls that we do have,
those figures could very easily be ten times higher or even a hundred, as they
were 20 years ago. The real problem today is destruction of habitat.

Destruction of habitat is a term that we come across so often that we don't
think about it any longer. Our brains say, 'tut-tut', and our eyes slide past the
words and on to the meaty bits. Television programmes show what is happening
but because all those forests are in a small box in the corner of the room they are
not real, they do not convey the immensity of the rape that is going on. The
only way to bring home to someone the enormous destruction is to show them,
and that is hardly possible due to the cost involved showing everybody. It is not
a lot of good writing to your top politicians because they are far more concerned
about their careers, nor can the conservation organisations do too much. They
are aware of the problem but their budgets are so limited that they have to
concentrate on parts of it, the parts that they see as being in greatest need of
protection. It is the uncaring man in the street who needs to be shown, and
nothing makes the point so well as driving across a country for hour after hour
after hour with the smell of smoke in your nostrils from one fire after another
where the forest is being destroyed in slash and burn operations. Or to walk for
mile after mile through a sterile, dark-grey landscape where each footfall raises a
puff of fine black ash, the result of slash and burn. There are laws everywhere to
stop it and still it is happening in every place where there are such laws. All over
the world one can see signs declaring protected areas, nature reserves, areas of
outstanding natural beauty, and behind the signs rise wisps of smoke from a
hundred fires.

'Illegal logging prohibited', said one sign that I saw, 'Guards patrolling to
prevent destruction.' A slash and burn operation was being conducted within 50
feet, the guard chatting and laughing with the crowd of locals who were lighting
the fires.

Khao Yai National Park is the environmental showpiece of Thailand. Nearly
all of it has been burnt. Katy Buri told me, 'We spent five days there and saw just
one animal, a deer, and this is our prime national park that is promoted as a
tourist attraction.' There are two reasons for this attitude. First, no-one cares.

Yes, you care, and I care, but not enough people in Third World countries
care. Their perception is not ours. They say, 'If he chops down that tree there
are plenty more, and if they are all destroyed what does it matter?' Consequently
the peasant sees no reason to object, the guard who is paid to protect does not
understand why he is protecting and the politician cannot understand what the
fuss is about. The second reason is that there are astronomical profits to be made
from destroying a rain forest, and don't let anyone tell you that it is being done
by the poor starving peasant who is trying to eke out a meagre living in the face
of starvation.

Those days are long gone. There are still starving peasants but they are not
destroying the forests, nor are they profiting from the carnage. Those that are
wrecking the world are the rich and the powerful who come along and see much
wealth in the form of timber and meat and skins and minerals, but to obtain all

this a man needs permits or at any rate, a nod and a wink, so he goes along to the government departments responsible for forests and by negotiating with individuals at all levels he starts work. Sometimes forestry department vehicles cart away his timber or politicians come along for a shoot as the land is cleared and before long there is a lunar landscape. A jungle is a noisy place, it is full of life. After it has gone there is only the sound of the wind which blows away the ash and the fine, rich top-soil and leaves the residue to be washed away in the next rainy season. You can actually watch it all happen. It does not take the sort of timespan that only geologists comprehend. One can watch timber being removed one week, undergrowth cut down the next and burnt the week after and the rains baring the countryside some days later leaving great red scars across the landscape.

When the forest has gone, one of two things happens: either the site is cultivated for a single season by the locals after which all the nutrients in the soil have disappeared, or the place is used for another money-making project such as rearing beef cattle. When this happens, needless to say the meat is not eaten by the starving peasants, but is exported to more affluent countries. It may be beef or bananas but the story is the same.

To someone who understands the vandalism it is so frustrating to pass this understanding to the uncaring. I said that the local people can only work the land till the nutrients in the soil are exhausted. A simple enough sentence, but just think how many educated, intelligent people in this country watch their houseplants die and wonder why, and when it is suggested that a bit of feeding mightn't come amiss they laugh and say that they had never thought of that though they had been religiously watering the things for years.

I recently wrote to an animal dealer in South East Asia and asked what animals he could supply. In return I received a phone call from a lady who explained that she was the Minister of the Interior of that country and, as such, responsible for exploiting natural resources. She was phoning, she explained, because she was a partner of the dealer to whom I had written. She then told me to ask what I would particularly like. I had only to say, she went on, as she would be able to quote me for anything. 'You tell me what you want. We can supply all animals or birds or insects, or if you have other business we can also supply timber or herbs or seeds or minerals. You see, we want to maximise profits from the forest which is no good to us. We want to get rid of it so that we can build a big tourist complex. Anything you want, you tell me.'

In South America, an old friend of mine tried to communicate to me his anguish at this wholesale eradication of the Amazon Rain Forest. Could I not publicise it when I got home? he asked me. I told him that I would do what I could but pretty well everyone is becoming desensitised to stories of disappearing jungles. However it was Katy Buri in Thailand who showed me a new habitat destruction story that I had not come across before. She told me that her son, Prasit, was distressed by the elimination of the mangrove forests. Why, I asked, should anyone want to destroy mangroves. I don't know much about the timber trade but I would not have thought that there was much demand for mangrove wood. 'Go with him and see for yourself,' Katy insisted, and I did. Prasit hired a small boat from a boatman who soon revealed that he knew the maze of creeks through the mangrove forest just as you and I know the streets where we live. At first the forest looked as it does anywhere in the world but as we drew closer it could be observed that the trees were only about half the height that one might have expected. Apart from that, all looked well. We drove around from one channel to the next identical one for hours in a temperature of over a hundred. I realised later that Prasit was making a point. All looked pretty normal until we turned a corner, and there in front of us was a grey bank—the first break in the eternal wall of mangroves. We ran the boat ashore, stepped up onto the bank and looked around. Before us was an empty expanse—a good mile across. Dug into it were lots and lots of square ponds full to the brim with sea water. In the distance, a digger was creating more ponds and to the left were a couple of low, corrugated iron buildings. Ten foot high poles stood around this huge nothing with large floodlights at the top of them and, except for the place where we had landed, the whole thing was screened from the water by the fringe of mangrove trees that we had been following for a considerable distance without my realising that this border was only a few yards deep. Prasit told me that the whole mangrove forest was like this, and I asked him to explain what was happening. He told me that this area was a prawn farm. The whole world loves prawns and the population of South East Asia alone consumes millions of them a year. This means that there is much money to be made from prawns. Enlightenment dawned. 'Ah' I exclaimed, 'They breed them here!' I was soon disillusioned. Each so-called prawn farm had gates that were lifted at the incoming tide. The water, containing prawns by the million, flowed into the ponds. The gates were closed and the prawns were trapped. No breeding was done anywhere, even though these places, and I soon found out that there are many of them, are known as prawn farms.

Whilst we talked, the workers wandered over to inspect us and Prasit asked if they would show me some of their stock. One of the men called out in the direction of the buildings and a teenage boy came forward carrying a net on his shoulder. He stood by us at the edge of the pond and gracefully tossed it into the water. Within a few seconds he hauled it out. It was full of prawns—a good dustbin full—but they were not what I had been expecting, the little crustaceans that we call prawns in Britain. They were magnificent animals, about one foot long, with blue feet and yellow joints on their otherwise grey bodies. The boy tipped them into a large plastic container so that we could examine them, and on closer inspection it became apparent that there were little prawns as well, millions of them. I don't know whether they were a separate species or the babies of the big ones but there were plenty of them.

The catch was tipped back and the boy repeated the manoeuvre at another pond with the same result, and then a third and a fourth. The whole place was teeming with prawns. The project must bring in a fortune which explained the floodlights around the perimeter. With the high market prices, prawn rustling was prevalent. I asked who owned the business and Prasit said that it was a syndicate of jewellers in Bangkok who were very wealthy and had many other businesses as well. 'They own that too,' he added, nodding at a nearby mountain, 'And they are clearing all the forest from it. Some of my ex-neighbours owned land on it and were bought out. Others who refused to sell were forced out and two or three were shot. The jewellers are powerful men.' Initially I might have treated his remarks with scepticism but by then I had got to know the Thais well enough to realise that what he said was entirely possible.

It emerged that all these prawn farms were sited illegally as it was against the law to destroy the mangrove forest, but apparently the appropriate government minister had implied that if he could not see them, he could not know they were there. Consequently the prawn farmers maintained the farce of leaving a fringe of mangrove forest between their activities and the water. Everyone knew they were there but no one could see them.

Letters to the editor of the *Bangkok Post* commonly complained of the despoilation of the rain forest and are always answered with wimpish comments on how difficult it is to achieve anything constructive, or else on odd occasions the Forestry Department proudly states that an area has now been declared officially protected. The Deputy Chief of the Forestry Department, Phairote Suwahnakom, is spoken of highly by Thai conservationists but he achieves nothing, despite his undoubted concern. What can the man do when some of the destructive projects around protected areas which encroach within their borders are government-initiated developments? Lest one should imagine that this sort of thing only happens elsewhere, let me remind you of the orchid-rich meadow on Mersea Island in Essex which was sprayed with herbicide in 1985 by the owner when he was prevented from building on the land.

When money is involved conservation comes a poor second, and this is nowhere more obvious than in Thailand which has lost 75 per cent of its forest in five years and each week there are reports in the papers about illegal logging. One can go on quoting statistics for ever but you have seen them all before; they have become meaningless. From the point of view of the animal trade, such destruction means that an awful lot of individual animals are killed by falling trees, fires and shotguns, and those that survive are captured and taken to the local markets. With no cover to hide in, whole communities of some species can be readily taken where previously only odd individuals would be removed. Then, of course, once the habitat has gone, so have the animals from that area and in time, altogether.

It would be wrong to suggest that trade in live animals never does harm to wild populations. Some species have become decidedly scarce as a direct result, but the destruction of habitat is by far the greater threat. It is certainly this that is going to cause the problems—and the trade in animal products, for when an animal is dead, it is dead for ever. Throughout the Third World, official blind eyes are turned to the disappearance of the forests but when a villager sells an animal that he has found in a dying jungle to a dealer, it is quite likely that the dealer cannot export it legally which results in a dead animal instead of giving it the chance to continue the species in a collection somewhere.

Some of the destruction we no longer think of with horror, it has been with us so long that we accept it. When I say this I am thinking particularly of Australia which is covered in rabbits and sheep, neither of which is native. Their presence has resulted in the destruction of large tracts of Australia. Where there are no sheep, there are fruit farms which are preyed upon by local birds who come along in flocks to munch their way through these goodies with the result that some birds, such as the Roseate Cockatoo, are not only shot as pests but have a bounty on their heads. Yet Australia will not allow the export of Roseate Cockatoos, or any other sort of native animal for that matter. The Australians erroneously seem to think there's something wrong with parrots and right with sheep.

I have been speaking throughout of private collectors rather than zoos. Western zoos fall conveniently into two major groups. There are those that are run by Zoological Trusts or similar bodies and are generally well-kept, do a great job of education and breeding, and take very little out of the wild; and there are the small commercial zoos which are generally an entirely different kettle of fish, and for the most part I have no time for them though I will be the first to admit that there are noble exceptions such as Birdland at Bourton-on-the-Water in Gloucestershire. Despite the knowing nudges and winks that one sees when the subject is mentioned, the first group take very few wild animals because more and more species are now being bred in captivity and the respectable zoos have exchange schemes. These zoos also have far too much to lose by handling the variety of illegal animals that they are offered annually. The small, commercial zoos are not necessarily so responsible nor averse to taking dodgy stock if conditions are right. Good zoos not only do a good job of conservation by breeding endangered animals in captivity but they do a great job by returning surplus animals to the wild. Perhaps the best known case is that of the Ne-ne Goose which was shot out in its homeland of Hawaii but was bred at Slimbridge Wildfowl Trust and returned home. Pere David's Deer are another nice example. They were only to be found in the grounds of the royal palace in Peking prior to the Boxer rebellion when they were all killed, except for a few that Pere David had smuggled out to the West. Today, all specimens of that particular species are captive-bred. But the story I like best is that of the Pink Pigeon that was hanging on by the skin of its beak in its home on Mauritius until Gerald Durrell at the Jersey Wildlife Preservation Trust bred the birds in captivity and was able to return some to the island whence their parents had come. Jersey has a great record of breeding endangered animals and even if you don't like zoos, you should go there; it's great and I promise you will enjoy it.

Jersey is also good at breeding tamarins and other South American primates. Some time ago, some specimens of Gold Headed Lion Tamarin were imported by a dealer into Belgium. In the past few years between 50 and 60 had been exported illegally from Brazil and it has been estimated that this represents between 25 and 50 per cent of all of them. Despite protests from Prince Philip, the World Wildlife Fund, the Brazilian government and the International Union for the Conservation of Nature, they were not repatriated. Protest grew and due to a lot of work by many individuals, including Jeremy Mallinson, the Director of Jersey Zoo who maintains the stud book for Lion Maned Tamarins, eventually the surviving animals were returned to Brazil on 30 November 1985 where they are being held at the Primate Rehabilitation Centre, not far from Rio de Janeiro until they can be released into a suitable bit of forest.

Frequently, such rare animals are found by peasants following forest destruction by international companies and their local representatives. The trouble with these concerns is that they have sufficient money to bulldoze over everybody brave enough to stand up to them. It takes a lot of money to take a big company to court, and they only need to maintain their defence long enough for the conservation bodies and concerned individuals to back down when their cash runs out, to win the case by default. There is such a case being fought in the courts at the moment which has resulted in one conservation group paying out $300,000 to date, and an individual paying another $100,000 and the whole palaver is not yet over. The international company involved is estimated to have already spent more than $1 million pursuing the case. All the involved parties on both sides are well aware that in this particular instance the conservationists are in the right. Most court cases involve a host of nuances and shades of grey but this one is unique in just being black and white. There is little doubt that black will win due to the greater depth of its pockets.

And in the end, does it all matter anyway?

Well, yes, it does. First, and most easily disposed of because you can argue it depending on your viewpoint, is the moral and aesthetic aspect. Many people could not care less if there are no more Giant Pandas in the world. But on the second point there can be no doubt, once the animals and plants have gone, they have gone forever and we have only recently developed the technology to investigate and extract from animals and especially plants, many compounds that are of use to man. In Madagascar there is a plant known as the Madagascar periwinkle. A drug obtained from this plant is now used to treat leukemia in children, and the plant is cultivated for this purpose. But, considering the rate at which Madagascan flora is being destroyed, the wild plant will have vanished in a very short time. Luckily we found it but there are going to be an awful lot that we are going to destroy before we do discover how to use them. And lastly, we do not know what the untold results of such destruction are going to be. In 1986, many of the waterways in Thailand dried up long before they normally do—long before the rains were due to replenish them. In March, the few measly little puddles in the beds of the rivers were being furiously pumped out by desperate farmers trying to save their crops, and all of them pointed out that each year, as the jungles were being wiped out, the situation was getting worse.

The solution, if there is one, lies in education. If one can persuade consumers that a rosewood coffee table is no more necessary than one made of pine, one is on the right track. At one time the pine coffee table might have looked cheap and nasty, but with today's techniques it can be made to resemble rosewood, though it will probably look nicer as pine anyway. And when all is said and done, it is only a device to keep this book off the floor.

Success has been achieved in some fields so that nowadays, it would be considered louche to wear the skin of a spotted cat in Britain and most people, however insensitive, would decline wearing a Leopard skin coat if only because of the vilification to which they would be subjected. But also, there will always be someone like the media star who arrived from New York at Heathrow airport and was photographed wearing a Leopard coat. Asked about this by a journalist she shrugged and said, 'I can afford a fur coat and if I want to wear one I will. I am not interested in the Leopards.' Yuk!

13. The Final Solution

There is no final solution. As long as there are people there will be trade in animals and animal products. In ten years or 50 years, the reports in the press will, I imagine, be much as they are now though the species involved may well be different. As with smoking, you will stop it only if you want to stop it badly enough and many countries just do not see the need to do that.

The colossal amount of live animals that used to enter Great Britain some years ago has declined but other markets are as demanding as ever. All the exporters with whom I have recently spoken hate sending consignments to London because legislation inspections are such a pain. In fact, many dealers will no longer even consider doing business with British dealers. However, it must be said that legislation and the current climate is definitely making dealers think of ways of re-shaping their business and most of them are conducting breeding programmes since every one of them is aware of CITES and its implications. Most of the supplying countries are signatories of CITES but the Convention and local legislation work with varying degrees of failure. The only real success story is in India which used to supply a large percentage of the animals in trade each year, and if I had been asked to guess I would never have thought that India would be the one place to knock the trade on the head as it can be a quite extraordinarily inefficient country where a way can be found round most troublesome laws. Knowing the place as well as I do, I should have taken into account the mentality of the bureaucrats in the offices and at the airports, who really do enjoy making a meal of paperwork and inspections. It must have very soon become apparent to dealers that they were not going to get away with consignments of protected species. As a result, the wildlife in India is now a delight to watch. Of all the places I recently visited, there are more birds and mammals to be casually seen in that country than anywhere else. There are far less lizards around than there used to be—perhaps the increased numbers of birds are having an effect on their numbers. This particular legislation has worked marvellously well and the Indians deserve congratulations for it.

Conservation legislation can, however, be counter-productive. It is now forbidden to import the traditional pet shop tortoise into Britain. They used to be taken from the wild in such huge numbers to be shipped in such terrible conditions that a stop was put on the trade. Now the populations have recovered and great hordes of the reptiles are munching their way through the crops of vegetables on the farms of the local peasants, who now plough them into the ground by the thousand in an attempt to keep down the numbers.

A birdwatching friend of mine returned recently from a holiday in Malta, and he was telling me how the Maltese seemed to have an intense dislike of flying animals, as they only needed to see a bird to reach for a gun. 'Still,' he finished, 'you can't do anything; that's the way they're brought up over there.' I am convinced that the only way to save wildlife is to make it commercial. When animals in their natural environment are worth pound notes or dollars, they will be preserved. One of the ways of doing this is to demonstrate to each country that foreign visitors will pay good money to come and see those beasts that the locals despise; but for such an approach, it is essential that the revenue from tourists must benefit every level of the population. It is the people in the country areas who often need to do the conserving, and if they feel that they are seeing no return for their effort because all the cash is vanishing into the pockets of the hotel owners in the capital, they will cease to bother and who can blame them?

Encouraging tourism of this sort solves many of the problems. It would provide employment for local people who could make and sell souvenirs, work in hotels and drive buses, and usefully help those villages in which the men have always existed by hunting and trapping. No one would be better than these chaps as guides to tour groups as they are superb naturalists. Having said all that, I am well aware of the hole in my argument because once an area becomes too popular with tourists it is ruined. It is not that the visitors trudging about through reserves do much harm as the animals soon adjust to that, it is rather that patches of land are cleared for monstrous, tower-block hotels, soft drinks stalls appear all over the place, nasty plastic souvenirs marked 'Made in Taiwan' are sold everywhere except Taiwan and the pimps and the touts move in. The trouble is that the hoteliers, the soft drink sellers and everybody else are not willing to take a modest profit and then open other centres elsewhere so that the hordes are evenly spread. Instead, they have to screw every last copper out of the visitor and the whole place becomes ever more tawdry. And, would you believe that there are actually people who like that sort of holiday? Natives of the Norfolk Broads were telling me last year that the punters on the hire boats go roaring along the waterways and shout to the local inhabitants to ask them to point out the right river to the next pub, throwing polystyrene cartons and beer cans overboard the while. Ee, there's nowt so queer as folk; why can't they all be like you and I?

I appreciate that there are many people who would not want to visit nature reserves in Rwanda or Thailand or Brazil, but there are an awful lot that do and every possible help should be given to the industry.

As to keeping animals in captivity, I feel that it is a need that is very basic within us. As I have said, I do not see any reason for not allowing caring, private, responsible animal keepers to take limited numbers of specimens from the wild for breeding programmes, though I do think that bulk trade with its attendant enormous wastage is not a good thing.

The trade in the products of wild animals is pretty crazy and I cannot find much justification for it, and I am positive that substitutes for all of them can be used. Synthetic musk is already commonplace, fake furs are everywhere and so good that even the closest scrutiny can fail to reveal whether the coat came from an animal or not. Sometimes only handling it will tell its origin. And when I visited a leather factory in Bangkok, although the place was full of Ostrich, lizard and pangolin skin, the proprietor showed me cattle skins that had been dyed and stamped to resemble other species, so that even when holding a fake next to the genuine article I could sometimes not differentiate. I asked Tony how difficult he found it, to which he replied that he could always tell when he was handling a piece of skin what animal it came from, but if the faking had been done well, once the skin was made up, it was frequently impossible to be sure.

In the years to come, there will certainly be more and more conservation legislation to ban trade in animals, and rightly so, and I would make a guess that in ten years time it will be impossible to import into the UK any wild animal except under special licence for zoos and similar establishments. I have even heard talk about banning the keeping of all exotic animals, including tropical fish bred in captivity, in Britain though I do not believe that that will ever happen.

The point must be brought home that such things matter to every one of us not just to those that are interested in animals. We are all guilty of exacerbating the problem without thinking. I refuse unnecessary paper bags in shops, which really annoys some unthinking assistants who come up with all sorts of wimpish excuses like, 'But it is the firm's policy,' or 'You might be stopped by Security on the way out'. I have noticed, however, that when I ask for a manager to make the point that he really must stop giving away all this useless paper, he will invariably back down 'just this once' when I tell him to give me my money back as I would rather buy the item from a shop with a more responsible attitude. Another example of this thoughtlessness was shown the other day by a sales rep who came to visit me after I had written to his firm about conservatories, as I was looking for one. The rep carefully went through all the specifications of his buildings which seemed like good buys, but when he proudly told me that the timber was all Philippine mahogany I told him to stop as I was not willing to buy a product containing mahogany. I explained that the tree is not cultivated, it is always cut down in the wild and it is such logging that is destroying the world's forest. He went off disgusted and shaking his head. He was far too well trained to say so, but he clearly thought I was a nut. I am not an extremist in any sense of the word but I have been lucky enough to have seen for myself the destruction that the demand for mahogany causes, and I care too much to add to it.

The other thing that must be looked at is the actual construction of new laws to protect our environment. People who know what they are talking about must be asked to draft the laws after which they can be knocked into shape by civil servants.

It is no good asking scientific experts for a report on what is wrong and then working out a bill from that, because the person who does so can get his emphasis wrong, misunderstand some facts and ignore others that to him seem unimportant. When I talk to lawmakers they say, 'But we do just what you are telling us to do'; that they don't is revealed the moment the relevant documents come out.

In a letter to me the other day, the zoologist C. H. Keeling says, 'If you have a Viper in your garden, know it is there and take steps to protect it, you can be in trouble with the Dangerous Wild Animals Act—while if you bundle it out you can be prosecuted under the Wildlife and Countryside Act!'

In the meantime, the live animal trade, both legal and illegal, continues with few problems and some people make a lot of money at it, though it must be said that more people make money from animal products than from live animals. Still, to the person who is willing to pay the price there is hardly a live animal that cannot be obtained. I imagine that a Giant Panda would be impossible and large mammals are a problem because of their size, but that leaves a heck of a lot of other beasties. I recently spoke to a smuggler whom I have known slightly for years. At one time his base was in the Far East but things got too hot for him and he now lives in the States. He sells all sorts of animals but like so many American dealers he specialises in parrots. He is still running the particular trade that was always his speciality. He is willing to supply for $100,000 or its equivalent in any major currency, any ten pairs of Australian parrots delivered to your door. He has contacts in Australia who collect the birds and when he receives information that they are available, he organises a boat to pick them up from a rendezvous on the coast. They are then laundered through another country so that they become ostensibly legal—well nearly legal—and then they go to Mexico before being taken across the border to the USA. When I talked to the man he had just received three such package deals and was keen to get one of them off to a customer who was most anxious as it had been a year since the order had been placed. Such consignments are only collected from Australia when there are enough orders to make the very complicated operation worthwhile and a consignment a few months ago had gone wrong. When the crates of birds are picked up from the trappers they are always weighted, and the boat carrying this particular consignment had been intercepted by an Australian Navy Patrol so the boxes had to be dumped overboard before they were spotted.

At one time this particular dealer used to have his own fast boat that was kept in Indonesia, but now, living in America as he does, he merely contacts his man in the area who goes to one of the boat skippers that regularly handle the job.

I earlier referred to the disappearance of wild genes before we have learnt to use them, and one of the fascinating things about the live animal trade is that even today a trapper sometimes brings in an animal that is completely new. You would think in this day and age that every species in the world had been catalogued but it is not so and new animals are being constantly discovered. Admittedly they are generally invertebrates that are easily overlooked but sometimes larger unknown animals are brought to light. Something like this happened to me in Georgetown, the capital of Guyana in South America when I was visiting Mr Lee who is a well-known dealer in the city. I was at his animal compound at Kissy, a little way from Georgetown, and as we talked we wandered around his collection. Much of his stock of smaller animals is housed in buildings rather like garden sheds on legs to keep them about 18 inches off the dusty ground which leaves a most convenient area beneath, when surrounded by wire netting, for keeping animals. We stopped at one building and turning to me, Mr Lee asked, 'Are you interested in any snakes?'

I asked him what he had.

'Oh, I have plenty of boas of course and one or two odds and ends, and a few Emerald Tree Boas', he ticked them off on his fingers as he spoke.

'And very many Anacondas.'

'I'd like to see your Anacondas,' I told him. 'Somebody has asked me if I could get hold of a couple.'

'Well, they are beneath this shed—have a look,' said Mr Lee with a gesture at the ground. 'And while you are looking, there is one other snake in there that I have never seen before. I have no idea what it is.'

That sounded interesting. Lee had been in the business for many years and I would have thought that he would have been familiar with every reptile in Guyana so if he didn't know the snake it must be something really special.

I got down on my knees and fiddled with the lock on the little wire-netting door. Looking up, I asked, 'What does this snake look like?'

'Oh, it is about three feet long,' Lee told me. 'It is green, bright green like an Emerald Tree Boa but it has a row of red spots surrounded by a yellow ring along each side. I have a feeling it is venomous and it is certainly arboreal.'

Unable to think of any South American snake that matched the description, I was fascinated to see what I would turn up.

The lock came undone with a rusty click and I pulled open the ramshackle door and lay on the ground so that I could slide under the shed. It was hot under there and before I had finished inching my way in the sweat was dripping off me. By the time I had wriggled as far as my hips I could see all around the enclosure. There was a heap of mouldy sacking in one corner and a large tin bath was sunk into a hole in the middle of the floor. This bath was full to the brim with green water with lumps of frothy scum floating on the top, and it stunk.

What the enclosure seemed not to contain was a single Anaconda, however. Thinking that they might be under the sacking I crept forward another couple of inches, banging my head on a beam above me as I did so. I moved the sacking this way and that but it seemed to hide no more than three beetles and a jet-propelled centipede that galloped over my hand and squeezed through the wire netting. I dropped the hessian and a cloud of dust wafted in my face. I sneezed twice and trying to twist round in my cramped position to face Mr Lee's legs I called out, 'I can't see any Anacondas; how many have you go in here?'

'About two hundred, I think.'

'Two hundred! I can't see one.'

I turned my head and cracked it again on a joist. I tried to rub it with my hand and as I did so, my fingers brushed against something above me that didn't feel like wood. I twisted around to try and see above me but it was pretty well impossible, so with a bit of grunting and heaving I turned over and, lying on my back, I looked up at the wooden beams a few inches from my face. Now I could see the Anacondas. They were all coiled up in amongst the framework that supported the floor of the shed. There were plenty of them and they were all peering down at me. As I turned my head, all the reptile heads turned as well to watch. The snakes varied in size from about four feet to about ten feet. The situation was a little delicate for I wasn't too pleased to find all these reptiles so close to my face. I like Anacondas and they don't go out of their way to savage people but they were close enough to make me wary.

'Mr Lee,' I called, 'I've found your Anacondas, but I see no sign of your bright green snake, are you sure it is in here?'

'Well, it was a day or two ago. I put it in there myself. Try in the pond.'

Pond! It looked more like liquid green jelly than water but if there was an unknown snake in there I was going to have to go fishing, so I wriggled back onto my tummy and gingerly put my hand into the water. I felt around slowly but could find nothing. It was odd, I thought: if there really was a snake in there I would have expected it to be swimming around or climbing out by now, but there was no sign. Eventually I felt something that could be a snake and I gripped it. I could not tell how far my hand was from its head and if it was venomous as Mr Lee suggested, it might turn around and bite but until I could see it there was not much to do, so with one quick movement I hauled it out and dropped it onto the ground. The violent movement covered me in green slime but I wiped it from my glasses and peered at my catch while the foul-smelling green liquid dripped from my beard. The effort was for nothing. The snake was dead. I backed out of the cage dragging it with me. When he saw me, Lee laughed like a drain but I only glanced at him sourly; and, squatting in a green puddle I examined the dead reptile. It was a shame, for even in death the animal was beautiful and as colourful as Lee had described it. I had no idea what it was and would have loved to pickle it in alcohol and take it back with me to be identified but sadly this was not possible. I would have needed a bottle at least as large as a Winchester and a good supply of spirit and I had neither. I made Lee promise that if ever he got another he would give me a ring but I've not heard that he has found any more.

It was that same evening I went collecting Marine Toads. These king-size amphibians have beautiful eyes and I wanted a few pairs. They can grow pretty huge and although it is said that when they come under enough stress they exude a white compound that is irritating, I have never known them to practise this anti-social habit. They are always impeccably behaved and are generally quite content to sit in the hand throbbing gently at you. Lee suggested to me that the best way to find several of these animals in the same place was to pay a nocturnal visit to the newly cut sugar cane fields on the outskirts of the capital. I thanked him and set off back to my hotel, a relic of the days when Guyana was British Guiana, and it was easy to imagine some curry-blowing colonel using the cavernous metal bath before retiring beneath the tentlike mosquito nets that were supported on strange metal arms that were swung out from the walls at night to support the voluminous marquee over the centre of the beds.

As it grew dark, I had a meal in the verandah restaurant and having just spent several uncomfortable days deep in the middle of nowhere, I decided that being back in civilisation I must order some chips. Guyana does not have potatoes and it is an offence to try and import them. I saw a man and his wife arrive in the country from Nijkerie in adjacent Surinam with a bag of potatoes and these were immediately confiscated and the couple were given a pretty nasty time. I was interested therefore to see what my chips were going to be. I would never have guessed that they would be made from banana, or to be more precise, plantain, but they were, and were acceptable too.

I finished the chips and drank my coffee while the last scraps of daylight disappeared. I had been warned not to go out on my own after dark as the city was supposed to be full of muggers and murderers but I hoped that where I was going there would be no baddies around. It is a pity that such nocturnal activities are now commonplace everywhere; they ruin towns that used to be so peaceful not many years ago.

On this occasion I was safe; the muggers had decided that there would be no profit in the now empty sugar cane fields but I did take the precaution of hiring a taxi to my destination and telling the driver to wait for my return. As I climbed from the vehicle, I wondered why Marine Toads wanted to congregate in this particular location as when the sugar cane is ready for harvesting the whole field is set alight to burn off all the leaves from the plants and to kill off all the creepy crawlies that take up residence in the fields during the growing season. After the burn and the subsequent harvesting the fields are pretty lifeless places. There were, however, wide waterfilled storm drains alongside so I suppose the toads came ashore from these.

When I say the fields are lifeless, what I mean is that they do not contain a wealth of small creatures for the amphibians to eat. I soon discovered that lifeless was definitely not the adjective to apply to the place that evening as it was the haunt of all the courting couples with nowhere else to go. I did not know this as I tucked some collecting bags into my belt and fitted my lamp onto my forehead. I set off without switching it on and I had not gone many paces before tripping over something soft which resulted in a muttered exclamation that meant, 'Go away and fall over someone else', followed by a female giggle. I apologised and went forward but the same thing happened before I had covered many feet, and again after that. It was amazing. The whole area was covered in people trying to find a bit of privacy for their lovemaking, as no doubt their families had for generations, only to have a dirty great toad collector come and boot them in the ribs.

It would have been easier to avoid them had they been white but they blended so well with the ground in the darkness. By this time, I found myself in a quandary as I had no way of extricating myself. In whichever direction I went, I found myself falling over people. In the end I decided that the only thing that I could possibly do would be to switch on my lamp for a couple of seconds, just long enough to find a way out of my mess. That was a distinctly unpopular move. Two startled black faces, not to mention other bits of anatomy, appeared briefly in my beam to be followed by a howl of protest as I quickly switched it off again. I really was rather bothered now as I visualised things getting nasty if everyone rose up in protest to drive me from the field, and I could hardly blame them. Luckily salvation was at hand. Somebody a few feet away had clearly realised that I wanted nothing more than to extricate myself from the muddle, someone moreover who obviously had infinitely better night vision than I had, for he called to me to walk in his direction so that he could point me towards the road.

Gratefully I called, 'I'm coming, I'm coming.'

'Me too,' growled a broad West Indian accent not far off, adding ruefully, 'If only I get de chance.' It probably did nothing to help the poor guy that his heartfelt comment resulted in peals of laughter from his girlfriend that continued until I reached the road.

After that I kept to the verges by the storm drains and despite the early setbacks I managed to collect some super Marine Toads in a very short time, so all in all I was pretty pleased with myself as I walked back to the taxi, and then with only a few feet to go I slipped and, despite scrabbling madly at everything within reach, I slid down the concrete side of the drain to land knee deep in water. Or at any rate, a mixture that contained water. It contained much else as well that was undoubtedly biologically fascinating but all I wanted to do was to get out of there and back to the hotel. I stumbled along the uneven bottom, lifting each foot with a sucking squelch till I came to some steps set into the bank, and climbed up these. I was feeling fairly uncomfortable by the time I found my taxi and, waking the driver, I climbed into the back, hoping that he was too dozy to realise that I smelt like a sewer. Fortunately he didn't comment and dropped me off a few minutes later at my hotel. I was dripping all over the place and felt that it would not be a good idea if I went in the front door and through the highly polished reception area, so I quietly walked to the back of the building where I knew there was a door only a few feet from my room. In a modern hotel I could not have got away with it as there are security men and automatic cameras and all sorts, but this particular establishment had not altered much in 50 years, and so I knew that my only obstacle would be the night watchman who sat where he could see both doors, but at this time of night he would certainly be asleep.

I eased the back door open, slid off my shoes, tugged my soggy socks from my feet and crept quietly to my room. It was such a delight to remove the smelly clothes and climb into the shower and a few minutes after I had done that I felt decidedly human again. I examined my toads which were lovely specimens and worth all the problems after all. I smiled happily and was climbing into bed when I noticed that there was now bright moonlight which was shining through the louvred shutters and casting stripes of light across the floor. On impulse I walked across to the windows and opened wide the shutters. Contentedly I looked out at the roofs of the houses reflecting the moonlight, and the single tall papaya tree, somehow more still at night time than during the day. I glanced down to the hibiscus bushes and then directly below my window at the ornamental lily pond which was surrounded by a low wall with a wide, flat capping. And sitting on this capping were 24 big, fat Marine Toads. The whole surface was covered in amphibians, from the toads and the giant South American Bullfrogs down to tiny little tree frogs that appeared slaty grey in the moonlight but which I knew were bright green. The noise of the shutters opening caused all the animals to freeze and for a second and a half they remained motionless, then as though at a signal the whole lot dived into the water and a couple of moments later the surface ripples had vanished, leaving only lots and lots of dark, wet frog shapes on the nearly white concrete.

Never mind, I thought as I climbed under the voluminous mosquito net, I got the toads I wanted and I was well pleased with them.

14. The Show Goes On

The scale of wildlife trading has declined over the years. None the less, the trade continues, and I receive reports from many sources around the world about what is happening today and browsing through them is an excellent way of overseeing the current picture.

Animal Skins Seized by Staff Reporter

In one of our major hauls of recent times, Calcutta officials seized 14 Leopard skins, and 125 wild cat skins from a house in the Tiretta Bazaar area of Central Calcutta late on Tuesday evening. The skins, collected from Orissa were to have been smuggled to Nepal.
The Statesman (8.4.86)—Newspaper cutting sent by David Whiting

* Of the hundred odd species of bird for sale last Saturday at the weekend market (Bangkok), I counted 62 species that are protected and 18 that can only be sold under the quota system. At least some of the stalls had more than their quotas allowed for.
Letter from a friend (1.5.86)

* Twenty-six eggs of the rare Lanner Falcon were recently smuggled into Manchester Airport on a flight from Agadir, Morocco.
The Guardian (17.3.86)

* The smuggling of South East Asian wildlife for sale in the United States has grown into a multi-million-dollar business, a US Attorney involved in its suppression told a reporter recently. Each case involved from $250,000 to over one million dollars worth of rare endangered species said Mr Jonathan Blackmer, a US Attorney.
Bangkok Post (6.11.84)

* I asked if I could buy a tiger skin and the man took me through New Market (Calcutta) to a tiny, shut up shop at the back of beyond. It was totally deserted but when it was opened up, it contained a variety of illegal skins.
Vic Watkins in conversation (2.6.86)

* Sir, I have just had the pleasure of spending three weeks in your beautiful country. The number of national parks in Thailand, their size, beauty and importance to wildlife is well known. I was therefore horrified to discover how little protection is given to the fauna within the parks.

During one hour I counted nine shot-gun shots within 300 metres of a park gate. My Thai companions reported these shots to the guards who said they had not heard the shots. In my opinion, this was impossible unless the guards were deaf or asleep.
Letter to the editor, *Bangkok Post* (12.12.85)

* Look, you can take the snakes (Papuan Green Tree Pythons) but if you're asked they never came from me, right?
A London dealer in conversation (1.6.86)

* The Chinese Crude Drugs Company has been running short of raw material as most of its sources have become scarce and subsequently officially protected. It has now announced plans to raise tigers, bears, leopards, snakes and other animals in captivity in order to harvest their bones, bile or blood for various tonics and elixirs.
Press release from a Chinese News Agency (May 1985)

* A West German egg thief has made his escape from Iceland while awaiting trial. Eight eggs were found in the possession of Peter Baly and his wife together with maps of nesting sites and incubation equipment. Baly escaped by stowing away on a German cargo vessel. The ship called at Esbjerg in Denmark but the captain refused to hand him over to the Police and landed him at Hamburg. There is little chance that a fine can be collected now although Baly already has a suspended sentence in Germany for stealing young falcons.
News from Iceland (June/July 1984)

* On 25 September 1985, snake collector Peter Murr from West Germany was detained in Greece for attempting to smuggle 70 Cyclades Blunt-nosed Vipers onto a ferry from the island of Milos bound for Piraeus. The snakes are of a protected endemic sub-species. Murr was later released, pending charges. All the snakes were released at several suitable wild locations on the island under police supervision.

The initial detective work leading to the arrest was carried out by amateur Dutch herpetologist Gaston Van Mook and David Stubbs of the UK.

It is estimated that over 1,000 of these snakes (perhaps ten to twenty percent of the population) are taken from the island each year.
Herpetofauna News (October 1985)

* What do you want to go to Greece to film wildlife for? There is no wildlife there!
Official of the Greek Embassy, London, on the phone (September 1985)

* Large scale encroachment threatens to turn the nation's last lowland rain forest in Tha Sae District of Chumphon Province, Thailand from a wildlife paradise to an ecological wasteland. Nearly 200 square kilometres of the reserved forest had been cleared by encroachers to cultivate cucumbers. The land was exploited for about a year after which the soil's fertility was exhausted.

It may now be too late to conserve the uniquely rich rain forest which supports more species of plants and animals. At least 25 species of birds and an immeasurable number of butterflies and other insects as well as frogs and

reptiles, are completely confined to the rain forests of the flat lowlands.
Bangkok Post (9.9.85)

* On his first trip to Germany, Tonge smuggled 40 parrots including African Greys, Blue-Fronted Amazons and Black Headed Caiques. Tonge accepted two of the parrots (as payment) which he had smuggled, then advertised the birds. He received an abundance of calls and earned £500 from the sale of the two parrots, he said.

On the second trip, Tonge returned with 36 birds and cleared customs with ease. He kept two Blue Fronted Amazon Parrots as his payment.

On his final trip, Tonge was caught. He said, 'I know that the person who I worked for is still running birds from the Continent using new couriers. There's a lot of money to be made all round.'
Sunday Times (23.5.86)

* 3.1 million cubic metres of timber and timber products valued at US $1.2 billion were exported from Peninsular Malaysia in 1983 the Malaysian Primary Industries Minister Datuk Paul Leong announced recently.

In view of the alarming current average logging rate of 300,000 hectares a year, the Malaysian authorities have directed that the annual logging rate be scaled down.
Sahabar Alam Malaysian (1984)

* I applied months ago, for a Department of the Environment permit to export the birds. Eventually, after much chasing, they wrote back to say that we had filled in the application form incorrectly. That's nonsense, I send the things off every week of the year—I know how to fill them in better than they do. Anyway I wrote back saying just that and in the end they replied, agreeing that we had filled in the form correctly after all but would I please fill in another once since they had mislaid the original!

You wouldn't believe the hassle. Even with perfectly legal species, they make life as difficult as they can for importers and exporters. Who do they think they are—after all, their job is to make sure the law is complied with.
A London dealer in conversation (16.3.86)

* The Management Authority of the Central African Republic has informed the CITES Secretariat of the theft of CITES Security Stamps. The last authentic permit of the CAE bearing a CITES Security Stamp was granted on 12 February 1985.
CITES Secretariat, Notification to the Parties, No. 340

* In October 1984, a Zimbabwean ornithologist, Adrian Lendrum and his son, Jeffrey, were convicted of stealing eggs of protected birds of prey and of fabricating entries in a nest record survey. Adrian Lendrum then invented data on the progress of stages of breeding. The effect has been to nullify all findings on one species and to devalue much of the data on the others. Both Lendrums were fined Z$4500 (£2650) and given four months suspended sentences. Adrian Lendrum was then arrested on 15 October on charges of smuggling eggs out of the country.
The Observer (21.10.84)

* William Robinson and Jonathan Wood were arrested at Los Angeles International Airport on 12 September 1984 when a customs inspector found 27 eggs of rare birds in their clothing.
Daily Telegraph (Australia) (31.10.85)

* I have just received a superb pair of Quetzals. They have come in from Costa Rica. If you know anyone who would like them then let me know and we can talk prices.
A dealer in Belgium during a phone conversation (10.4.86)

* A Briton, John Slaytor, is to go on trial in Canada accused of heading a sophisticated rare bird smuggling ring. They allegedly set up links to supply wild birds from Britain, Iceland and Finland to the USA and Saudi Arabia. Wildlife officers say rare Gyrfalcons—worth up to £75,000 (US $107,500) each, ended up in the hands of members of the Saudi Royal family.
Mail on Sunday (14.7.85)

* A Zimbabwean who smuggled two rhino horns, worth more than Z$49,000 (US$29,945) into the country from Mozambique was jailed on 7 March 1986 for four years.

Duwariti Aliphasi, 62, was arrested while trying to sell the horns to an official of the Zimbabwean Department of National Parks and Wildlife Management.
The Zimbabwe Herald (3.8.86)

* From: Guidelines for Transport and Preparation for Shipment of Live Wild Animals and Plants.

Packer's Guidelines: General Welfare

1.1. Birds should have priority over merchandise.
1.2. Only birds in good health should be transported.
1.3. Birds should not be sedated.
1.4. Birds should be transported in semi-darkness.
1.5. Birds of different species should not be transported in the same container.
1.6. Unless birds of the same species are known to be compatible with one another, they should not be transported in the same container.
1.7. Birds should be disturbed as little as possible.
1.8. Birds that have become sick, or have been injured during transport, should receive veterinary treatment as soon as possible, and if necessary, should be humanely destroyed. A record of such occurrences should be kept.
1.9. Sick or dead birds should be removed from containers when feasible, and a record kept.
1.10. Any rest periods prescribed by a veterinarian should be complied with.
1.11. The frequency and type of feeding and watering natural to the birds should be adhered to during transport and should be clearly specified on the labelling.
1.12. To avoid cross-infection, and for health and hygiene reasons, human contact with birds should be avoided, and they should not be housed near foodstuffs or in places to which unauthorised persons have access.

1.13. No bird should be transported with radioactive material or other substances dangerous to health.

1.14. Containers should be secured to the aircraft, rail wagon, lorry or ship to avoid any possible movement, and should, at all times, be maintained in a horizontal position.

* SPECIAL : Black Palm Cockatoo, 'Goliath', super tame, $4,500. Also taking orders on all other types of black cockatoos and other rare birds.
If it's not extinct we can get it. If it is, we will still try.
Time needed for endangered species.
Extract from an advertisement for 'PARROT JUNGLE' in *New York Times* (8.4.79)

* I've got a couple of dozen 'under the counter' chipmunks arriving from the continent next week. They'll come in through Felixstowe and if you want to meet the lorry as soon as it has left the docks, I'll tell the driver to let you have whatever you want and we can settle up later.
East London dealer during a phone conversation (April 1986)

* Arowanas? You can get them with no problems. I saw about 80 at a fish importer's [place] the other day. They import them from Singapore when they are very young with the yolksacs still attached and sell them as a novelty.
Aquarium fish supplier (Essex) in conversation (May 1986)

15. Tailpiece

Education is the only way to stop the worst abuses to animals. After all, if a country fails to honour its commitments to CITES, what can the rest of the world do? Not much, as was shown by the CITES Secretariat's Notification to the Parties No. 366 last year, which urged all Parties to prohibit trade in CITES species, with or through the United Arab Emirates. Although the UAE has joined CITES in 1975 it was apparently doing nothing to implement the Convention and was known to be facilitating trade in violation of CITES.

Another country that is so careless about taking CITES responsibilities seriously is Japan. So much so that the Duke of Edinburgh had a moan at them on the subject when he was last there.

Do you remember the case of the Frilled Lizards? In the Spring of 1984 a Japanese television commercial screened a shot of a Frilled Lizard. Overnight the animal became a star. Japan went lizard mad and quick-thinking entrepreneurs promptly started to import as many as they could find, even though the lizard is protected in all the countries from which it was purchased. It is known that over 50 specimens were imported into Japan and put on show to the public. The poor old lizards were carted about the country on promotional tours in supermarkets, safari parks and department stores and while thousands of visitors piled in to these places to look at reptiles, the promoters were taking £3,000 a day in entrance fees—a sum that turned out to be peanuts when compared with the profits from the toys, the T-shirts and the badges.

One of the promoters is the Director of the Insect Museum in Utsunomiya. He is only entitled to import insect specimens, but he still managed to get hold of 12 Frilled Lizards. Another importer, Mr Naotsugu Shoji, was associated with a reptile and amphibian dealership in Tokyo, and bought his animals via the Netherlands and perhaps other countries as well. Further supplies of Frilled Lizards arrived for other importers and the picture became very obscure as everyone started laying down smokescreens to confuse the issue. The mania, while it lasted, demonstrates how easily protection laws can be flouted when large profits can be made by commercial exploitation of an animal.

There is a footnote to that story; when I was in Jakarta I did not even think of mentioning Frilled Lizards to the dealers, but even so, one of them offered to get some for me from Irian Jaya. All of those that ended up in Japan came from Irian Jaya or New Guinea, or Australia via Indonesia.

I must finish by relating the tale of Reginald Gant.

Animal dealers are extraordinarily sensitive people who will not reveal to an outsider anything about their business. They do not generally slam shut a door, they simply talk about all sorts of things that are perfectly innocuous, even when they are people who refuse to involve themselves in illegal practices, simply to hide their success or otherwise from competitors or from misunderstanding by people that they see as interfering do-gooders.

If they do handle smuggling deals there is no way at all that a layman will discover what they are up to.

So when I started to do my research I decided that the only way to approach the many dealers with whom I had no contact was to establish myself as another dealer. I wanted to call myself Reginald Perrin but then I thought that someone in Miami or Singapore was bound to have seen the series on television so my daughter suggested the name Reginald Gant, and Reginald Gant I became.

I spika da lingo so there was no problem passing myself off as a dealer and I think I was only rumbled on one occasions when a dealer saw me in deep conversation with a well-known local conservationist who was cordially hated by all the exporters. So Reginald Gant was most useful, though at times he was a pain in the neck when I forgot about him. On one occasion I even became two partners, John Gant and Reginald Nichol!

Acknowledgements

It is boringly repeated by every writer, but it is none the less true, that a book cannot be written without help from many people. They really are the book; the writer merely records what they say.

If I was to add details to the names of the people who did help me, we would need another book just for the acknowledgements, so I must be content with just listing them. In doing so I thank all of them for their inestimable help without which this book would not have happened.

Asia

Nasir Ali
Mohn Aphinives
Naresh Bedi
Ramesh Bedi
Herr Sogor
Katy Buri
Koret Buri
Prasit Buri
Rachit Buri
Chuck Darsono
Marjorie Doggett
Shahnawaz Khan
Norman Lewis
Terence Loh Peck Soon
Low Siang Huat
Rudolf Maengkom
Mok Ah Leong
Andy Ng
Komain Nukulphanitwipat
Oi
Pisit Na Patalung
Kampeng Ploenth
Herman Rijicsen
Ilsa Sharp
Somsak
Eddie Subarus
Frankie Sulemain
Yon
Pat Young

Africa

Abdullah
Mohammed Ali
Mohammed Amin
Ayub
Ian Douglas-Hamilton
Esmond Bradley-Martin
Chryssee Bradley-Martin
Ashok Mukerjee
Noora
William Obe
Prudence Patel
Ibrahim Rachman
Paddy Reilly
Diane Simmons
Franz Sitter
Sally Tully
Peter Whitehead
Simon Wong

The Americas

Jackie Clay
Eileen Opatut

Ardith Eudey
Ricardo Gonzales
Gerraro A Huertas Al
Bernie Levine
David Mack
Shirley McGreal
Russell Mittermeier
Greta Nilsson

Alvaro Posada-Salazar
Augusto Ruschi
Jose Sanchez
Christine Stevens
Geza Teleki
Mike Tsalikis
Rosalia Vargas
John Walsh

Europe
Gaby Auer
Rene Corten
Ram Dhan
Anton Fernhart
Wolfgang Frey

Dieter Kaiser
George Munro
David Potter
Herr Wirth

Great Britain
David Attenborough
Jon Barzdo
David Bellamy
Colin Booty
John Burton
Adam Cade
Mark Cawardine
Sue Cormack
Gerald Durrell
John Fisher
Rosamund Fisher
Alistair Gammell
Chris Harbard
Reginald Hardy
Carol Haslam
Ivan Hattingh
Rob Hepworth
Tim Inskipp
Craig Johnson

Rosemary Low
Jeremy Mallinson
Virginia McKenna
Ian McPhail
Ed Milner
Mark O'Shea
Michael O'Sullivan
Trina Paskell
Colin Platt
Barry Riley
Peter Robinson
Thomas Schultze-Westrum
Patricia Spanner
Tim Thomas
Alan Thornton
Vic Watkins
Ann Webb
David Whiting
Joe Williams

And to all the other people whose names I never knew, but especially those whose names I cannot reveal for a variety of reasons, thank you.

Appendix 1

COUNTRIES WHICH ARE PARTIES TO CITES

Afghanistan—entry into force 28 January 1986
Argentina 8 April 1981
Algeria 21 February 1984
Australia 27 October 1976
Austria 27 April 1982
Bahamas 18 September 1979
Bangladesh 18 February 1982
Belgium 1 January 1984
Benin 28 May 1984
Bolivia 4 October 1979
Botswana 12 February 1978
Brazil 4 November 1975
Cameroon 3 September 1981
Canada 9 July 1975
Central African Republic 25 November 1980
Chile 1 July 1975
China, People's Republic of 8 April 1981
Colombia 29 November 1981
Congo 1 May 1983
Costa Rica 28 September 1975
Cyprus 1 July 1975
Denmark 24 October 1977
Ecuador 1 July 1975
Egypt 4 April 1978
Finland 8 August 1976
France 9 August 1978
Gambia 24 November 1977
German Democratic Republic 7 January 1976
Germany, Federal Republic of 20 June 1976
Ghana 12 February 1976
Guatemala 5 February 1976
Guinea 20 December 1981
Guyana 25 August 1977
Honduras 13 June 1985
Hungary 27 August 1985
India 18 October 1976
Indonesia 28 March 1979
Iran 1 November 1976

Israel 17 March 1980
Italy 31 December 1979
Japan 4 November 1980
Jordan 14 March 1979
Kenya 13 March 1979
Liberia 9 June 1981
Liechtenstein 28 February 1980
Luxembourg 12 March 1984
Madagascar 18 November 1975
Malawi 6 May 1982
Malaysia 18 January 1978
Mauritius 27 July 1975
Monaco 18 July 1978
Morocco 14 January 1976
Mozambique 23 June 1981
Nepal 16 September 1975
Netherlands 18 July 1984
Nicaragua 4 November 1977
Niger 7 December 1975
Nigeria 1 July 1975
Norway 25 October 1976
Pakistan 19 July 1976
Panama 15 November 1978
Papua New Guinea 11 March 1976
Paraguay 13 February 1977
Peru 25 September 1975
Philippines 16 November 1981
Portugal 11 March 1981
Rwanda 18 January 1981
Saint Lucia 15 March 1983
Senegal 3 November 1977
Seychelles 9 May 1977
Somalia 2 March 1986
South Africa 13 October 1975
Sri Lanka 2 August 1979
Sudan 24 January 1983
Suriname 15 February 1981
Sweden 1 July 1975

Switzerland 1 July 1975
Tanzania 27 February 1980
Thailand 21 April 1983
Togo 21 January 1979
Trinidad & Tobago 18 April 1984
Tunisia 1 July 1975
Union of Soviet Socialist Republics
8 December 1976
United Arab Emirates 1 July 1975
United Kingdom 31 October 1976
United States of America 1 July 1975
Uruguay 1 July 1975
Venezuela 22 January 1978

Zaire 18 October 1976
Zambia 22 February 1981
Zimbabwe 17 August 1981

Signatory States not yet Ratified

Ireland 1 November 1974
Kampuchea 7 December 1973
Kuwait 9 April 1973
Lesotho 17 July 1974
Poland 8 October 1973
Vietnam 3 March 1973

Appendix 2
CITES, THE CONVENTION ON INTERNATIONAL TRADE IN ENDANGERED SPECIES

CITES, The Convention on International Trade in Endangered Species, is without doubt the most important document affecting the trade so, although it makes desperately dull reading, it is worth going through.

Animals referred to within the text are placed on CITES Schedules 1, 2 or 3 depending on their need for protection. The position of an animal might well be changed as its status alters, and geographical races of an animal might be on different schedules.

CITES:
The Convention on International Trade in Endangered Species

The Contracting States,

Recognizing that wild fauna and flora in their many beautiful and varied forms are an irreplaceable part of the natural systems of the earth which must be protected for this and the generations to come;

Conscious of the ever-growing value of wild fauna and flora from aesthetic, scientific, cultural, recreational and economic points of view;

Recognizing that peoples and States are and should be the best protectors of their own wild fauna and flora;

Recognizing, in addition, that international cooperation is essential for the protection of certain species of wild fauna and flora against over-exploitation through international trade;

Convinced of the urgency of taking appropriate measures to this end;

Have agreed as follows:

Article I

Definitions

For the purpose of the present Convention, unless the context otherwise requires:

(a) "Species" means any species, subspecies, or geographically separate population thereof;

(b) "Specimen" means:

(i) any animal or plant, whether alive or dead;

(ii) in the case of an animal: for species included in Appendices I and II, any readily recognizable part or derivative thereof; and for species included in Appendix III, any readily recognizable part or derivative thereof specified in Appendix III in relation to the species; and

(iii) in the case of a plant: for species included in Appendix I, any readily recognizable part or derivative thereof; and for species included in Appendices II and III, any readily recognizable part or derivative thereof specified in Appendices II and III in relation to the species;

(c) "Trade" means export, re-export, import and introduction from the sea;

(d) "Re-export" means export of any specimen that has previously been imported;

(e) "Introduction from the sea" means transportation into a State of specimens of any species which were taken in the marine environment not under the jurisdiction of any State;

(f) "Scientific Authority" means a national scientific authority designated in accordance with Article IX;

(g) "Management Authority" means a national management authority designated in accordance with Article IX;

(h) "Party" means a State for which the present Convention has entered into force.

Article II

Fundamental Principles

1. Appendix I shall include all species threatened with extinction which are or may be affected by trade. Trade in specimens of these species must be subject to particularly strict regulation in order not to endanger further their survival and must only be authorized in exceptional circumstances.

2. Appendix II shall include:

(a) all species which although not necessarily now threatened with extinction may become so unless trade in specimens of such species is subject to strict regulation in order to avoid utilization incompatible with their survival; and

(b) other species which must be subject to regulation in order that trade in specimens of certain species referred to in sub-paragraph (a) of this paragraph may be brought under effective control.

3. Appendix III shall include all species which any Party identified as being subject to regulation within its jurisdiction for the purpose of preventing or restricting exploitation, and as needing the cooperation of other parties in the control of trade.

4. The Parties shall not allow trade in specimens of species included in Appendices I, II and III except in accordance with the provisions of the present Convention.

Article III

Regulation of Trade in Specimens of Species included in Appendix I

1. All trade in specimens of species included in Appendix I shall be in accordance with the provisions of this Article.

2. The export of any specimen of a species included in Appendix I shall require the prior grant and presentation of an export permit. An export permit shall only be granted when the following conditions have been met:

(a) a Scientific Authority of the State of export has advised that such export will not be detrimental to the survival of that species;

(b) a Management Authority of the State of export is satisfied that the specimen was not obtained in contravention of the laws of that State for the protection of fauna and flora;

(c) a Management Authority of the State of export is satisfied that any living specimen will be so prepared and shipped as to minimize the risk of injury, damage to health or cruel treatment; and

(d) a Management Authority of the State of export is satisfied that an import permit has been granted for the specimen.

3. The import of any specimen of a species included in Appendix I shall require the prior grant and presentation of an import permit and either an export permit or a re-export certificate. An import permit shall only be granted when the following conditions have been met:

(a) a Scientific Authority of the State of import has advised that the import will be for purposes which are not detrimental to the survival of the species involved;

(b) a Scientific Authority of the State of import is satisfied that the proposed recipient of a living specimen is suitably equipped to house and care for it; and

(c) a Management Authority of the State of import is satisfied that the specimen is not to be used for primarily commercial purposes.

4. The re-export of any specimen of a species included in Appendix I shall require the prior grant and presentation of a re-export certificate. A re-export certificate shall only be granted when the following conditions have been met:

(a) a Management Authority of the State of re-export is satisfied that the specimen was imported into that State in accordance with the provisions of the present Convention;

(b) a Management Authority of the State of re-export is satisfied that any living specimen will be so prepared and shipped as to minimize the risk of injury, damage to health or cruel treatment; and

(c) a Management Authority of the State of re-export is satisfied that an import permit has been granted for any living specimen.

5. The introduction from the sea of any specimen of a species included in Appendix I shall require the prior grant of a certificate from a Management Authority of the State of introduction. A certificate shall only be granted when the following conditions have been met:

(a) a Scientific Authority of the State of introduction advises that the introduction will not be detrimental to the survival of the species involved;

(b) a Management Authority of the State of introduction is satisfied that the proposed recipient of a living specimen is suitably equipped to house and care for it; and

(c) a Management Authority of the State of introduction is satisfied that the specimen is not to be used for primarily commercial purposes.

Article IV

Regulation of Trade in Specimens of Species included in Appendix II

1. All trade in specimens of species included in Appendix II shall be in accordance with the provisions of this Article.

2. The export of any specimen of a species included in Appendix II shall require the prior grant and presentation of an export permit. An export permit shall only be granted when the following conditions have been met:

(a) a Scientific Authority of the State of export has advised that such export will not be detrimental to the survival of that species;

(b) a Management Authority of the State of export is satisfied that the specimen was not obtained in contravention of the laws of that State for the protection of fauna and flora; and

(c) a Management Authority of the State of export is satisfied that any living specimen will be so prepared and shipped as to minimize the risk of injury, damage to health or cruel treatment.

3. A Scientific Authority in each Party shall monitor both the export permits granted by that State for specimens of species included in Appendix II and the actual exports of such specimens. Whenever a Scientific Authority

determines that the export of specimens of any such species should be limited in order to maintain that species throughout its range at a level consistent with its role in the ecosystems in which it occurs and well above the level at which that species might become eligible for inclusion in Appendix I, the Scientific Authority shall advise the appropriate Management Authority of suitable measures to be taken to limit the grant of export permits for specimens of that species.

4. The import of any specimen of a species included in Appendix II shall require the prior presentation of either an export permit or a re-export certificate.

5. The re-export of any specimen of a species included in Appendix II shall require the prior grant and presentation of a re-export certificate. A re-export certificate shall only be granted when the following conditions have been met:

(a) a Management Authority of the State of re-export is satisfied that the specimen was imported into that State in accordance with the provisions of the present Convention; and

(b) a Management Authority of the State of re-export is satisfied that any living specimen will be so prepared and shipped as to minimize the risk of injury, damage to health or cruel treatment.

6. The introduction from the sea of any specimen of a species included in Appendix II shall require the prior grant of a certificate from a Management Authority of the State of introduction. A certificate shall only be granted when the following conditions have been met:

(a) a Scientific Authority of the State of introduction advises that the introduction will not be detrimental to the survival of the species involved; and

(b) a Management Authority of the State of introduction is satisfied that any living specimen will be so handled as to minimize the risk of injury, damage to health or cruel treatment.

7. Certificates referred to in paragraph 6 of this Article may be granted on the advice of a Scientific Authority, in consultation with other national scientific authorities or, when appropriate, international scientific authorities, in respect of periods not exceeding one year for total numbers of specimens to be introduced in such periods.

Article V

Regulation of Trade in Specimens of Species included in Appendix III

1. All trade in specimens of species included in Appendix III shall be in accordance with the provisions of this Article.

2. The export of any specimen of a species included in Appendix III from any State which has included that species in Appendix III shall require the prior grant and presentation of an export permit. An export permit shall only be granted when the following conditions have been met:

(a) a Management Authority of the State of export is satisfied that the specimen was not obtained in contravention of the laws of that State for the protection of fauna and flora; and

(b) a Management Authority of the State of export is satisfied that any living specimen will be so prepared and shipped as to minimize the risk of injury, damage to health or cruel treatment.

3. The import of any specimen of a species included in Appendix III shall require, except in circumstances to which paragraph 4 of this Article applies, the prior presentation of a certificate of origin and, where the import is from a State which has included that species in Appendix III, an export permit.

4. In the case of re-export, a certificate granted by the Management Authority of the State of re-export that the specimen was processed in that State or is being re-exported shall be accepted by the State of import as evidence that the provisions of the present Convention have been complied with in respect of the specimen concerned.

Article VI

Permits and Certificates

1. Permits and certificates granted under the provisions of Articles III, IV, and V shall be in accordance with the provisions of this Article.

2. An export permit shall contain the information specified in the model set forth in Appendix IV, and may only be used for export within a period of six months from the date on which it was granted.

3. Each permit or certificate shall contain the title of the present Convention, the name and any identifying stamp of the Management Authority granting it and a control number assigned by the Management Authority.

4. Any copies of a permit or certificate issued by a Management Authority shall be clearly marked as copies only and no such copy may be used in place of the original, except to the extent endorsed thereon.

5. A separate permit or certificate shall be required for each consignment of specimens.

6. A Management Authority of the State of import of any specimen shall cancel and retain the export permit or re-export certificate and any corresponding import permit presented in respect of the import of that specimen.

7. Where appropriate and feasible a Management Authority may affix a mark upon any specimen to assist in identifying the specimen. For these purposes "mark" means any indelible imprint, lead seal or other suitable means of identifying a specimen, designed in such a way as to render its imitation by unauthorized persons as difficult as possible.

Article VII

Exemptions and Other Special Provisions Relating to Trade

1. The provisions of Articles III, IV and V shall not apply to the transit or trans-shipment of specimens through or in the territory of a Party while the specimens remain in Customs control.

2. Where a Management Authority of the State of export or re-export is satisfied that a specimen was acquired before the provisions of the present Convention applied to that specimen, the provisions of Articles III, IV and V shall not apply to that specimen where the Management Authority issues a certificate to that effect.

3. The provisions of Articles III, IV and V shall not apply to specimens that are personal or household effects. This exemption shall not apply where:

(a) in the case of specimens of a species included in Appendix I, they were acquired by the owner outside his State of usual residence, and are being exported into that State; or

(b) in the case of specimens of species included in Appendix II:

(i) they were acquired by the owner outside his State of usual residence and in a State where removal from the wild occurred;

(ii) they are being imported into the owner's State of usual residence; and

(iii) the State where removal from the wild occurred requires the prior grant of export permits before any export of such specimens;

unless a Management Authority is satisfied that the specimens were acquired before the provisions of the present Convention applied to such specimens.

4. Specimens of an animal species included in Appendix I bred in captivity for commercial purpose, or of a plant species included in Appendix I artificially propagated for commercial purposes, shall be deemed to be specimens of species included in Appendix II.

5. Where a Management Authority of the State of export is satisfied that any specimen of

an animal species was bred in captivity or any specimen of a plant species was artificially propagated, or is a part of such an animal or plant or was derived therefrom, a certificate by that Management Authority to that effect shall be accepted in lieu of any of the permits or certificates required under the provisions of Articles III, IV or V.

6. The provisions of Articles III, IV and V shall not apply to the non-commercial loan, donation or exchange between scientists or scientific institutions registered by a Management Authority of their State, of herbarium specimens, other preserved, dried or embedded museum specimens, and live plant material which carry a label issued or approved by a Management Authority.

7. A Management Authority of any State may waive the requirements of Articles III, IV and V and allow the movement without permits or certificates of specimens which form part of a travelling zoo, circus, menagerie, plant exhibition or other travelling exhibition provided that:

(a) the exporter or importer registers full details of such specimens with that Management Authority;

(b) the specimens are in either of the categories specified in paragraphs 2 or 5 of this Article; and

(c) the Management Authority is satisfied that any living specimen will be so transported and cared for as to minimize the risk of injury, damage to health or cruel treatment.

Article VIII

Measures to be Taken by the Parties

1. The Parties shall take appropriate measures to enforce the provisions of the present Convention and to prohibit trade in specimens in violation thereof. These shall include measures:

(a) to penalize trade in, or possession of, such specimens, or both; and

(b) to provide for the confiscation or return to the State of export of such specimens.

2. In addition to the measures taken under paragraph 1 of this Article, a Party may, when it deems it necessary, provide for any method of internal reimbursement for expenses incurred as a result of the confiscation of a specimen traded in violation of the measures taken in the application of the provisions of the present Convention.

3. As far as possible, the Parties shall ensure that specimens shall pass through any formalities required for trade with a minimum of delay. To facilitate such passage, a Party may designate ports of exit and ports of entry at which specimens must be presented for clearance. The Parties shall ensure further that all living specimens, during any period of transit, holding or shipment, are properly cared for so as to minimize the risk of injury, damage to health or cruel treatment.

4. Where a living specimen is confiscated as a result of measures referred to in paragraph 1 of this Article:

(a) the specimen shall be entrusted to a Management Authority of the State of confiscation;

(b) the Management Authority shall, after consultation with the State of export, return the specimen to that State at the expense of that State, or to a rescue centre or such other place as the Management Authority deems appropriate and consistent with the purposes of the present Convention; and

(c) the Management Authority may obtain the advice of a Scientific Authority, or may, whenever it considers it desirable, consult the Secretariat in order to facilitate the decision under subparagraph (b) of this paragraph, including the choice of a rescue centre or other place.

5. A rescue centre as referred to in paragraph 4 of this Article means an institution designated by a Management Authority to look after the welfare of living specimens, particularly those that have been confiscated.

6. Each Party shall maintain records of trade in specimens of species included in Appendices I, II and III which shall cover:

(a) the names and addresses of exporters and importers; and

(b) the number and type of permits and certificates granted; the States with which such trade occurred; the numbers or quantities and types of specimens, names of species as included in Appendices I, II and III and, where applicable, the size and sex of the specimens in question.

7. Each Party shall prepare periodic reports on its implementation of the present Convention and shall transmit to the Secretariat:

(a) an annual report containing a summary of the information specified in sub-paragraph (b) of paragraph 6 of this Article; and

(b) a biennial report on legislative, regulatory and administrative measures taken to enforce the provisions of the present Convention.

8. The information referred to in paragraph 7 of this Article shall be available to the public where this is not inconsistent with the law of the Party concerned.

Article IX

Management and Scientific Authorities

1. Each Party shall designate for the purpose of the present Convention:

(a) one or more Management Authorities competent to grant permits or certificates on behalf of that Party; and

(b) one or more Scientific Authorities.

2. A State depositing an instrument of ratification, acceptance, approval or accession shall at that time inform the Depositary Government of the name and address of the Management Authority recognized to communicate with other Parties and with the Secretariat.

3. Any changes in the designations or authorizations under the provisions of this Article shall be communicated by the Party concerned to the Secretariat for transmission to all other Parties.

4. Any Management Authority referred to in paragraph 2 of this Article shall if so requested by the Secretariat or the Management Authority of another Party, communicate to it impression of stamps, seals or other devices used to authenticate permits or certificates.

Article X

Trade with States not Party to the Convention

Where export or re-export is to, or import is from, a State not a party to the present Convention, comparable documentation issued by the competent authorities in that State which substantially conforms with the requirements of the present Convention for permits and certificates may be accepted in lieu thereof by any Party.

Article XI

Conference of the Parties

1. The Secretariat shall call a meeting of the Conference of the Parties not later than two years after the entry into force of the present Convention.

2. Thereafter the Secretariat shall convene regular meetings at least once every two years, unless the Conference decides otherwise, and extraordinary meetings at any time on the written request of at least one-third of the Parties.

3. At meetings, whether regular or extraordinary, the Parties shall review the implementation of the present Convention and may:

(a) make such provision as may be necessary to enable the Secretariat to carry out its duties;

(b) consider and adopt amendments to Appendices I and II in accordance with Article XV;

(c) review the progress made towards the restoration and conservation of the species included in Appendices I, II and III;

(d) receive and consider any reports presented by the Secretariat or by any Party; and

(e) where appropriate, make recommendations for improving the effectiveness of the present Convention.

4. At each regular meeting, the Parties may determine the time and venue of the next regular meeting to be held in accordance with the provisions of paragraph 2 of this Article.

5. At any meeting, the Parties may determine and adopt rules of procedure for the meeting.

6. The United Nations, its Specialized Agencies and the International Atomic Energy Agency, as well as any State not a Party to the present Convention, may be represented at meetings of the Conference by observers, who shall have the right to participate but not to vote.

7. Any body or agency technically qualified in protection, conservation or management of wild fauna and flora, in the following categories, which has informed the Secretariat of its desire to be represented at meetings of the Conference by observers, shall be admitted unless at least one-third of the Parties present object:

(a) international agencies or bodies, either governmental or non-governmental, and national governmental agencies and bodies; and

(b) national non governmental agencies or bodies which have been approved for this purpose by the State in which they are located.

Once admitted, these observers shall have the right to participate but not to vote.

Article XII

The Secretariat

1. Upon entry into force of the present Convention, a Secretariat shall be provided by the Executive Director of the United Nations Environment Programme. To the extent and in the manner he considers appropriate, he may be assisted by suitable inter-governmental or non-governmental, international or non-governmental, international or national agencies and bodies technically qualified in protection, conservation and management of wild fauna and flora.

2. The functions of the Secretariat shall be:

(a) to arrange for and service meetings of the Parties;

(b) to perform the functions entrusted to it under the provisions of Articles XV and XVI of the present Convention;

(c) to undertake scientific and technical

studies in accordance with programmes authorized by the Conference of the Parties as will contribute to the implementation of the present Convention, including studies concerning standards for appropriate preparation and shipment of living specimens and the means of identifying specimens;

(d) to study the reports of Parties and to request from Parties such further information with respect thereto as it deems necessary to ensure implementation of the present Convention;

(e) to invite the attention of the Parties to any matter pertaining to the aims of the present Convention;

(f) to publish periodically and distribute to the Parties current editions of Appendices I, II and III together with any information which will facilitate identification of specimens of species included in those Appendices.

(g) to prepare annual reports to the Parties on its work and on the implementation of the present Convention and such other reports as meetings of the Parties may request;

(h) to make recommendations for the implementation of the aims and provisions of the present Convention, including the exchange of information of a scientific or technical nature;

(i) to perform any other function as may be entrusted to it by the Parties.

Article XIII

International Measures

1. When the Secretariat in the light of information received is satisfied that any species included in Appendices I or II is being affected adversely by trade in specimens of that species or that the provisions of the present Convention are not being effectively implemented, it shall communicate such information to the authorized Management Authority of the Party or Parties concerned.

2. When any Party receives a communication as indicated in paragraph 1 of this Article, it shall, as soon as possible, inform the Secretariat of any relevant facts insofar as its laws permit and, where appropriate, propose remedial action. Where the Party considers that an inquiry is desirable, such inquiry may be carried out by one or more persons expressly authorized by the Party.

3. The information provided by the Party or resulting from any inquiry as specified in paragraph 2 of this Article shall be reviewed by the next Conference of the Parties which may make whatever recommendations it deems appropriate.

Article XIV

Effect on Domestic Legislation and International Conventions

1. The provisions of the present Convention shall in no way affect the right of Parties to adopt:

(a) stricter domestic measures regarding the conditions for trade, taking, possession or transport of specimens of species included in Appendices I, II and III, or the complete prohibition thereof; or

(b) domestic measures restricting or prohibiting trade, taking, possession, or transport of species not included in Appendices I, II or III.

2. The provisions of the present Convention shall in no way affect the provisions of any domestic measures or the obligations of Parties deriving from any treaty, convention, or international agreement relating to other aspects of trade, taking, possession, or transport of specimens which is in force or subsequently may enter into force for any Party including any measure pertaining to the Customs, public health, veterinary or plant quarantine fields.

3. The provisions of the present Convention shall in no way affect the provisions of, or the obligations deriving from, any treaty, convention or international agreement concluded or which may be concluded between States creating a union or regional trade agreement establishing or maintaining a common external customs control and removing customs control between the parties thereto insofar as they relate to trade among the States members of that union agreement.

4. A State Party to the present Convention, which is also a party to any other treaty, convention or international agreement which is in force at the time of the coming into force of the present Convention and under the provisions of which protection is afforded to marine species included in Appendix II, shall be relieved of the obligation imposed on it under the provisions of the present Convention with respect to trade in specimens of species included in Appendix II that are taken by ships registered in that State and in accordance with the provisions of such other treaty, convention or international agreement.

5. Notwithstanding the provisions of Articles III, IV and V, any export of a specimen taken in accordance with paragraph 4 of this Article shall only require a certificate from a Management Authority of the State of introduction to the effect that the specimen was taken in accordance with the provisions of the other treaty, convention or international agreement in question.

6. Nothing in the present Convention shall prejudice the codification and development of the law of the sea by the United Nations Conference on the Law of the Sea convened pursuant to Resolution 2750 C(XXV) of the General Assembly of the United Nations nor the present or future claims and legal views of any State concerning the law of the sea and the nature and extent of coastal and flag State jurisdiction.

Article XV

Amendments to Appendices I and II

1. The following provisions shall apply in relation to amendments to Appendices I and II at meetings of the Conference of the Parties:

(a) Any Party may propose an amendment to Appendix I or II for consideration at the next meeting. The text of the proposed amendment shall be communicated to the Secretariat at least 150 days before the meeting. The Secretariat shall consult the other Parties and interested bodies on the amendment in accordance with the provisions of subparagraph (b) and (c) of paragraph 2 of this Article and shall communicate the response to all Parties not later than 30 days before the meeting.

(b) Amendments shall be adopted by a two-thirds majority of Parties present and voting. For these purposes "Parties present and voting" means Parties present and casting an affirmative or negative vote. Parties abstaining from voting shall not be counted among the two-thirds required for adopting an amendment.

(c) Amendments adopted at a meeting shall enter into force 90 days after that meeting for all Parties except those which make a reservation in accordance with paragraph 3 of this Article.

2. The following provisions shall apply in relation to amendments to Appendices I and II between meetings of the Conference of the Parties:

(a) Any Party may propose an amendment to Appendix I or II for consideration between meetings by the postal procedures set forth in this paragraph.

(b) For marine species, the Secretariat shall, upon receiving the text of the proposed amendment, immediately communicate it to the Parties. It shall also consult intergovernmental bodies having a function in relation to those species especially with a view to obtaining scientific data these bodies may be able to provide and to ensuring coordination with any conservation measures enforced by such bodies. The Secretariat shall communicate the views expressed and data provided by these bodies and its own findings and recommendations to the Parties as soon as possible.

(c) For species other than marine species, the Secretariat shall, upon receiving the text of the proposed amendment, immediately communicate it to the Parties, and, as soon as possible thereafter, its own recommendations.

(d) Any Party may, within 60 days of the date on which the Secretariat communicated its recommendations to the Parties under subparagraphs (b) or (c) of this paragraph, transmit to the Secretariat any comments on the proposed amendment together with any relevant scientific data and information.

(e) The Secretariat shall communicate the replies received together with its own recommendations to the Parties as soon as possible.

(f) If no objection to the proposed amendment is received by the Secretariat within 30 days of the date the replies and recommendations were communicated under the provisions of sub-paragraph (e) of this paragraph, the amendment shall enter into force 90 days later for all Parties except those which make a reservation in accordance with paragraph 3 of this Article.

(g) If an objection by any Party is received by the Secretariat, the proposed amendment shall be submitted to a postal vote in accordance with the provisions of sub-paragraphs (h), (i) and (j) of this paragraph.

(h) The Secretariat shall notify the Parties that notification of objection has been received.

(i) Unless the Secretariat receives the votes for, against or in abstention from at least one-half of the Parties within 60 days of the date of notification under sub-paragraph (h) of this paragraph, the proposed amendment shall be referred to the next meeting of the Conference for further consideration.

(j) Provided that votes are received from one-half of the Parties, the amendment shall be adopted by a two-thirds majority of Parties casting an affirmative or negative vote.

(k) The Secretariat shall notify all Parties of the result of the vote.

(l) If the proposed amendment is adopted it shall enter into force 90 days after the date of the notification by the Secretariat of its acceptance for all Parties except those which make a reservation in accordance with paragraph 3 of this Article.

3. During the period of 90 days provided for by sub-paragraph (c) of paragraph 1 or sub-paragraph (l) of paragraph 2 of this Article any Party may by notification in writing to the Depositary Government make a reservation with respect to the amendment. Until such reservation is withdrawn the Party shall be treated as a State not a Party to the present

Convention with respect to trade in the species concerned.

Article XVI

Appendix III and Amendments thereto

1. Any party may at any time submit to the Secretariat a list of species which it identifies as being subject to regulation within its jurisdiction for the purpose mentioned in paragraph 3 of Article II. Appendix III shall include the names of the Parties submitting the species for inclusion therein, the scientific names of the species so submitted, and any parts or derivatives of the animals or plants concerned that are specified in relation to the species for the purposes of sub-paragraph (b) of Article I.

2. Each list submitted under the provisions of paragraph 1 of this Article shall be communicated to the Parties by the Secretariat as soon as possible after receiving it. The list shall take effect as part of Appendix III 90 days after the date of such communication. At any time after the communication of such list, any Party may by notification in writing to the Depositary Government enter a reservation with respect to any species or any parts or derivatives, and until such reservation is withdrawn, the State shall be treated as a State not a Party to the present Convention with respect to trade in the species or part or derivative concerned.

3. A Party which has submitted a species for inclusion in Appendix III may withdraw it at any time by notification to the Secretariat which shall communicate the withdrawal to all Parties. The withdrawal shall take effect 30 days after the date of such communication.

4. Any Party submitting a list under the provisions of paragraph 1 of this Article shall submit to the Secretariat a copy of all domestic laws and regulations applicable to the protection of such species, together with any interpretations which the Party may deem appropriate or the Secretariat may request. The Party shall, for as long as the species in question is included in Appendix III, submit any amendment of such laws and regulations or any new interpretations as they are adopted.

Article XVII

Amendment of the Convention

1. An extraordinary meeting of the Conference of the Parties shall be convened by the Secretariat on the written request of at least one-third of the Parties to consider and adopt amendments to the present Convention. Such amendments shall be adopted by a two-thirds majority of Parties present and voting. For these purposes "Parties present and voting" means Parties present and casting an affirmative or negative vote. Parties abstaining from voting shall not be counted among the two-thirds required for adopting an amendment.

2. The text of any proposed amendment shall be communicated by the Secretariat to all Parties at least 90 days before the meeting.

3. An amendment shall enter into force for the Parties which have accepted it 60 days after two-thirds of the Parties have deposited an instrument of acceptance of the amendment with the Depositary Government. Thereafter, the amendment shall enter into force for any other Party 60 days after that Party deposits its instrument of acceptance of the amendment.

Article XVIII

Resolution of Disputes

1. Any dispute which may arise between two or more Parties with respect to the interpretation or application of the provisions of the present Convention shall be subject to negotiation between the Parties involved in the dispute.

2. If the dispute cannot be resolved in accordance with paragraph 1 of this Article, the Parties may, by mutual consent, submit the dispute to arbitration, in particular that of the Permanent Court of Arbitration at The Hague and the Parties submitting the dispute shall be bound by the arbitral decision.

Article XIX

Signature

The present Convention shall be open for signature at Washington until 30th April 1973 and thereafter at Berne until 31st December 1974.

Article XX

Ratification, Acceptance, Approval

The present Convention shall be subject to ratification, acceptance or approval. Instruments of ratification, acceptance or approval shall be deposited with the Government of the Swiss Confederation which shall be the Depositary Government.

Article XXI

Accession

The present Convention shall be open indefinitely for accession. Instruments of accession shall be deposited with the Depositary Government.

Article XXII

Entry into Force

1. The present Convention shall enter into force 90 days after the date of deposit of the tenth instrument of ratification, acceptance, approval or accession, with the Depositary Government.

2. For each State which ratifies, accepts or approves the present Convention or accedes thereto after the deposit of the tenth instrument of ratification, acceptance, approval or accession, the present Convention shall enter into force 90 days after the deposit by such State of its instrument of ratification, acceptance, approval or accession.

Article XXIII

Reservations

1. The provisions of the present Convention shall not be subject to general reservations. Specific reservations may be entered in accordance with the provisions of this Article and Articles XV and XVI.

2. Any State may, on depositing its instrument of ratification, acceptance, approval or accession, enter a specific reservation with regard to:

　(a) any species included in Appendix I, II or III; or

　(b) any parts or derivatives specified in relation to a species concluded in Appendix III.

3. Until a Party withdraws its reservation entered under the provisions of this Article, it shall be treated as a State not a party to the present Convention with respect to trade in the particular species or parts or derivatives specified in such reservation.

Article XXIV

Denunciation

Any Party may denounce the present Convention by written notification to the Depositary Government at any time. The denuncia-tion shall take effect twelve months after the Depositary Government has received the notification.

Article XXV

Depositary

1. The original of the present Convention, in the Chinese, English, French, Russian and Spanish languages, each version being equally authentic, shall be deposited with the Depositary Government, which shall transmit certified copies thereof to all States that have signed it or deposited instruments of accession to it.

2. The Depositary Government shall inform all signatory and acceding States and the Secretariat of signatures, deposit of instruments of ratification, acceptance, approval or accession, entry into force of the present Convention, amendments thereto, entry and withdrawal of reservations and notifications of denunciation.

3. As soon as the present Convention enters into force, a certified copy thereof shall be transmitted by the Depositary Government to the Secretariat of the United Nations for registration and publication in accordance with Article 102 of the Charter of the United Nations.

In witness whereof the undersigned Plenipotentiaries, being duly authorized to that effect, have signed the present Convention.

Done at Washington this third day of March, One Thousand Nine Hundred and Seventy-three.

Appendix 3

RARE, ENDANGERED OR THREATENED ANIMALS KNOWN TO HAVE BEEN TRADED WITHIN RECENT YEARS

This list has been compiled either from personal sightings, written information, dealers' price lists or personal conversations with dealers and collectors. The animals in question were all wild-caught, but may have been either traded live or as animal products. There were plenty of other species available also but those listed here are the less common species.

MAMMALS

Anteater, Collared, *Tamandua tetradactyla*
Anteater, Giant, *Myrmecophaga tridactyla*
Anteater, Scaly, *Manis temmincki*
Antelope, Saiga, *Saiga tatarica*
Armadillo, Brazilian Three-banded, *Tolypeutes tricinctus*
Armadillo, Fairy, *Chlamphorus truncatus*
Armadillo, Giant, *Priodontes giganteus*
Babirusa, *Babyrousa babyrussa*
Banteng, *Bos javanicus*
Bear, Asiatic, *Selenarctos thibetamus*
Bear, Himalayan, *Ursus arctos isabellinus*
Bear, Polar, *Ursus maritima*
Bear, Sloth, *Melursus ursinus*
Bear, Spectacled, *Tremarctos ornatus*
Bear, Sun, *Helarctos malayanus*
Blackbuck, *Antilope cervicapra*
Bobcat, *Felis rufus*
Brocket, Red, *Mazama americana*
Bushbaby, *Galago* spp.
Cacomistle, Central American, *Bassariscus sumichrasti*
Caracal, *Felis caracal*
Cat, Bornean Marbled, *Felis badia*
Cat, Flat-headed, *Felis planiceps*
Cat, Golden or Temminck's, *Felis temmincki*
Cat, Iriomote, *Prionailurus iriomotensis*

Cat, Leopard, *Felis bengalensis*
Cat, Little Spotted or Tiger, *Felis tigrina*
Cat, Marbled, *Felis marmorata*
Cat, Rusty-spotted, *Felis rubiginosa*
Cat, Sand, *Felis margarita*
Cheetah, *Acinonyx jubatus*
Chevrotain, Water, *Hyemoschus aquaticus*
Chimpanzee, *Pan troglodytes*
Chimpanzee, Pygmy, *Pan paniscus*
Chincillas, Chinchillidae spp.
Civet, African, *Viverra civetta*
Civet, Banded Palm, *Hemilagus derbyanus*
Civet, Large-spotted, *Viverra megaspila*
Coati, *Nasua nasua*
Coatimundi, *Nasua narica*
Colobus, Black, *Colobus satanus*
Colobus, Red, *Colobus badius*
Cougar, *Felis concolor*
Deer, Brow-antlered, *Cervus eldi*
Deer, Hog, *Axis porcinus annamiticus*
Deer, Marsh, *Blastocerus dichotomus*
Deer, Musk, *Moschus moschiferus*
Deer, Sika, *Cervus nippon*
Deer, Swamp, *Cervus duvauceli*
Deer, White-tailed, *Odocoileus virginianus*
Drill, *Papio leucophaeus*
Dugong, *Dugong dugon*
Duiker, Blue, *Cephalophus monticola*
Eland, *Taurotragus derbianus*
Elephant, African, *Loxodonta africana*
Elephant, Asian, *Elaphas maximus*
Flying Fox, *Pteropus* spp.
Fox, Fennec, *Fennecus zerda*
Fox, Grey, *Dusicyon griseus*
Gazelle, Arabian, *Gazella gazella*
Gelada, *Theropithecus gelada*
Gibbons, *Hylobates* spp.
Gibbon, Black, *Hylobates concolor*
Gibbon, Javan, *Hylobates moloch*
Gibbon, Pileated, *Hylobates pileatus*
Gorilla, *Gorilla gorilla*

Grison, Central American, *Galictus allamandi*
Guanaco, *Lama guanacon*
Hartebeest, *Alcelaphus buselaphus*
Impala, *Aepyceros melampus*
Jaguar, *Panthera onca*
Jaguarundi, *Felis yagouaroundi*
Kangaroo, Red, *Megeleia rufa*
Langur, Capped, *Presbytis pileatus*
Langur, Douc, *Pygathrix nemaeus*
Langur, Entellus, *Presbytis entellus*
Langur, Golden, *Presbytis geei*
Langur, Nilgiri, *Presbytis johni*
Langur, Pig-tailed, *Simias concolor*
Leopard, *Panthera pardus*
Leopard, Clouded, *Neofelis nebulosa*
Leopard, Snow, *Panthera uncia*
Linsang, Banded, *Prionodon linsang*
Linsang, Spotted, *Prionodon pardicolor*
Loris, Lesser Slow, *Nycticebus pygmaeus*
Lynx, *Lynx canadensis*
Macaque, Japanese, *Macaca fuscata*
Macaque, Lion-tailed, *Macaca silenus*
Macaque, Stump-tailed, *Macaca arctoides*
Macaque, Toque, *Macaca sinica*
Mandrill, *Papio sphinx*
Margay, *Felis wiedii*
Markhor, *Capra falconeri*
Marmoset, Cotton-top, *Saguinus oedipus*
Marmoset, Goeldi's, *Callimico goeldii*
Marmoset, Golden Lion, *Leontopithecus rosalia*
Marmoset, Golden-headed, *Leontopithecus chrysomelas*
Marmoset, White, *Callithrix argentata*
Marmoset, White-eared, *Callithrix aurita*
Monkey, Black Howler, *Alouatta nigra*
Monkey, Brown Howler, *Alouatta fusca*
Monkey, Central American Squirrel or Red-Backed, *Saimiri oerstedi*
Monkey, Diana, *Cercopithecus diana*
Monkey, Howler, *Alouatta villosa*

Monkey, Spider, *Ateles geoffroyi*
Monkey, Woolly, *Lagothrix lagothicha*
Muntjac, *Muntiacus* spp.
Ocelot, *Felis pardalis*
Orang Utan, *Pongo pygmaeus*
Otter, Cameroon Clawless, *Aonyx microdon*
Otter, European, *Lutra lutra*
Otter, Giant, *Pteronura brasiliensis*
Otter, River, *Lutra canadensis*
Pangolin, Chinese, *Manis pentadactyla*
Pangolin, Indian, *Manis crassicaudata*
Pangolin, Malayan, *Manis javanica*
Peccary, Collared, *Tayassu tajacu*
Porcupines, Crested, *Hystrix* spp.
Porpoises, all spp.
Pudu, Southern, *Pudu pudu*
Rhinoceros, Black, *Diceros bicornis*
Rhinoceros, Great Indian, *Rhinoceros unicornis*
Rhinoceros, Sumatran, *Didermocerus sumatrensis*
Rhinoceros, White, *Ceratotherium simum*
Saki, White-nosed, *Chiropotes albinasus*
Siamang, *Symphalangus syndactylus*
Sloth, Three-toed Brazilian, *Bradypus torquatus*
Squirrel, Four-striped Ground, *Lariscus hosei*
Squirrel, Oriental Giant, *Ratufa* spp.
Squirrel, Southern Flying, *Glaucomys volans*
Tamarin, Emperor, *Saguinus imperator*
Tapir, Brazilian, *Tapirus terrestris*
Tapir, Malayan, *Tapirus indicus*
Tiger, *Panthera tigris*
Uakari, *Cacajao calvus*
Uakari, Black-headed, *Cacajao melanocephalus*
Vicuna, *Lama vicugna*
Wolf, Maned, *Chrysocyon brachyurus*
Wolverine, *Gulo gulo*

BIRDS

Barbet, Toucan, *Semnornis ramphastinus*
Bird, Secretary, *Sagittarus serpentarius*
Birds of Paradise, *Paradisaeidae* spp.
Birds of Prey, Falconiformes
Blackbird, Yellow-headed, *Xanthocephalus xanthocephalus*
Blackbird, Yellow-shouldered, *Agelaius xanthomus*
Caracara, *Polyborus cheriway*
Cardinal, Yellow, *Gubernatrix cristata*

Cockatoos, all spp.
Cock-of-the-Rock, Andean, *Rupicola peruviana*
Cock-of-the-Rock, Guianan, *Rupicola rupicola*
Curassow, *Crax* spp.
Doves and Pigeons, *Columbidae* spp.
Ducks and Geese, *Anatidae* spp.
Eagles, *Aquila* spp.
Eagle, Crested, *Morphnus guianensis*

Eagle, Golden, *Aquila chrysaetos*
Eagle, Harpy, *Harpia harpyia*
Eagle, Philippine, *Pithecophaga jefferyi*
Egret, Cattle, *Bubulcus ibis*
Egret, Great, *Casmerodius albus*
Egret, Little, *Egretta garzetta*
Falcon, Peregrine, *Falco peregrinus*
Finches, *Fringillidae* spp.
Flamingo, Andean, *Phoenicoparrus andinus*
Flamingo, Greater, *Phoenicopterus ruber*
Flamingo, James', *Phoenicoparrus jamesi*
Gallinule, Purple, *Porphyrula martinica*
Heron, Black-crowned Night, *Nycticorax nycticorax*
Heron, Goliath, *Ardea goliath*
Hornbill, Great Pied, *Buceros bicornis*
Hornbill, Helmeted, *Rhinoplas vigil*
Hornbill, Rufous, *Buceros hydrocorax*
(Hummingbird) Black Barbthroat, *Threnetes grzimeki*
(Hummingbird) Black Inca, *Coeligena prunellei*
(Hummingbird) Black-billed Hermit, *Phaethornis nigrirostris*
Hummingbird, Broad-bellied, *Cynathus latirostris*
(Hummingbird) Chilean Woodstar, *Eulidia yarrellii*
Hummingbird, Violet-crowned, *Amazilia violiceps ellioti*
Hummingbird, White-eared, *Hylocharis leucotis*
Ibis, Sacred, *Threskionis aethiopica*
Lammergeier, *Gypaetus barbatus*
Macaw, Caninde, *Ara caninde*
Macaw, Spix's, *Cyanopsitta spixii*
Merlin, *Falco columbarius*
Owls, all spp.
Owl, Barn, *Tyto alba*
Owl, Scops, *Otus elegans botelensis*
Owl, Short-eared, *Asio flammeus*
Parrots, Parakeets, Psittaciformes, all spp.
Parrot, Grey, *Psittacus erithacus*
Parrot, Thick-billed, *Rhynchopsitta pachyrhyncha*

Parrot, Vasa, *Coracopsis nigra*
Parrot, Vinaceous, *Amazona vinacea*
Peafowl, Green, *Pavo muticus*
Pelican, White, *Pelecanus erythrorhynchos*
Penguin, Humboldt, *Spheniscus humbolti*
Penguin, Jackass, *Spheniscus demersus*
Pheasant, Blood, *Ithaginus cruentus*
Pheasant, Grey Peacock, *Polyplectron bicalcaratum*
Pheasant, Himalayan Monal, *Lophophorus impejanus*
Pheasant, Imperial, *Lophura imperialis*
Pheasant, Malay Peacock, *Polyplectron malacense*
Pigeon, Nicobar, *Caloenas nicobarica*
Pigeon, Victoria Crowned, *Goura victoria*
Quetzal, Resplendent, *Pharomacrus mocinno*
Raven, *Corvux corax*
Rhea, Darwin's, *Pterocnemia pennata*
Rhea, Greater, *Rhea americana*
Rock-fowl, White-necked, *Picathartes gymnocephalus*
Siskin, Red, *Spinus cucullatus*
Starling, Rothschild's, *Leucopsar rothschildi*
Stork, Marabou, *Leptoptilos crumeniferus*
Stork, Saddlebill, *Ephippiorhynchus senegalensis*
Swan, Black-necked, *Cygnus melancoryphus*
Swan, Coscoroba, *Coscoroba coscoroba*
Tanager, Azure-rumped, *Tangara cabanisi*
Tanager, Seven-coloured, *Tangara fastuosa*
Tern, Arctic, *Sterna paradisaea*
Tern, Caspian, *Hydroprogne caspia*
Tern, Common, *Sterna hirundo*
Toucan, Keel-billed, *Rhamphastos sulphuratus*
Turacos, Musophagidae spp.
Turaco, Knysna, *Turaco corythaix*
Turaco, Purple-crested, *Gallirex prophyreolophus*
Umbrellabird, Long-wattled, *Cephalopteruis penduliger*

REPTILES

Alligator, Chinese, *Alligator sinensis*
Anaconda, Yellow, *Eunectes notaeus*
Anole, Giant, *Anolis roosevelti*
Boas, Boidae spp.
Boa, Cuban, *Epicrates angulifer angulifer*
Boa, Jamaican, *Epicrates subflavus*

Boas, Madagascar, *Acrantophis* spp.
Boa, Rubber, *Charina bottae*
Caiman, Black, *Melanosuchus niger*
Caiman, Spectacled, *Caiman crocodilus*
Chameleons, *Chamaeleo* spp.
Chuckwalla, *Sauromalus varius*

Cobra, *Naja* spp.
Cobra, False, *Cyclagras gigas*
Constrictor, Boa, *Constrictor constrictor*
Crocodiles, Crocodylidae spp.
Crocodile, Estuarine or Saltwater,
Crocodylus porosus
Crocodile, Mugger, *Crocodylus palustris*
Crocodile, New Guinea, *Crocodylus
novaeguineae*
Crocodile, Siamese, *Crocodylus siamensis*
Crocodile, West African Dwarf,
Osteolaemus tetraspis
Gavial, False, *Tomistoma schlegelii*
Geckos, Day, *Phelsuma* spp.
Iguanas, Green, *Iguana* spp.
Iguana, Rhinoceros, *Cyclura cornuta*
Kingsnake, Sonora Mountain,
Lampropeltis pyromelana pyromelana
Kingsnake, Speckled, *Lampropeltis getulus*
Lizard, Caiman, *Dracaena guianensis*
Lizard, Glass, *Ophisaurus attenuatus*
Lizard, Sail-fin, *Hydrosaurus pustulatus*
Monitors, *Varanus* spp.
Monitor, Bengal, *Varanus bengalensis*
Monitor, Yellow, *Varanus flavescens*

Mussurana, *Pseudoboa cloelia*
Pythons, *Python* spp.
Python, Indian, *Python molurus*
Skink, Five-lined, *Eumeces fasciatus*
Snake, Corn, *Elaphe guttata*
Snake, Hognose, *Heterodon* spp.
Snake, Indigo, *Drymarchon corais*
Snake, Rainbow, *Farancia erytrogramma*
Snake, Rat, *Elaphe obsoleta*
Tegus, *Tupinambis* spp.
Tortoises, Testudinidae spp.
Tortoise, Mediterranean Spur-thighed,
Testudo graeca graeca
Tortoise, Radiated, *Geochelone radiata*
Turtle, Burmese Swamp, *Morenia ocellata*
Turtle, Green Sea, *Chelonia mydas*
Turtle, Hawksbill, *Eretmochelys imbricata*
Turtle, Loggerhead, *Caretta caretta*
Turtles, Marine, Cheloniidae spp.
Turtle, Olive Ridley, *Lepidochelys olivacea*
Turtle, Side-necked, *Pelusios* spp.
Turtle, Spotted, *Clemmys guttata*
Turtle, Stinkpot, *Stenotherus odoratus*

AMPHIBIANS
Hellbender, *Cryptobranchus alleganiensis
alleganiensis*
Peeper, Spring, *Hyla crucifer*

Appendix 4

ORGANISATIONS INVOLVED WITH WILDLIFE TRADE

Listed below are a few organisations that are in some way involved with wildlife trade. Hopefully their position will be obvious from their names.

American Association of Zoological Parks and Aquariums: Oglebay Park, Wheeling WV 26003, USA

American Tarantula Society: 564 Boulevard, New Milford, NJ 07646, USA

Animal Research & Conservation Center: P.O. Box 5047 Church Street Station, New York, NY 10242, USA

Animal Welfare Institute: P.O. Box 3650, Washington, DC 20007, USA

Association of Aquarists: 31 Overstrand, Aston Clinton, Bucks, UK

Association of British Wild Animal Keepers: 21 Northcote Road, Clifton, Bristol BS8 3HB, UK

Association of Responsible Animal Keepers: 13 Pound Place, Shalford, Guildford, Surrey, GU4 8HH, UK

Bolivian Wildlife Society (PB): Tan-yr-allt, Llantilio Crossenny, Gwent, NP7 8TH, Wales, UK

British Chelonian Group: 105 Burnham Lane, Slough, Berks., UK

British Herpetological Society: c/o The Zoological Society of London, Regent's Park, London NW1 4RY, UK

British Tarantula Society: 34 Phillimore Place, Radlett, Herts., UK

The Chipperfield Organisation: Heatherset, Chilworth Road, Southampton, Hants, UK

CITES Secretariat: 6 Rue du Maupas, Case Postale 78, 1000 Lausanne 9, Switzerland

Compassion in World Farming: 20 Lavant Street, Petersfield, Hants, GU32 3EW, UK

Conchological Society of Great Britain & Ireland: 51 Wychwood Avenue, Luton, Beds. LU2 7HT, UK

Department of the Environment: UK CITES Management Authority, Tollgate House, Houlton Street, Bristol, BS2 9DJ, UK

Environmental Investigation Agency: 23b Highbury Crescent, London N5 1RX, UK

Fauna & Flora Preservation Society: c/o The Zoological Society of London, Regent's Park, London NW1, UK

Foreign Bird Importers Association: c/o B. Riley, PTA, 151 Pampisford Road, South Croydon, Surrey, UK

Friends of the Earth (USA), 529 Commercial Street, San Francisco, CA 94111, USA

Fur Traders Association: Fur Trade House, Little Trinity Lane, London EC4, UK

Greenpeace (UK): 36 Graham Street, London N1 8LL, UK

Greenpeace (USA): P.O. Box 4793, Santa Barbara, CA 93103, USA

International Council for Bird Preservation: c/o Wildlife Trade Monitoring Unit, IUCN Conservation Monitoring Centre, 219C Huntingdon Road, Cambridge CB3 0DL, UK

International Primate Protection League (UK): 19–25 Argyll Street, London W1V 2DU, UK

International Primate Protection League (USA): P.O. Drawer X, Summerville, SC 29483, USA

International Union for the Conservation of Nature & Natural Resources: 1196 Gland, Switzerland

Marine Conservation Society: 4 Gloucester Road, Ross-on-Wye, Herefordshire HR9 5BU, UK

Ministry of Agriculture, Fisheries & Food (Animal Health Division): Hook Rise, Tolworth, Surrey, UK

National Audubon Society: 950 Third Ave., New York, NY 10022, USA

New York Zoological Society, Bronx, NY 10460, USA

Organisation of Fish Importers: Haycliffe Mills, Haycliffe Lane, Bradford, West Yorkshire ED5 7ET, UK

People's Trust for Endangered Species: Hamble House, Meadron, Godalming, Surrey GU7 3JX, UK

Pet Trades Association: 151 Pampisford Road, South Croydon, Surrey, UK

Raptor Research & Rehabilitation Program: Department of Veterinary Biology, College of Veterinary Medicine, University of Minnesota, St Paul, MN 55108, USA

Royal Society for the Prevention of Cruelty to Animals: The Manor House, The Causeway, Horsham, Sussex RH12 1HG, UK

Royal Society for the Protection of Birds: The Lodge, Sandy, Bedfordshire SG19 2DL, UK

TRAFFIC (Australia): P.O. Box 799, Manly 2095, New South Wales, Australia

TRAFFIC (Germany): World Wildlife Fund, Deutschland, Sophienstrasse 44, D-6000 Frankfurt am Main 90, West Germany

TRAFFIC (Japan): 6th Floor, 39 Mori Building, 2-4-5 Azabudai, Minato-ku, Tokyo 106, Japan

TRAFFIC (Netherlands): Postbus 7, 3700 AA Zeist, Holland

TRAFFIC (South America): Carlos Roxlo 1496/301, Montevideo, Uruguay

TRAFFIC (UK): Wildlife Trade Monitoring Unit, IUCN Conservation Monitoring Centre, 219C Huntingdon Road, Cambridge CB3 0DL, UK

TRAFFIC (USA): 1255 23rd Street, NW, Washington, DC 20037, USA

World Society for the Protection of Animals (Canada): 215 Lakeshore Blvd. E, Suite 113, Toronto, Ontario MSA BWG, Canada

World Society for the Protection of Animals (Colombia): Calle 74 No 9-13, Of. 202, Aptdo Aereo 75002, Bogota, Colombia

World Society for the Protection of Animals (Costa Rica): Aptdo, 516, Heredia, Costa Rica

World Society for the Protection of Animals (UK): 106 Jermyn Street, London SW1Y 6EE, UK

World Society for the Protection of Animals (USA): 29 Perkins Street, P.O. Box 190, Boston MA 02130, USA

World Wildlife Fund (Headquarters): 1196, Gland, Switzerland

World Wildlife Fund (UK): Panda House, 11-13 Ockford Road, Godalming, Surrey, GU7 1QU, UK

World Wildlife Fund (USA): 1601 Connecticut Avenue, NW, Washington, DC 20009, USA

Zoo Check: 67 Glebe Place, London SW3, UK

Zoological Society of London: Regent's Park, London NW1 4RY, UK

Bibliography

African Elephants, CITES & the Ivory Trade, E. B. Martin, J. Caldwell & J. Barzdo (CITES Secretariat, 1986)

Alien Animals—The Story of Imported Wildlife, The, George Laycock (Ballantine Books, 1986)

All Heaven in a Rage, Tim Inskipp (Royal Society for the Protection of Birds, 1975)

Amphibians of Europe, D. Ballasina (David & Charles, 1984)

And Then There Were None: America's Vanishing Wildlife, N. Leen (Holt, Rinehart & Winston, 1973)

Animal Connection, The, Jean-Yves Domalain (William Morrow & Co., 1977)

Audubon Society Field Guide to North American Reptiles & Amphibians, The, J. L. Behler & F. W. King (Knopf, 1979)

Aves do Brasil, Augusto Ruschi (Editoria Rios Ltda, 1979)

Bangkok Post, many issues (Thailand)

BBC Wildlife, many issues, Editor: Rosamund Kidman-Cox (BBC Enterprises Ltd & Wildlife Publications Ltd.)

The Bird Business, Greta Nilsson (Animal Welfare Institute, 2nd edn, 1981)

Birds Illustrated, many issues, Managing Editor: Annette Preece (Royal Society for the Protection of Birds)

Breeding Endangered Species in Captivity, Editor: R. D. Martin (Academic Press, 1975)

Business Times, 18 June 1985 (Singapore)

Care & Management of Wild Mammals in Captivity, The, Lee Crandall (Chicago University Press, 1964)

Checklist: Wildlife of Bangladesh, R. Khan (Dhaka University, 1982)

Commercialism of Domestically Produced Raptors, Robert Berry (The North American Raptor Breeders Association, 1983)

Complete Checklist of Birds of the World, A, Richard Howard & Alick Moore (Oxford University Press, 1980)

Dangerous to Man, Roger Caras (Holt, Rinehart & Winston, 1975)

Directory of Crocodilian Farming Operations, A, R. Duxmore, J. Barzdo, S. Broad & D. Jones (IUCN Conservation Monitoring Centre, 1985)

Doomsday Book of Animals, David Day (Viking Press, 1981)

Durrell in Russia, Gerald Durrell & Lee Durrell (Macdonald, 1986)

El Tiempo, 6 July 1985 (Colombia)

Encyclopedia of Cage & Aviary Birds, Cyril H. Rogers (Macmillan Publishing Co., 1975)

Endangered One, The, James A. Cox (Crown Publishing Co., 1975)

Endangered Parrots, Rosemary Low (Blandford Press, 1984)

Endangered Species Handbook, The, Greta Nilsson et al. (Animal Welfare Institute, 1983)

Extinct & Vanishing Mammals of the Western Hemisphere, Glover P. Allen (Cooper Square Publications, 1972)

Extinction: The Causes & Consequences of the Disappearance of Species, Paul & Anne Ehrlick (Victor Gollancz, 1982)

Facts About Furs, Greta Nilsson, Christine Stevens & John Gleiber (Animal Welfare Institute, 1980)

Field Guide to the Larger Mammals of Africa, J. Dorst & P. Dandelot (William Collins & Sons, 1972)

Handbook of Living Primates, J. R. Napier & P. H. Napier (Academic Press, 1967)
Handbook of the Birds of India & Pakistan, Salim Ali & S. D. Ripley (Oxford University Press, 1968–74)
Herpetofauna News, David Stubbs (October 1985)
In Defence of Animals, Editor: Peter Singer (Basil Blackwell, Ltd, 1985)
Indonesian Handbook, Bill Dalton (Moon Publications, 1978)
International Primate Trade, vol. 1, Editors: David Mack & Russell A. Mittermeier (TRAFFIC USA, 1984)
International Trade in Wildlife, Tim Inskipp & S. Wells (Earthscan, 1979)
International Wildlife Law, Simon Lyster (Grotius Publications Ltd, 1985)
Japanese Ivory Industry, The, Esmond Bradley Martin (World Wildlife Fund, Japan, 1985)
Last Chance on Earth, A Requiem for Wildlife, Roger Caras (Chilton, 1966)
Latin American Wildlife Trade Laws, Kathryn Fuller & Byron Swift (TRAFFIC USA, 1985)
Let Them Live. A Worldwide Survey of Animals Threatened with Extinction, Kai Curry-Lindahl (William Morrow & Co., 1972)
Mail on Sunday, 14 July 1985 (London)
Mammal Species of the World, A Taxonomic & Geographic Reference, Editors: J. Honacki, K. Kinman & J. Koeppl (Allen Press Inc. & the Association of Systematics Collections, 1982)
Man & Beast, C. W. Hume (Universities Federation for Animal Welfare, 1982)
Man Kind? Our Incredible War on Wildlife, Amory Cleveland (Harper & Row, 1974)
Mulu—The Rain Forest, Robin Hanbury-Tenison (Weidenfeld & Nicolson, 1980)
National Geographic Magazine, many issues (National Geographic Society)
Oryx, many issues (The Flora & Fauna Preservation Society)
Parrots of South America, The, Rosemary Low (John Gifford, 1972)
Parrots of the World, J. Forshaw (TFH Publications, 1977)
Plants of Khao Yai National Park, Editor: Prof. Dr Tem Smitinand (Friends of Khao Yai National Park Association, Thailand, 1977)
Politics of Extinction. The Shocking Story of the World's Endangered Wildlife, The, Lewis Regenstein (Macmillan, 1975)
Red Data Book, The IUCN Amphibia-Reptilia (Part 1), Compiler: Brian Groombridge (IUCN, 1982)
Red Data Book, The IUCN Fish (Volume 4 Pisces), Compiler: R. Miller (IUCN, 1977)
Red Data Book, The IUCN Invertebrate, Compilers: Susan Wells, Robert Pyle & Mark Collins (IUCN, 1983)
Red Data Book, The IUCN Mammal (Part 1), Compilers: Jane Thornback & Martin Jenkins (IUCN, 1981)
Red Data Book of Endangered Birds of the World, The (International Council for Bird Preservation, 1980)
Red Data Book, South African Reptiles & Amphibians, Compiler: G. McLachlan (IUCN, 1978)
Rhino Exploitation, Esmond Bradley Martin (World Wildlife Fund, Hong Kong, 1984)
Saving the Animals, Bernard Stonehouse (Weidenfeld & Nicolson, 1987)
Silent Spring, Rachel Carson (Fawcett World Library, 1970)
Sinking Ark: A New Look at the Problem of Disappearing Species, Norman Myers (Pergamon Press, 1979)
Soft-billed Birds, Clive Roots (Gifford, 1970)
Some Butterflies of Khao Yai National Park, Robert Nuhn & Philip Reeves (Friends of Khao Yai National Park Association, Thailand, 1980)
Squirrel Monkey, The, Editors: L. A. Rosenblum & R. W. Cooper (Academic Press, 1968)
The Star, 15 November 1985 (Malaysia)
Status Survey of Otters & Spotted Cats in Latin America, W. Metquist (University of Idaho, 1984)
Straits Times (Singapore)
Sunday Times (London)
TRAFFIC Bulletin, many issues, Compiler: Kim Lochen (Wildlife Trade Monitoring Unit)

Transport of Live Animals by Air from Calcutta & Bangkok Airports, Colin Platt (International Society for the Protection of Animals, 1974)

'Utilization (Export) of Indonesian Wildlife', Charles J. Darsono (unpublished paper, 1979)

Vanishing Birds of the World, Tim Halliday (Holt, Rinehart & Winston, 1978)

Why Big Fierce Animals are Rare—An Ecologist's Perspective, P. Colinvaux (Princeton University Press, 1979)

Wildlife Crisis, HRH Prince Philip & James Fisher (Cowles Book Co., 1970)

Wildlife Resources & Economic Development, S. K. Eltringham (John Wiley & Sons, 1985)

World Birdwatch, various issues (Cambridge)

World Checklist of Threatened Amphibians & Reptiles, B. Groonbride (Nature Conservancy Council, 1983)

World's Disappearing Wildlife, The, Maurice Buron & Robert Burton (Marshall Cavendish, 1978)

In addition to the books and other publications listed above I have also dipped into heaps of other sources of information. Many of these I knew already, some were shown to me by friends in different parts of the world and cuttings from others were posted to me by contacts everywhere. But they were all valuable sources of information, as were the following publications:

Agscene
Animal Kingdom
Avicultural Magazine
Auk
Bird Talk
Birds International
Cage & Aviary Birds
Conservation News of South East Asia
Daily Telegraph
Dodo
Guardian, The
International Primate Protection League Newsletter
International Wildlife
International Zoo Yearbook
Malayan Nature Journal

Miami Herald
Natural History Bulletin of the Siam Society
Nature
New Scientist
Newsletter of the Marine Conservation Society
New York Herald Tribune
New York Times
Observer
Pet Business
Ratel
San Diego Evening Tribune
Tiger Paper
Times of India
World Wildlife Fund News
Zoonooz

Another great source of pointers that enabled me to dig out a variety of stories were the press releases that I received from:

Bolivian Wildlife Society
Department of the Environment
Environmental Investigation Agency
Friends of the Earth
Greenpeace
Her Majesty's Customs & Excise Department
Lynx
Primary Protection Department, Singapore
Royal Society for the Prevention of Cruelty to Animals
Royal Society for the Protection of Birds
United States Department of Agriculture
United States Fish & Wildlife Service
World Society for the Protection of Animals
World Wildlife Fund

Index
OF SPECIES MENTIONED WITHIN THE TEXT

Note: Numbers in bold type denote illustrations. C denotes Colour Plate.